LOMA LINDA MESSAGES

By
Ellen G. White

**PRINTED IN
THE UNITED STATES OF AMERICA**

World rights reserved. This book or any portion thereof may not be copied or reproduced in any form or manner whatever, except as provided by law, without the written permission of the publisher, except by a reviewer who may quote brief passages in a review.

The author assumes full responsibility for the accuracy of all facts and quotations as cited in this book.

Facsimile Reproduction

As this book played a formative role in the development of Christian thought and the publisher feels that this book, with its candor and depth, still holds significance for the church today. Therefore the publisher has chosen to reproduce this historical classic from an original copy. Frequent variations in the quality of the print are unavoidable due to the condition of the original. Thus the print may look darker or lighter or appear to be missing detail, more in some places than in others.

Copyright © 2004, 2015 TEACH Services, Inc.
ISBN-13: 978-1-57258-287-3
Library of Congress Control Number: 2004100755

Published by

TEACH Services, Inc.
P U B L I S H I N G
www.TEACHServices.com • (800) 367-1844

Introduction

The merciful hand of God was obviously present in the work of E. G. White. After she had labored in Australia for nine years, the Lord instructed her to return to the United States. She made her trip back to America in 1900 and established her home in Elmshaven, a few miles from St. Helena, in northwestern California. As ever, she was full of zeal for the promotion of the Gospel. In many of her writings she urged the leadership and lay members to resort to medical missionary work as an entering wedge for bringing present truth to the world.

Medical missionary work was already established in Battle Creek, Michigan, and also in St. Helena, California, but Ellen White saw a need for opening a medical center in Southern California. She requested Elder John A. Burden to help find a suitable place for the establishment of the medical work.

At her suggestion Elder Burden looked for a property a little distance from each of the three cities of Riverside, Redlands, and San Bernardino. Elder Burden and his committee found a place in Loma Linda, in 1904, priced at $110,000.00. As the brethren prayed, the price of this property was reduced. A year later, this same property was available for $40,000.00. Ellen White urged the reluctant brethren to approve this purchase. In May 1905 Elder Burden made a $1,000.00 deposit on the property. The contributions came in miraculously from unexpected sources, and before the end of 1905 the property was payed off.

The Sanitarium was opened in October 1905. In November 1905 Julia A. White, M.D., made plans for nursing education. In 1906 the institution was named "Loma Linda College of Medical Evangelists," which began its program under the leadership of educator Warren E. Howell.

Ellen White was earnestly engaged in bringing out a number of books. Her pressing bookwork was frequently interrupted by her repeated visits to Loma Linda to encourage the work there, which she personally had helped establish. Ellen White wrote numerous pages of God-given instructions for this new institution, many of which are contained in this book.

The counsels coming through the pen of inspiration reveal the goals that are to be achieved through the medical work. If these directions are carefully followed, God's people will reach in the art of preventing and treating disease a distinction which will place them upon the highest platform in medical knowledge.

This collection of Ellen White's writings is a reprint of the 1935 edition, which was re-edited in 1957 in the hope of arousing God's people to their responsibility of the hour, that they may follow His blueprint in the medical missionary work.

—The Publishers.

CONTENTS

Section I

Loma Linda—A Medical Missionary Training Center	1
Work for Southern California	22
Work for Redlands, Riverside, and San Bernardino	36
Work for Los Angeles and San Diego	39
To Our Brethren and Sisters in Southern California	41
Glendale Sanitarium	44
Work for Cities	46
Medical Missionary Work	53
Perils of Last Days	75
Cultivate Both Mental and Physical Powers	76
Economy To Be Used	77
Simplicity Without Display	78

Section II

Individual Responsibility	83
Value of Counsel	98
Unity in Work	99
Hedging up Way for Others	106
General Instruction	109

Section III

Training Physicians and Nurses	138
Kind of Workers Needed in Our Medical Institutions	144
Location of Schools and Sanitariums	157
Kind of Students Needed in Our Institutions	165
Work for Students	170
Amusements	170
Competing with Worldly Medical Schools	171
Conforming to Legal Requirements	172
Unequally Yoked Together	173
Higher Education	178
Word of God Basis of All Education	182
Kind of Teachers	183
Care Workers Should Have for Own Health	186
Out-of-door Work for Patients	187
Dealing with Sanitarium Workers	189
Use of Drugs in Our Institutions	191

Section IV

Money for Work	196
Debt and Borrowing Money	201
"Christ's Object Lessons" and "Ministry of Healing"	204
Physicians' Salaries	210
Store, Bakery and Health Foods	216
Use of Loma Linda Land	222
Work for W.C.T.U.	225
General Index	237

In the year 1905, Seventh-day Adventists, in response to the urgings of Ellen G. White, purchased property in southern California known as Loma Linda, and began sanitarium work. In 1909 the *College of Medical Evangelists* came to birth in harmony with her early declarations that physicians would be trained in this place, which was to become a "great educational center."

Section I

Loma Linda
A Medical Missionary Training Center

Redlands and Riverside have been presented to me as places that should be worked. These two places should not longer be neglected. I hope soon to see an earnest effort put forth in their behalf. Will you please consider the advisability of establishing a sanitarium in the vicinity of these towns, with treatment rooms in each place to act as feeders to the institution?

We cannot afford to allow these places to go unwarned. —*April 12, 1905. (p. 142, pars. 2, 3 first)*

Your letter has just been read. I had no sooner finished reading it than I said, "I will consult no one; for I have no question at all about the matter." I advised Willie to send you a telegram without spending time to ask the advice of the brethren. Secure the property by all means, so that it can be held, and then obtain all the money you can and make sufficient payments to hold the place. This is the very property that we ought to have. Do not delay; for it is just what is needed. As soon as it is secured, a working force can begin operations in it. I think that sufficient help can be secured to carry this matter through. I want you to be sure to lose no time in securing the right to purchase the property. We will do our utmost to help you raise the money. I know that Redlands and Riverside are to be worked, and I pray that the Lord may be gracious, and not allow anyone else to get this property instead of us. —*May 14, 1905. (p. 150, par. 1)*

We hope to see you soon now; but in regard to the purchase of "Loma Linda" I will say, "Go ahead." I hope to be able to help by giving the proceeds from a certain number of copies of "Ministry of Healing." I can do no more, except to borrow. I wish the place purchased. Do not neglect to tell me all I ought to know. I have been looking over your descriptive letter, and I am well satisfied that the place is one we ought to have. It is cheap at forty thousand dollars. We will not leave you, but will stand back of you, and help you to raise the means. In regard to the right man to manage the institution, I am confident that we shall find some one when the right time comes. —*May 31, 1905. (p. 160 all)*

I am much encouraged by the letters that I have received from you regarding Loma Linda. From your description of the place, I believe it meets the representation which I have seen, of what we should seek for as sanitarium locations. Such a place was presented to me a few miles from an important city. The city has recently been built up. —*June 2, 1905. (p. 161, par. 1)*

On our way to Los Angeles, we stopped off at Loma Linda, and visited the property that we have purchased for sanitarium work. We were taken through the different buildings. There is one large main building, which was built for sanitarium work and is well adapted for that purpose. Some changes will have to be made regarding bath and treatment facilities, but otherwise, everything is in readiness for us to begin work at once.

Until this recent visit, I have never before seen such a place with my natural eyes, but four years ago such a place was presented before me as one of those that would come into our possession if we moved wisely. It is a wonderful place in which to begin work for Redlands and Riverside. We must make decided efforts to secure helpers who will do most faithful medical missionary work. If God will bless the treatments given and Christ will let His healing power be felt, a wonderful work will be accomplished. —*June 23, 1905. (p. 165, pars. 1, 2)*

I have a great desire that you may both be greatly blessed in your work in the new sanitarium. I hope that Brother _____ will move understandingly in reference to the sanitariums already in operation and also in regard to the new sanitarium. I pray that the Lord may provide suitable people to connect with this institution, people who will be a genuine strength to the institution.

Do not be discouraged if in any wise there is some cutting across of your plans, and if you are somewhat hindered. But I hope that we shall never again have to meet the hindrance that we have met in the past because of the way in which things have been conducted in some lines in Southern California. I have seen the hold-back principles followed, and I have seen the displeasure of the Lord because of this. If the same spirit is manifested, I shall not consent to keep silent as I have done. —*June 25, 1905. (p. 168, pars. 1, 2)*

I wish to present before our people the blessings that the Lord has placed within our reach by enabling us to obtain possession of the beautiful sanitarium property known as Loma Linda. This property lies sixty miles east of Los Angeles, on the main line of the Southern Pacific Railway. Its name, Loma Linda—"beautiful hill"—describes the place. Of the seventy-six acres comprised in the property, about thirty-five form a beautiful hill, which rises one hundred and twenty-five feet above the valley. Upon this hill the sanitarium building is situated.

The main building is a well-planned structure of sixty-four rooms, having three stories and a basement. It is completely furnished, heated by steam, and lighted by electricity. It is surrounded with large pepper trees and other shade trees.

About ten rods away and on the highest part of the hill there is a group of five cottages. The central cottage has nine beautiful living rooms and two bathrooms. In the basement is a heating plant for the five cottages.

Prettily grouped around this larger cottage are four smaller ones, having four rooms each, with bath and toilet. An interesting feature of three of these cottages is that each room has its veranda with broad windows running to the floor, so that the beds can be wheeled right out on the veranda, and the patients can sleep in the open air.

Between these cottages and the main building, there is a recreation

A Medical Missionary Training Center

building, which can be used as a gymnasium and for class rooms and meetings.

In all there are ninety rooms, the buildings are furnished throughout, and ready for use.

There is a post office in the main building, and most of the trains stop at the railway station, about forty rods from the sanitarium.

The seventy-six acres of hill and valley land are well cultivated and will furnish much fruit and many vegetables for the institution. Fifteen acres of the valley land are in alfalfa hay. Eight acres are in good bearing orange orchards. Many acres of land around the cottages and the main building are laid out in lawns, drives, and walks.

There are horses and carriages, cows and poultry, farming implements and wagons. The buildings and grounds are abundantly supplied with excellent water.

This property is now in our possession. It cost the company from whom we purchased it about 140,000.00. They erected the buildings and ran the place for a time as a sanitarium. Then they tried to operate it as a tourist hotel. But this plan did not succeed, and they decided to sell. It was closed last April, and as the stockholders became more anxious to sell, it was offered to us for $40,000.00 and for this amount our brethren have purchased it. —*July 1905. (pp. 179, 180 to par. 7)*

O, how I long to see the sick and suffering coming to this institution! It is one of the most perfect places for a sanitarium that I have ever seen, and I thank our heavenly Father for giving us such a place. It is provided with almost everything necessary for sanitarium work, and it is the very place in which sanitarium work can be carried forward on right lines, by faithful physicians and managers.

The buildings are all ready, and work must be begun in them as soon as we can secure the necessary physicians and nurses. I am anxious to see the work started. For some time I have been looking for just such a place as this, with good buildings, all ready for occupancy, surrounded by shade trees and orchards. When I saw Loma Linda, I said, Thank the Lord. This is the very place we have been hoping to find. —*July 1905. (p. 181, pars. 2, 3)*

The character of the buildings, the terraced hill, covered by graceful pepper trees, the profusion of flowers and shrubs, the tall shade trees, the orchards and fields—all combine to make this place meet fully the descriptions that I have given in the past, of the place presented to me as the most perfect for sanitarium work. Everything at Loma Linda is fresh and wholesome and attractive. The patients could live out of doors a large part of the time. The land will serve as a school for the education of patients. By out-door exercises and working in the soil, men and women will regain their health. Rational methods for the cure of disease will be used in a variety of ways. Drugs will be discarded. —*July 1905. (p. 182, par. 1)*

I have just enjoyed the pleasure of reading your good letters. Brother _____ from Battle Creek spent Sabbath and Sunday with us here at Loma Linda. He was astonished that such beautiful premises and such complete equipment could be purchased at so low a price as that for which we have secured this property.

We regard this place as one especially provided for us by the Lord. Some of the brethren had spoken to me of Loma Linda as a popular health resort, conducted as a hotel, but it was not considered possible that we would be able to pay so much as it was supposed they would ask. I had supposed we would be obliged to erect buildings for sanitarium work in the vicinity of the beautiful cities of Redlands and Riverside.

Last spring I asked Brother _____ to look carefully for any opening to secure property suitable for a sanitarium in this vicinity. While I was in Washington he wrote to me describing the beauty of Loma Linda, and stated the everything connected with the place was offered to us for forty thousand dollars.

When I read the description of the property as written by Brother _____, I recognized it as answering fully to an ideal sanitarium property such as had been presented to me. I received the letter on Friday afternoon, and I told W. C. White to telegraph Brother _____ immediately that he should secure the place. One of our brethren sent another telegram contrary to this. Some of the men connected with the conference thought that such a large place would be like an elephant on their hands. I was so burdened that for several nights I could not sleep. I feared lest the enemy might, through unbelief, keep this property out of our hands.

In the meanwhile Brother _____ had been obliged to tell the men that we would be unable to purchase the property. But when he received from me a letter of good cheer and hope, and an assurance that this was the place for which I had long been looking, to correspond with places such as the Lord had shown me would be offered to us at a small part of their original cost. Brother _____ in fear and trembling, returned to the agent, and told him we would purchase the place. Had he been an hour later, the opportunity might have been lost; for they were sending men to offer the property to other parties.

The main building contains four stories. In its entrance is a most beautiful sun-parlor. There is also a large parlor, carpeted with the very best body brussels. The furniture in the house is of first class quality—not fancy, but durable and very handsome. We could not have furnished the building as expensively as it has been furnished by others. In the main building the furniture cost twelve hundred dollars, and has been in use less than two years.

The long halls are carpeted with fine brussels carpet, and there are carpets and rugs for the various rooms throughout the building. There is a large roll of rubber carpet that can be used wherever it is thought best. The matresses on the beds look like new ones. There are two feather pillows, sheets, blankets, quilts, and spreads for every bed. Every room contains chairs, substantial but very comfortable.

A Medical Missionary Training Center 5

Besides the main building, in which there are about sixty rooms that can be used by patients, there are four, four-roomed cottages setting back on higher ground. Some of these are so arranged that each room is connected with a private veranda, where in warm weather a bed can be rolled from the room through the large windows. Besides the four cottages with four rooms each, there is a two-story cottage with nine beautiful rooms, and splendidly furnished. This of itself is quite a large building.

Between the cottages and the main building is what they called the amusement building. This has been used for a bowling alley and a billiard hall. The billiard tables will be sold and with a few alterations the building may be made into a good meeting-house.

There are seventy-six acres of land in this property. Quite a portion of it is set out in orchard. They raise oranges, lemons, grapefruit, peaches, apples, plums, pears, etc. I am having strawberries from the second crop and they are very nice.

Five horses, three cows, about a hundred hens and a few turkeys were purchased with the place. There were also a number of hogs, which have since been sold.

About one hundred and fifty thousand dollars has been expended in making the property what it is at present; and forty thousand dollars seems very reasonable for such complete equipment as we find here. It would be a heavy tax if we had to pay interest on such an amount, but we believe that our brethren will raise this money, and that we shall soon be free from debt. Every dollar is to be expended with great care. Something must be done to furnish treatment rooms, but this need not incur great expense.

The city of Redlands is five miles from the institution. This city is one of the most beautiful cities in America. When President Roosevelt visited Redlands about two years ago, he expressed the thought that it was as near like heaven as any place he had ever seen. The purchase of Loma Linda will help to give us an influence with the people of this city.

The more we realize of the advantages of this location, the more certain we feel that we are in the line of duty. We shall now endeavor to secure the very best help possible to conduct the work of this institution. Some of the outside stairways need to be painted, and other work must be done before we are ready to open the institution.

For a time we had to work against fearfulness and unbelief in the minds of some of our brethren. There are some who will always be found holding back when any advance move is to be made.

Last June a meeting was called at Los Angeles to consider the question of the purchasing of Loma Linda. I was very glad that Elder _____ was present. When some expressed themselves as thinking it unwise for the Conference to incur further indebtedness by such a heavy investment, Elder _____ spoke right to the point, urging them to follow the manifest leadings of God.

I also bore my testimony that the Lord would bless us if we would act by faith. There are some who seem to consider it a virtue to talk unbelief and to hold back when there should be an advance. We are hoping that there may be connected with the work in Southern California men who will act in faith.

Only a few were present at this meeting, but they expressed themselves as favoring the purchase of the property, and they pledged eleven hundred dollars as a gift to start the enterprise.

Last Sunday afternoon quite a number of our brethren from neighboring churches met on the lawn under the trees just back of the main building, and brother _____ says they had an excellent meeting. One man said he had gone to the camp-meeting in Los Angeles as an unbeliever, but had been convicted of the Sabbath truth. He seemed very happy, and made a donation of one hundred dollars to Loma Linda. We shall now endeavor to secure the necessary means so that we shall not have to carry a heavy burden of interest on borrowed money.

Let us praise the Lord that He is making it possible for us to obtain such advantages, where we can help the sick to take their minds away from themselves, and delight in the beauty of God's handiwork. —*August 29, 1905. (pp. 205-209)*

For a long time we have desired to see a work begun in Redlands. Now, in the providence of God, we have come into possession of Loma Linda. This will give us an influence in Redlands and Riverside, enabling us to find openings for the proclamation of present truth. This beautiful property was offered to us at a very low price. It is completely furnished. We have only to take possession. We trust that our people will rally to the support of this institution, that it may not be burdened with a large interest-bearing debt. —*September 9, 1905. (p. 213, par. 3)*

I write to urge you to connect with our sanitarium work at Loma Linda. In the providence of God, this property has passed into our hands. The securing of this sanitarium thoroughly equipped and furnished, is one of the most wonderful providences that the Lord has opened before us. It is difficult to comprehend all that this transaction means to us. —*September 15, 1905. (p. 219, par. 1)*

I am continually thankful to our heavenly Father that in His providence we have been favored to secure this beautiful location for a health resort. It answers perfectly to the representation that was given me,—a main building and cottages so well fitted with windows. The surroundings are very attractive. Praise the Lord for His goodness and mercy expressed to us amidst the difficulties we have to meet. —*December 10, 1905. (p. 250, par. 1 the lines underscored)*

This property came into our possession in such a way that we know the hand of the Lord was in the matter. Loma Linda is one of the most perfect places for a sanitarium that I have ever seen; and I thank our heavenly Father for giving us such a place. It is provided with

A Medical Missionary Training Center

almost everything necessary for sanitarium work, and it is the very place in which sanitarium work can be carried forward in right lines by faithful physicians and managers. —*December 19, 1905. (p. 265, par. 4)*

Sunday, April 15, 1906, the beautiful buildings and grounds at the Loma Linda Sanitarium were solemnly dedicated to the service of God. —*(p. 279, par. 1)*

The extensive view of valley and mountain is magnificent. One of the chief advantages of the institution at Loma Linda is the pleasing variety of charming scenery on every side.

But more important than magnificent scenery and beautiful buildings and spacious grounds, is the close proximity of this institution to a densely populated district, and the opportunity thus afforded of communicating to many, many people a knowledge of the third angel's message. We are to have clear spiritual discernment, else we shall fail of understanding the opening providences of God that are preparing the way for us to enlighten the world. The great crisis is just before us. Now is the time for us to sound the warning message, by the agencies that God has given us for this purpose. Let us remember that one most important agency is our medical missionary work. Never are we to lose sight of the great object for which our sanitariums are established—the advancement of God's closing work in the earth.

Loma Linda is to be not only a sanitarium, but an educational center. With the possession of this place comes the weighty responsibility of making the work of the institution educational in character. A school is to be established here for the training of gospel medical missionary evangelists.

Much is involved in this work, and it is very essential that a right beginning be made. The Lord has a special work to be done in this part of the field. —*April 15, 1906. (p. 282, pars. 1-4)*

"I thank the Lord with heart and soul and voice that He has brought Loma Linda to our notice, and that we might obtain it. I thank the Lord that He has sent you to help me carry out in a determined effort that which He designed should be a gret blessing to us. Redlands will be a center and so also will Loma Linda. A school will be established as soon as possible, and the Lord will open the way."

"I am certainly thankful to our heavenly Father that in His providence we have been favored to secure this beautiful location as a health resort. It answers perfectly to the representation that was given me. Praise the Lord for His goodness and mercy expressed to us amidst the many difficulties we have to meet. The Lord is our Helper, and constant Guide. I say to you my brother, Jesus will be to us a present helper in every time of need. In regard to the school, I would say, Make it all you possibly can in the education of nurses and physicians."

Make the school especially strong for nurses and physicians. Thousands of workers are to be qualified with all the ability of physicians, to labor not as physicians, but as medical missionary evangelists. —*November 1, 1905. (p. 283 all but first par.)*

The Lord has instructed me that it would be a mistake for us to plan for the production of a large quantity of health foods at Loma Linda, to be distributed through commercial channels. Loma Linda is a place that has been especially ordained of God to make a good impression upon the minds of many who have not had the light of present truth. Every phase of the work in this place, every movement made, should be so fully in harmony with the sacred character of present truth as to create a deep spiritual impression.

Everything connected with the institution at Loma Linda should, so far as possible, be unmingled with commercialism. Nothing should be allowed to come in that would in any wise lessen the favorable impression you are striving to make. If we manifest a genuine faith in eternal realities, this will have a far-reaching effect on the minds of others. We must allow nothing to hinder our efforts for the saving of souls. God requires us to leave impressions that will help awaken unbelievers to a realization of their duty. Let us use voice and pen in helping those who need clear discernment. —*May 6, 1906. (p. 286, pars. 2, 3)*

Be careful not to do anything that would restrict the work at Loma Linda. It is in the order of God that this property has been secured, and He has given instruction that a school should be connected with the sanitarium. A special work is to be done there in qualifying young men and women to be efficient medical missionary workers. They are to be taught how to treat the sick without the use of drugs. Such an education requires an experience in practical work.

The work at Loma Linda demands immediate consideration. Preparations must be made for the school to be opened as soon as possible. Our young men and young women are to find in Loma Linda a school where they can receive a medical missionary training, and where they will not be brought under the influence of some who are seeking to undermine the truth. —*August 19, 1906. (p. 315, pars. 3, 4)*

The students are to unite faithfully in the medical work, keeping their physical powers in the most perfect condition possible, and laboring under the instruction of the great Medical Missionary. The healing of the sick and the ministry of the Word are to go hand in hand.

There is to be a thorough education in Bible truth. The word of God is spirit and life. We need constantly to look to Jesus. The efficiency of every worker is largely determined by the education and training he receives. In our educational institutions there is to be a higher class of education than can be found elsewhere. The students are to be treated kindly, tenderly, and interestedly. —*August 19, 1906. (p. 316, par. 1)*

In the carrying forward of the educational work at Loma Linda, our brethren must constantly guard against the efforts of the enemy to bring in a spirit of criticism and alienation between brethren. —*August 19, 1906. (p. 317, par. 1)*

A Medical Missionary Training Center

A sanitarium has been established at Loma Linda, and this is in the providence of God. Some know how difficult it has been to accomplish the work that has been done. But the work at Loma Linda is not yet perfected. More money must be raised in order to make this place a center for the training of medical missionary evangelists. —*August 19, 1906. (p. 318, par. 1)*

Brethren _____ and _____, the work of the school and the sanitarium will be a blessing, the one to the other. Each must act its individual part, but both must blend together; then the interests of both will be advanced. If there is cooperation between the educational work and the work of the sanitarium, we can heartily recommend that the higher education be carried on in the sanitarium grounds for this is the Lord's plan. If the men at the head of this enterprise plan for the usefulness of these institutions, each helping the other, there is nothing to hinder the operations of the school. As the work grows, buildings may have to be prepared. —*September 14, 1906. (p. 322, par. 2)*

Loma Linda is to be not only a sanitarium but an educational center. With the possession of this place comes the mighty responsibility of making the work of the institution educational in character. The school that is to be established at Loma Linda is to stand in the freedom of the truth. —*May 6, 1906. (p. 290, par. 3)*

There is a large work to be done. Sanitariums are to be carried on in many lands. When facilities are added to sanitariums that have been set in operation, let the additions be most thoroughly and firmly constructed; but there should be no large expenditure of means to secure every advantage at the beginning. While at Loma Linda it is necessary to add some treatment rooms and other rooms, yet I would counsel you not to add anything that would greatly increase the labor and expense of operating the institution. Build no more than is positively necessary. —*May 6, 1906. (p. 294, pars. 3, 4)*

For forty thousand dollars our brethren secured at Loma Linda, buildings and land that cost originally one hundred and fifty thousand dollars. These buildings were furnished completely, far more elegantly than we would have furnished them.

The Lord has worked wonderfully in bringing us into possession of this place. Here is a center from which light is to shine into the surrounding cities of Redlands, Riverside, San Bernardino, Colton and other places nearby.

It has been found necessary to provide additional bathroom facilities at Loma Linda, and to make some changes greatly needed; and a small bakery should be added. We are in need of means to accomplish that which must be done, and we pray the Lord to put it into the heart of our brethren and sisters to help in this time of necessity. —*May 19, 1907. (p. 355, pars. 3-5)*

For years the Lord has instructed us that we should have a sanitarium in the vicinity of San Diego, where many thousands of tourists come every year. A valuable property was procured at National City at a very small part of its original cost. There an important work is to be done in caring for the sick, and in reaching many with the light of truth. At the Paradise Valley Sanitarium also it was found necessary to add to the original building, and obligations have been made that must soon be met. The Lord has blessed this institution, and some have been converted to the truth as the result of the work already done.

At Glendale, a few miles from Los Angeles, we purchased a sanitarium at about one fourth its real value. This institution is at the present time full of patients. It is well equipped for work, and is in a position of influence. Its need is not so pressing as that of the sanitariums at Loma Linda and National City.

The establishment of these three institutions has brought a heavy financial burden to our people in Southern California. Yet they have cheerfully responded to the calls for means that have been made. Brother _____, Dr. _____ and others connected with these sanitariums have invested all they could spare, that the work might not be hindered.

We have none too many sanitariums. There is need for every one that has been established. In these institutions we are endeavoring to carry the work earnestly and solidly in harmony with the instruction the Lord has given in regard to sanitarium work. They are to stand as a means of teaching the truth in these great centers of tourist resort. —*May 19, 1907. (p. 356, pars. 1-4)*

At out request, Brother _____ is going East to attend some of our camp-meetings, where he may come in contact with many of our brethren and sisters, and lay before them the opportunities for assisting these important branches of the Lord's work. We unite in asking those who have means to spare, to consider the matter of investing some of their money in these institutions; thus helping to provide necessary facilities, that a thorough work may be done in caring for the sick who are coming to Southern California to search for health.

May the Lord give ability to help and a willing mind. —*May 19, 1907. (p. 357, par. 1)*

The Lord wants His people in these days to believe that He will do as great things for them as He did for the children of Israel in their journey from Egypt to Canaan. We are to have an educated faith that will not hesitate to follow His instructions in the most difficult experiences. "Go forward," is the command of God to His people.

Faith and cheerful obedience are needed to bring the Lord's designs to pass. When He points out the necessity of establishing the work in the places where it will have influence, the people are to walk and work by faith. By their godly conversation, their humility, their prayers and earnest efforts, they should strive to bring the people to appreciate the good work that the Lord has established among them. It was the Lord's purpose that the Loma Linda Sanitarium should become the property of our people, and He brought it about at a time when the rivers of difficulty were full and overflowing their banks.

A Medical Missionary Training Center

The working of private interests for the gaining of personal ends is one thing. In this men may follow their own judgment. But the carrying forward of the Lord's work in the earth is entirely another matter. When He designates that a certain property should be secured for the advancement of His cause and the building up of His work, whether it be for sanitarium or school work, or for any other branch, He will make the doing of that work possible, if those who have experience will show their faith and trust in His purposes, and will move forward promptly to secure the advantages He points out. While we are not to seek to wrest property from any man, yet when advantages are offered, we should be wide awake to see the advantage, that we may make plans for the building of the work. And when we have done this, we should exert every energy to secure the free-will offerings of God's people for the support of these new plants. —*September 19, 1907. (p. 479, pars. 1-3)*

I am bidden to say to the sanitarium family, let your social meetings, and all your religious exercises be characterized by a deep earnestness and a joy that expresses the love of God in the soul. Such meetings will be profitable to all; for they will bind heart to heart. Let there be earnest seasons of prayer; for prayer will give strength to the religious experience. Confess Christ openly and bravely, and manifest at all times the meekness of Christ.

The Lord would have the family of workers at Loma Linda channels of light. If we will keep the heart and mind opened heavenward, cherishing the comfort of His grace in the heart, the presence of Christ will be revealed. Let earnestness and zeal come into your lives. Make no backward movements. The Lord is our Helper, our Guide, our Shield, our exceeding great reward. Do not allow levity to come into your experience, but cultivate cheerfulness; for this is an excellent grace. We cannot afford to be unmindful of our words and deportment. —*August 29, 1907. (p. 432, pars. 2, 3)*

Here (at Loma Linda) we have ideal advantages for a school and for a sanitarium. Here are advantages for the patients. I have been instructed that here we should have a school, conducted on the principles of the ancient schools of the prophets. It may not be carried on, in every respect, as are the schools of the world, but it is to be especially adapted for those who desire to devote their lives, not to commercial pursuits, but to unselfish service for the Master.

We want a school of the highest order—a school where the Word of God will be regarded as essential, and where obedience to its teachings will be taught. For the carrying forward of such a school, we must have carefully selected educators. Our young people are not to be wholly dependent on the schools where they are told, "If you wish to complete our course of instruction, you must take this study, or some other study,"—studies that perhaps would be of no practical benefit to those whose only desire is to give to the world God's message of health and peace. In the education that many receive there are not only subjects that are non-essential, but much that is decidedly objectionable. We should endeavor to give instruction that will prepare students quickly for service to their fellow men. —*October 30, 1907. (p. 535, pars. 1, 2)*

Physicians are to receive their education here. Here they are to receive such a mould that when they go out to labor, they will not seek to grasp the very highest wages, or else do nothing. —*October 30, 1907. (p. 536, par. 2)*

I feel a deep interest that careful study shall be given to the needs of our institutions at Loma Linda, and that the right moves may be made. In the carrying forward of the work ot this place, men of talent and of decided spirituality are needed.

We may, in the work of educating our nurses, reach a high standard in the knowledge of the true science of healing. That which is of most importance is that the students be taught how to truly represent the principles of health reform. Teach the students to pursue this line of study faithfully, combined with other essential lines of education. The grace of Jesus Christ will give wisdom to all who will follow the Lord's plan of true education.

Let the students follow closely the example of the One who purchased the human race with the costly price of His own life. Let them appeal to the Saviour, and depend upon Him as the One who heals all manner of diseases. The Lord would have the workers make special efforts to point the sick and suffering to the great Physician who made the human body. He would have all become obedient children to the faith, that they may come with confidence and ask for bodily restoration. Many who come to our sanitariums will be blessed as they learn the truth concerning the Word of God, many who would never learn it through any other medium. —*November 3, 1907. (p. 557, pars. 1-3)*

For more than a year the light has been coming to me that here at Loma Linda we should have a school of the highest order, and that the very best talent should be obtained, in order to prepare young men and young women for medical missionary work. This work we are desirous of seeing accomplished. It should not be necessary for students to be placed under the influence of teachers who do not obey the law of God. —*November 3, 1907. (p. 562, par. 1)*

In Loma Linda we have an advantageous center for the carrying on of various missionary enterprises. We can see that it was in the providence of God that this sanitarium was placed in the possession of our people. We should appreciate Loma Linda as a place which the Lord foresaw we should need, and which He gave. —*December 1907. (p. 579, par. 4)*

I am instructed to say to you, "Let every soul earnestly seek the Lord." We all need to understand clearly what is our duty, that we may make no false moves. We need to hold fast the experiences which in the past the Lord has given us. I have a great desire to see success attend every movement we shall make.

There is a very precious work to be done in connection with the interests of the sanitarium and school at Loma Linda; and this will be done when we all work to that end. The Word of God is to be our

A Medical Missionary Training Center

lesson book. In the unity that is coming in among our people we can see that God is working in our midst.

"Therefore be ye not unwise, but understanding what the will of the Lord is." Let us walk and work circumspectly. Let humble prayers go up to God, and let us seek Him with the whole heart. Then the Lord will open the way for us to lay wise plans. My brethren, speak to yourselves in psalms, and hymns, and spiritual songs, "singing and making melody in your hearts to the Lord, giving thanks always for all things unto the Lord."

Ever bear in mind that heaven is interested in every question that agitates your mind in regard to your school and sanitarium. Both are to be strengthened. The Lord is our helper and our God; let us look to Him to open the way for carrying out of our plans.

We must have a church at Loma Linda, that those in the sanitarium and school may have a suitable place in which to meet for worship; but this should not be an expensive building. We shall build a neat, modest, but roomy chapel, that will show that we believe we are living in the closing days of this earth's history, in a time when many of the cities because of their sins will be cast down and their lofty buildings destroyed.

In our school at Loma Linda many can be educated to work as missionaries in the cause of Health and Temperance. The best teachers are to be employed in this educational work, not men who esteem highly their own capabilities, but men who will walk circumspectly, depending wholly upon the Lord.

Small cottages will have to be built at little cost to accommodate the teachers and students; for these are to gain all the advantage possible from the lectures given at the Sanitarium. This work should go forward as fast as means for it can be obtained.

If the teachers in medical lines will stand in their lot and place, we shall see a good work done. My soul is drawn out in earnest prayer to God that He will preserve the honest in heart from being led astray by those who are themselves in confusion and darkness.

Teachers are to be prepared for many lines of work. Schools are to be established in places where no efforts have been made. Missionaries are needed to go to other states where little work has been done. Truth, Bible truth, is to be presented in many places. Christ is represented as identifying Himself with all the needy upon earth when He said, "Inasmuch as ye have done it unto one of the least of these, My brethren, ye have done it unto Me."

All should put forth efforts to enlarge their experience. We are in a most critical situation; but Christ identifies Himself with our necessities. Christians are to learn daily of Christ. Spiritual sinew and muscle are now needed to work out right principles in every city and town and village. Varied talents are to be appreciated and cultivated, and with all we need true wisdom. We may not see our need of counseling with God; but the true Christian in every place will inquire what is the will of the Lord concerning his individual work.

All heaven is interested in the work of preparation to be done in our schools. Let the talent that is among us be combined wisely for the accomplishment of the greatest good. "Ye are God's husbandry; ye are God's building." Then link up the powers that God has given for the doing of the special work He designs to have done. If self is kept humble, the transforming grace of Christ and His wisdom will blend heart to heart. Let us make our gifts and offerings with a single heart. Let us draw upon our talents, remembering that for this purpose they were given. To every man God has given his work; and He would have this work done intelligently. The Lord will make it possible for each to do a work that can be accepted by Him.

The Lord expects all, by acts of self-denial, to help in the upbuilding of His work. In the house of worship to be erected and the additional schoolrooms that will be needed, let all be willing to do their best, willing to deny themselves the unnecessary expenditures for display, that they may have means to give to the cause of God. The work of promulgating the principles of health reform, which the Lord has outlined to us, must be accomplished. When we study the self-denial of Christ, and make His life our example, truth and righteousness will prevail among us. We will esteem as of highest value the ornament of a meek and quiet spirit, which is in the sight of God of great price. —*April 28, 1908. (pp. 673-675)*

Loma Linda has been specified to me as a very important place, and one which demands the best Bible teacher we can supply. There are promising youth here who are to be qualified to fill important positions in the work. They should have the best class of instructors, and capable Bible teachers who understand the truths of the Word. The truth and righteousness revealed in the Word of God is to be the stronghold of our workers.

There has been given me an outline of the work that must be done at Loma Linda, and I know that we must give to that place our best labors. The Lord wants the wisest talent there, for by means of our very best educational talent we are to train our ministerial laborers. The work is to be carried after the Lord's order, and not according to the suppositions of man. —*June 20, 1908. (p. 695, pars. 3, 4)*

We hope that in the school established at Loma Linda many will be qualified to go forth and impart the knowledge of truth they have here received. A quick work will the Lord do in our world, for Satan is preparing his forces to seek to overcome the remnant people who love God and keep His commandments. He points to the smallness of their numbers, and flatters his followers that his larger army can outnumber the believers. We know how powerful are the hosts of Satan; but God is more powerful than they. Our risen Saviour is all-sufficient for our needs. —*April 12, 1909. (p. 721, par. 2)*

"Loma Linda is to be not only a sanitarium, but an *educational center*. With the possession of this place comes the weighty responsibility of making the work of the institution, educational in character. A school is to be established here for the training of gospel,

A Medical Missionary Training Center

medical missionary, evangelists." "In regard to the school I would say, Make it all you possibly can in the education of nurses and physicians." "Thousands of workers are to be qualified with all the ability of physicians, to labor, not as physicians, but as medical missionary evangelists." —*October 1903. (p. 733, par. 3)*

"There is a very precious work to be done in connection with the interests of the sanitarium and school at Loma Linda, and this will be done when all work to that end... Ever bear in mind that heaven is interested in every question that agitates your mind in regard to your school and sanitarium. Both are to be strengthened.... In our school at Loma Linda many can be educated to work as missionaries in the cause of Health and Temperance. The best teachers are to be employed in this educational work. Not men who esteem highly their own capabilities, but men who will walk circumspectly, depending wholly upon the Lord." —*April 23, 1908. (p. 735, par. 2)*

I feel a decided interest in the work at Loma Linda, and I desire that it shall exert a powerful influence for the truth. Your success depends upon the blessing of God, not upon the views of men who are opposed to the law of God. When they see that God blesses us, then people will be led to give consideration to the truths we teach. —*September 20, 1909. (p. 755, par. 2)*

You have the Word which tells you that God's commandment-keeping people are to have His special favor, and that they are to be sanctified through obedience to the truth. Shall we unite ourselves with those that are full of error, who have no respect for God's commandments, and shall our students go forth to obtain the finishing touches of their education from them?

Whatever plan you follow, take your position that you will not unite with those that do not respect God's commandments.

We shall have a school of our own. But we are not to be dependent upon the world; we must place our dependence upon a power that is higher than all human power. If we honor God, He will honor us. —*September 20, 1909. (p. 756, pars. 2, 4, 6)*

_____: "The governments of earth provide that if we conduct a medical school, we must take a charter from the government. That in itself has nothing to do with how the school is conducted. It is required, however, that certain studies shall be taught. There are ten required subjects. Physiology is one. It is required that those who labor as physicians shall be proficient in these studies. In starting our sanitariums for the care of the sick, we must secure a charter from the government; our printing office must do the same. Would the securing of a charter for a medical school, where our students might obtain an education, militate against our dependence upon God?"

E. G. White: No, I do not see that it would. Only see that you do not consult men above God. If you can gain force and influence that will make your work more effective without tying yourselves to worldly men, that would be right.

_____: "That is the vital point, where we have been hanging for three years. The only thing that we have asked for in this matter is to take advantage of the government provision that would give standing room for our students when they are qualified."

E. G. White: I do not see anything wrong in that, as long as you do not in any way lift men above the Lord God of Israel, or throw discredit upon His power.

_____: "In planning our course of study, we have tried to follow the light in the Testimonies, and in doing so it has led us away from the requirements of the world. The world will not recognize us as standing with them. We will have to stand distinct, by ourselves."

E. G. White: We shall always have to stand distinct. God desires us to be separate.

_____: "It has seemed to me from the very first, that we were to stand by ourselves in a distinct light, following the light that God has given with reference to physical healing; and that when we do that, God will open the way before us, and give us prestige with the people. But if we deviate and connect with these other schools, we would find ourselves being thrown more and more into the very things that they are doing, and our students would be molded after their similitude instead of after the similitude of the truth."

E. G. White: That is what I am trying to guard against all the time. As we read the Bible we see that God is dishonored when His people go to any worldly power, or put their trust in a worldly power. That is where God's people spoiled their history. You must arrange the matter the best you can, but that which is presented to me is that you are not to acknowledge any power as above that of our God. Our influence is to be acknowledged of God, because we keep His commandments, and His commandments are not grievous.

_____: "Jesus said at one time, 'The scribes and Pharisees sit in Moses' seat: all therefore whatsoever they bid you observe, that observe and do; but do not ye after their works.' Now the law says that a man shall not practice medicine unless he has a diploma from a college, and unless he has passed the examination of the state board, and has a certificate. The law would not recognize the diplomas of our physicians unless they have studied some things that we do not think are really essential. For instance, in their preparation they have to study a number of things that we think they might get along without; but we can teach them. We do not have to teach these subjects in their way; we can teach them in our way. When it comes to the study of drugs, they teach how to give them. We teach the dangers of using them, and how to get along without them. In some other schools they teach geology on the evolution basis. We can teach geology and show that evolution is false."

E. G. White: Well, you must plan these details yourselves. I have told you what I have received, but these details you will have to work out for yourselves.

A Medical Missionary Training Center

_____: "It seems clear to me that any standing we can lawfully have without compromising, is not out of harmony with God's plan."

E. G. White: No, it is not. All I can say is that I have had very distinct light, however, that there is danger of our limiting the power of the Holy One of Israel. He is the God of the universe. Our influence is dependent upon our carrying out the Word of the living God. We weaken our powers by not placing our dependence upon God, and taking hold of His strength. This is our privilege. —*September 1909. (pp. 757-759, pars. 1-3)*

And not only should our larger training schools give this preparatory instruction to those who contemplate taking a medical course, but we must also do all that is essential for the perfecting of the courses of study offered by our Loma Linda College of Medical Evangelists as pointed out about the time this school was founded. —*October 1, 1909. (p. 765 part of par. 2)*

The representation of the great Teacher is to be considered an all-sufficient revelation. Those in our ranks who qualify as physicians are to receive only such education as is in harmony with these divine truths. Some have advised that students should, after taking some work at Loma Linda, complete their medical education in worldly colleges. But this is not in harmony with the Lord's plan. God is our wisdom, our sanctification, and our righteousness. Facilities should be provided at Loma Linda, that the necessary instruction in medical lines may be given by instructors who fear the Lord, and who are in harmony with His plans for the treatment of the sick.

I have not a word to say in favor of the world's ideas of higher education in any school that we shall organize for the training of physicians. There is danger in their attaching themselves to worldly institutions, and working under the ministrations of worldly physicians. Satan is giving his orders to those whom he has led to depart from the faith. I would now advise that none of our young people attach themselves to worldly medical institutions in the hope of gaining better success, or stronger influence as physicians. —*October 11, 1909. (p. 789, pars. 1, 2)*

The light given me is, we must provide that which is essential to qualify our youth who desire to be physicians, so that they may intelligently fit themselves to be able to stand the examinations required to prove their efficiency as physicians. They should be taught to treat understandingly the cases of those who are diseased, so that the door will be closed for any sensible physician to imagine that we are not giving in our school the instruction necessary for properly qualifying young men and young women to do the work of a physician. Continually the students who are graduated are to advance in knowledge, for practice makes perfect. —*January 1910. (p. 847, par. 1)*

The medical school at Loma Linda is to be of the highest order; because those who are in that school have the privilege of maintaining a living connection with the wisest of all physicians, from Whom there is communicated knowledge of a superior order. And for the special preparation of those of our youth who have clear convictions of their duty to obtain a medical education that will enable them to pass the examinations required by law of all who practice as regularly qualified physicians, we are to supply whatever may be required, so that these youth need not be compelled to go to medical schools conducted by men not of our faith. Thus we shall close a door that the enemy would be pleased to have left open; and our young men and young women, whose spiritual interests the Lord desires us to safeguard, will not feel compelled to connect with unbelievers in order to obtain a thorough training along medical lines. —*January 1910. (p. 848, par. 1)*

It is the favorable situation of the property, that makes Loma Linda an ideal place for the recovery of the sick and for the warning of many who might otherwise never hear the truth for this time. It is God's plan that Loma Linda shall be not only a sanitarium, but a special center for the training of gospel medical missionary evangelists. —*January 27, 1910. (p. 854, par. 3)*

Are you prepared for it? Are you preparing? Are you preparing to give an account of yourself before you shall go to rest in the night season? Have you called to mind what you can do to glorify God? Now here is this institution and we are glad we have it. It is just what we wanted and now we want to act our individual part in it, every one of us. We believe in Jesus Christ that He is our Saviour and that He will bear our sins; and we want to glorify His name. But many who are coming into position just as soon as they consider that they are looked upon as those who can help—they grow into such large proportions that they cannot handle themselves nor anybody else. We want to be humble workers for Jehovah. We have to face the future of this work; we have to face it. We want those who come to this institution to obtain just as much blessing as they possibly can obtain. We want them to receive instruction and light and physical health and understanding; so that when they return to their homes they can treat their own families and their own sick, and no doubt many consider this a great advantage. —*April 5, 1910. (p. 889, par. 3)*

At Loma Linda, at Washington, at Wahroonga, Australia, and in many other sanitariums established for the promulgation of the work of the third angel's message there are to come to the physicians and to the teachers new ideas, a new understanding of the principles that must govern the medical work. An education is to be given that is altogether in harmony with the teachings of the Word of God. —*April 27, 1910. (p. 901, par. 2)*

"With the possession of this place comes the weighty responsibility of making the work of the institution educational in character. Loma Linda is to be not only a sanitarium, but an educational center. A school is to be established here for the training of gospel medical missionary evangelists. Much is involved in this work, and it is very essential that a right beginning be made."

"Some of the students are to be educated as physicians. It is not necessary for our students to go to Ann Arbor for a medical education. They may obtain at our schools all that is essential to perform the work for this time." —*June 1905. (p. 904, pars. 3, 4)*

Today with Sister _____, and again with my son, I rode around the Loma Linda grounds, and took more particular notice of them than ever before; and I feel very thankful that we have such a place. Surely we ought to be a grateful people because God has brought us into possession of this beautiful place.

In our meetings during this council, we have been speaking of the higher education. What is the higher education? It is to understand Christ's words and teachings, and to follow on to know the Lord. It is to know that His going forth is prepared as the morning.

Today, as I looked over the place more thoroughly than ever before, and saw the grounds, the drives, and the cottages that were standing before we came here, I felt gratitude in my heart toward God, that through His providence we had been brought into possession of Loma Linda. I felt thankful also to see the improvements that have been made since we have had the place, and I thought how important it is that we make every move in accordance with the will of God. —*April 20, 1911. (p. 929, pars. 1, 2)*

The Lord is well pleased with what you have already done here at Loma Linda. When one sees the prosperity that has attended the work, and the spirit of consecration that prevails, the conviction deepens that you are working in harmony with God.

I desire that all the work of this place shall be a correct representation of what our health institutions should be. Let everything that we lay our hands to, show the result of the moving of the Spirit of God upon the human heart. This will be evidence that we have the higher education. Workers whose hearts are in obedience to the movings of the Spirit of God will make this place what God desires it to be. I am surprised, happily surprised, to see everything looking so well. It is beyond my expectations. And now let every one strive to keep it so, and labor for improvements. —*April 20, 1911. (p. 931, pars. 2, 3)*

The proper development of the work at Loma Linda calls for prayerful thought and planning, that the instruction which the Lord has given concerning the work there may be fulfilled. Our people in the Eastern and Middle States, as well as those on the Pacific Coast, should feel an intense interest that a special work be done at Loma Linda at the present time. It fills me with anxiety to think that any who seek to obtain the benefits of the education that Loma Linda can give, should be turned away because the buildings are insufficient to give them a place. That some patients have had to be turned away from the sanitarium has caused me sorrow. The work of the Medical College at Loma Linda must not be crippled for lack of room. There must be some way devised to enlarge quickly the buildings for the rooming of students, so that those who seek a training may not be turned away.

The students at Loma Linda are seeking for an education that is after the Lord's order, an education that will help them to develop into successful teachers and laborers for others. When their education there is completed, they should be able to go forth and join the intelligent workers in the world's great harvest fields who are carrying forward the work of reform that is to prepare a people to stand in the day of Christ's coming. Everywhere workers are needed who know how to combat disease and give skillful care to the sick and suffering. We should do all in our power to enable those who desire to be thus fitted for service, to gain the necessary training. I am instructed that those among us who have means should become God's agencies in this work. —*August 29, 1911. (p. 959, pars. 1, 2)*

Whenever I look at the buildings, the fields, and the orchards here at Loma Linda, I am thankful that we have this beautiful place, thankful for every foot of land that we control. By and by you will see, if you do not understand it now, that the securing of the land was essential. It may not appear to you now that it was necessary for us to secure so large a tract, but I am instructed that our work here must be carried forward on broad lines and in solid unity. That the will of the Lord may be done in this place, we must be in a position where we can understand His pleasure in regard to our words and actions, where we may be always helping forward that work which is most essential. During the night it was again impressed upon my mind that it was through the providence of God we obtained this place when we did. Also that the branching out and enlargement that we have done, and the development of the work as it stands today, is what the Lord would have us do. —*May 28, 1912. (p. 990, par. 2)*

The work to be carried on here at Loma Linda is a great work. To carry it forward successfully every one of us must stand in right relation to God, all striving to be learners in the school of Christ. We are not to stand in the position of persons looking for some opportunity to differ from one another. We are not to cherish differences of opinion and keep them to the front; but we are to seek to be of one mind, one heart, one spirit; because there is One who stands at our head, and it is His character that we are to represent in our labors and association together. —*March 28, 1912. (p. 992, par. 1)*

Let us all strive to make of Loma Linda just what God means it should be. This is the principle thing I have to say—Make of this place what God would have you make of it. Every one of you is under bounded duty to God to labor in harmony, and to press the battle to the gate. If unbelievers come in and talk of their doubts and fears, remember that Satan is not dead. He has agencies through whom he works; but shall we become discouraged because of this? Oh, no! Christ, our Saviour, lives and reigns. Let us not look on the dark side. As soon as we yield to the temptation to do this, we shall have plenty of company. But there is nothing to be gained by looking on the dark side. What we want is courage in the Lord. And we

A Medical Missionary Training Center

want to follow on to know the Lord, that we may know that His going forth is prepared as the morning. This is not going back into darkness. You know how the morning is prepared. If you follow on to know the Lord every day, you will increase in brightness, in courage, in faith, and the Lord Jesus will be to you a present help in every time of need. —*November 9, 1912. (p. 1015, par. 2)*

We received your letter today. I wish to say that I cannot ask the Conference to invest in a sanitarium in Redlands. They have enough responsibilities to carry without taking upon them others. If you in Los Angeles will do your best, we will do our best. If you will do nothing, say so, and we will do nothing. If you will work intelligently, as we know you can, then we will do what we can. But if you do nothing, waiting for the Conference, you will lose your chances. If you are going to depend on the Conference purchasing it, I have no hope of your obtaining it.

Can you give us definite terms of payment? Then we shall know what to tell the people. I am anxious to secure the place for a sanitarium; but if you cannot state anything definite as to the terms of payment, we are left without any certain information. —*May 24, 1905. (p. 154, pars. 1, 2)*

"Loma Linda is to be not only a sanitarium but an educational center. A school is to be established here for the training of Gospel Medical Missionary Evangelists. With the possession of this place comes the weighty responsibility of making the work of the institution educational in character. In regard to the school I would say, Make it especially strong in the education of nurses and physicians." —*August 1909. (p. 747, par. 3)*

Work for Southern California

I have always felt a deep interest in the work in Southern California. For more than twenty years this part of the State has been represented to me as an important field. Our people should be ready to meet those who come and go, and speak to them the words of life. They should scatter the publications containing present truth. The Lord will do great things for those who co-operate with Him. —*September 9, 1905. (p. 214, par. 4)*

God sees our dangers, and knows the weight of our burdens. He remembers that we are in need of His strength, and those who make Him their trust will be enabled to resist every temptation. We shall have enemies who will plot against us because they know not the value that God places on those whom He has chosen. But the Lord God knoweth them that are His. However misrepresented and misjudged these may be, if they walk humbly before Him, He will give them help in time of need. They may be compassed with discouragements; but He who knows what is the mind of the Spirit, knows all who love Him, and will honor them. —*(p. 239, par. 4)*

In the work in Southern California, we need men of earnest determined faith, and unshaken courage in the Lord. Our time to work is short, and we are to labor with unflagging zeal. I earnestly hope that you will decide to come to our assistance. Please consider this matter carefully, because we need your help. —*H. 245, 1905. (p. 240, par. 1)*

By unmistakable representations, the Lord has given evidence that a great work is to be done in Southern California. —*1905. (p. 241, par. 2)*

If you see your way clear to labor a portion of this winter in Southern California, I think I could be with you and I will help you all I can to open up the work. If you will gather about you a group of workers and do, for a time in Southern California, a work similar to that which you have done in New York and Nashville, praying and working and doing the will of the Lord, God will not fail to show Himself your Helper, for you will be following where He has marked out the way.

I do not propose that you divorce yourself permanently from the work in the cities of the Southern States; but I ask you to come and help us start the work of training true medical missionaries in this very fruitful field, Southern California. —*1905. (p. 248, pars. 4, 5)*

For years we have wrestled to see the work of God advanced in Southern California. At one time we found such narrow, prescribed plans that the work could not move forward. Then when an effort was made to advance, it resulted in large outlay, and in extravagant plans that were altogether out of order. Then followed a pressure for money, and the work was held back. —*1906. (p. 317, par. 4)*

The Lord has given me a message for the laborers in the Southern California Conferences. The Lord Jesus wants us to believe that He

Work for Southern California

is our Wisdom, and Sanctification, and Redemption. Influences are appearing among us that are decidedly opposed to the healthy development of the work which the Lord would have carried in straight lines. —*August 15, 1907. (p. 387, par. 1)*

A message has been given me for our people in Southern California. God bids you, "Arise and shine." Now, just now, let every believing soul study to comprehend the words of Christ, "Ye are the light of the world." It is no time now to become weakened and discouraged. This is a time for every soul to humble his heart before God in confession of mistakes and sins, and to wait upon the Lord that his spiritual strength may be renewed.

Day by day God's faithful, commandment-keeping people are to become better prepared to let their light shine forth amid the moral darkness of a world that is rapidly filling up its cup of apostasy, and becoming as it was in the days of Noah. Knowing the times, we are to set in operation every agency that can be employed in doing missionary work for Christ. The great aim of those who profess to believe the third angel's message, should be to bring all their powers into active service in the cause of God.

Not all are called to engage in the same line of labor, but to every man and woman who enters the service of Christ, are given responsibilities to bear, and a special work to do. My brethren and sisters, Christ sends you this message, "Search the scriptures; for in them ye think ye have eternal life; and they are they which testify of Me." Humble your hearts before God, and seek counsel of Him who never makes a mistake. Under His guidance you will never go astray. You need to seek as you have never sought before for an understanding of the word of God. Pray that the Lord will open your understanding, and turn your whole heart to the One who has bought you with an infinite price. You are Christ's purchased possession. Ask Him to tell you what He would have you do.

Letters come to me from near and from far, asking for definite instruction in regard to individual duty. I gladly refer these inquirers to the words of Christ, spoken just before His ascension to heaven, "And Jesus came and spake unto them, saying, All power is given unto Me in heaven and in earth. Go ye therefore, and teach all nations, baptizing them in the name of the Father, and of the Son, and of the Holy Ghost: teaching them to observe all things whatsoever I have commanded you: and, lo, I am with you alway, even unto the end of the world."

Before leaving them, the Saviour outlined to His disciples the work in which they were to engage. They did not yet fully comprehend the mission to which, as followers of Christ, they had given themselves. "Then opened He their understanding, that they might understand the Scriptures, and said unto them, Thus it is written, and thus it behooved Christ to suffer, and to rise from the dead the third day; and that repentance and remission of sins should be preached in His name among all nations, beginning at Jerusalem. And ye are witnesses of these things. And, behold, I send the promise of My Father upon you: but tarry ye in the city of Jerusalem, until ye be endued with power from on high."

As the Lord's missionaries, a great work was before the disciples; but they were to be witnesses for Christ first in Jerusalem where His enemies thought to extinguish the torch of truth that had been lighted. In their cruel murder of the Saviour, and by the false reports they had circulated regarding His resurrection, they thought to remove all witness to the truth. But these falsehoods were to be met by the positive testimony of the disciples. They had talked with Christ after His resurrection; they had been eye-witnesses of His ascension.

The enemies of Christ had supposed that the disciples would be intimidated by the events that had taken place, and would give up their faith in the Messiah. They were astonished when they saw with what boldness these humble followers took up the work where Christ had laid it down. Multitudes from many parts of the world were gathered at Jerusalem at the time of the crucifixion of Christ, and these had heard the false reports regarding the Messiah. Before these multitudes the disciples, with the power of the Holy Spirit resting upon them, bore witness to the truth of the words of Christ, "I am the Resurrection and the Life." The gospel message heard by these representatives of other nations, was carried by them to their homes; the scenes they had witnessed at the crucifixion of Christ and on the day of Pentecost were related; and the message of repentance and remission of sins preached in Christ's name, was carried to many places.

In the words of the Saviour, "Go ye therefore, and teach all nations," the work of the followers of Christ in every age was outlined. There is a promise for us in His assurance, "All power is given unto Me in heaven and in earth." Brethren, shall we not take up our work, not seeking to carry burdens which the Lord has not committed to us, but doing that to which we are called, with a spirit of thoroughness, earnestness, and willingness? If we do our work faithfully, the Lord will complete His part of the contract, fulfilling the promise of His presence, "Lo, I am with you alway, even unto the end of the world." Let us not allow our faith to waver, but putting our dependence in God, let us teach all things whatsoever He has commanded. Day by day we need to receive divine instruction. I pray that every laborer may ask, and believe, and receive, the promise, "Lo, I am with you alway."

O, how much less we are doing as a people than we should be doing! Even those in responsible positions do not realize their privileges and duties. And how weak seem my words, how inadequate to set before God's people what He requires of them. I am distressed as I see the work developing, and note how difficult it is to support the agencies appointed for the diffusion of the light of the gospel. The Lord demands more of His people than they are doing.

The invitation is given to all, "Come unto Me, all ye that labor and are heavy laden, and I will give you rest. Take My yoke upon you, and learn of Me; for I am meek and lowly in heart: and ye shall find rest unto your souls. For My yoke is easy and My burden is light."

Work for Southern California

Those who have a part in the work and cause of God should be careful that they strike no discordant notes. There are some who have been laboring in the Southern California Conference who need to lay off the armor for a while until they learn Christ's method of working. They need to be converted, for they give the impression to others that they consider all the other workers out of harmony with them. Thus the seeds of dissension and strife are sown. When these workers take upon them the yoke of Christ, and learn of Him Who is meek and lowly in heart, they will return to God in acceptable service the talents He has lent them, and in doing this they will find rest unto their souls. They will hunger and thirst after righteousness, and their desire will be satisfied in a new and living experience. They will become daily students of the Word of God; and guided by the light shining from that Word, they will follow on to know the Lord, whose going forth is prepared as the morning.

No worker is to consider it his duty to administer reproof, to point out existing evils, and stop with this. Such work does not accomplish any good, but only disheartens and discourages. Plain, sensible, intelligent discourses should be preached to the churches, that will show the need of seeking the Lord in prayer, and of opening the heart to the Light of life, and that will lead church members to engage in humble work for God. To every man God has given a work; to each worker who engages in service for Him, He gives a part to act in communicating light and truth.

The appointed leaders of our churches need themselves to seek the Lord with humble, broken hearts; then they will discern their own defects of character. They need to present their cases before the Lord, asking, What shall I do that I may comprehend my individual duty? What shall I do that I may meet the mind and will of God? And when you have asked this question, my brethren, do not yield the point until you have surrendered soul, body, and spirit to God. Then God can stamp His image on your soul.

God placed His church in the earth that it might be the light of the world. But the self-indulgent course of many church members, and the rising up of self to take the lines of control, have resulted in diffusing darkness rather than light. God's professing people need to seek Him in sincere sorrow of heart, because there is so little life in the church, so little effort put forth to let the light shine in good works. "We are laborers together with God," the apostle Paul declares: "Ye are God's husbandry; ye are God's building." God designs that life-giving beams shall, through the individual members of the church, shine forth to the world. Receiving that light from the Source of all light, they are to reflect that light to others. But this can be done only as the church draws near to God and lives in close connection with the Giver of life and light. The purity and simplicity of Christ, revealed in the lives of His humble followers will witness to the possession of genuine piety. The believer who is imbued with a true missionary spirit, will be a living epistle, known and read of all men. He is a partaker of the divine nature and therefore escapes the corruptions that are in the world through lust.

The field is the world. Christ declares, "Go ye into all the world, and preach the gospel to every creature." My brethren, you would increase your pleasure in the Lord if you would practice self-denial. If you would resolve to love God truly and keep His commandments, you would discern the duties that devolve upon you as laborers together with God. You would willingly bring Him your offerings. You would faithfully and joyfully tithe your income, that His work in home and foreign fields might be advanced. The truth would go forth from your lips in no feigned words. Your zeal and piety would be greatly increased, and the unbelieving world would see that you have been in communion with God, and have learned of Him.

When this is your experience, no words of censure or blame will fall from your lips for those who are your fellow workers because you are taught of God, and are learning to speak the words of Christ. Your earnest prayers for pardon for your own defects, and for the blessing of God upon your efforts, will show that your lips have been converted. And this will touch the cold hearts of unbelievers. They will distinguish between the human and the divine.

We read that on the day of Pentecost, when the Holy Spirit descended upon the disciples, no man said that aught that he possessed was his own. All they owned was held for the advancement of the wonderful reformation. And thousands were converted in a day. When the same spirit actuates believers today and they give back to God His own with the same liberality, wide and far-reaching work will be accomplished.

The Spirit of the Lord has been working with His people, and many have given liberally for the upbuilding of the kingdom of God on the earth. Brethren, let us take hold anew, holding ourselves and all that we have in readiness to meet the demands of the cause of God upon us. —*August 29, 1907. (pp. 424-430)*

I have a message to bear to some who held positions of responsibility in the Southern California Conference. They are losing from their experience that true fervor which the presence of the Holy Spirit gives, and which would teach them to subdue self and walk humbly in the way of Christ. The responsible worker who will not become a humble follower of Christ will do great harm to the cause of God by molding and fashioning the experience of the conference to a common, worldly standard. The sacred work that we handle, if performed in a spirit of consecration, will never cheapen the experience of a single soul.

The men who stand as presidents of conferences, or as leaders in any part of the solemn work of giving the last gospel message, must cultivate and cherish broad views and ideas. It is the privilege of all who bear responsibilities in the work of the gospel, to be apt learners in Christ's school. The professed follower of Christ must not be led by the dictates of his own will; his mind must be trained to think Christ's thoughts, and enlightened to comprehend the will and way of God. Such a believer will be a follower of Christ's methods of work.

A mistake has been made in the course that has been followed to clear the San Fernando school from debt. When the school property was first purchased, and the minds of our people were upon it, only a feeble effort was made to raise the money spent in its purchase. But after the sanitariums were purchased, and the sympathy and financial strength of the people were needed to put them in working order, there were some who made the school debt the matter of first consideration, and who, by criticism of the sanitarium work and management, discouraged the brethren from giving them the full support that they needed.

The Lord did not call upon the president of the conference to make it his first work to gather up the gifts of our people for the school. There was necessity just then of giving first attention to the requirements of the sanitariums. —*September 12, 1907. (pp. 469, 470 to par. 2)*

The Lord sends His messages to correct the erring, however highly they may regard themselves. He asks that they submit their judgment to His control. Every soul must be under discipline to God. To occupy an exalted position is not always evidence that the Lord has placed an individual in that position. It is the works, not position, that testify to the value of a man. Hereditary traits of character need to be overcome. A man cannot safely be entrusted with the control of others, unless he himself is under the sanctification of the Holy Spirit.

In the spirit of meekness and lowliness of heart, all methods and plans should be submitted to wise counselors for their prayerful consideration and their endorsement. Otherwise, a restless, speculative energy and ambition may make an evil mark upon the cause of God, and subvert and hinder the very work that the Lord has declared should be done in this conference.

In order that the great work of sanctification that needs to be carried forward in the churches of Southern California may be accomplished, the minds and wills of our ministers, physicians, and teachers should be united—their hearts blending in one spirit to give the trumpet a certain sound. Let every voice proclaim distinctly the third angel's message. In word and act let those who are proclaiming the message reveal that they are numbered among those "that keep the commandments of God, and the faith of Jesus."

If this had been done faithfully, with the Word of the living God as the great lesson-book, the third angel's message would have gone with greater power. Had all God's ministers, as faithful stewards of the grace of God, called upon the world to hear the last note of warning, giving the trumpet a certain sound, thousands more might have been converted, and added their voices in proclaiming the message to the world. In distinct notes of solemn warning, is to be given the closing message that will prepare a people to receive the seal of the living God.

Satan is working to fill minds with the spirit of ambition and commercialism. Those whose minds are thus diverted will lose their opportunity of giving the last message to the world.

If a faithful work had been done during the last few years that have gone into eternity, thousands of souls would now be found with Bibles in their hands, reading the Word of God, and praying for light and guidance. Many of these would be engaged in the work of hunting for souls, and fitting up a people to stand in the great day of God. But some who ought to be missionaries are filled with the spirit of commercialism and with an ambition to secure for themselves certain advantages. The truth becomes to them a dead letter, not practiced nor obeyed.

Jehovah is the true God. Let Him be feared and reverenced. —*1907. (pp. 564, 565)*

Southern California is a field that should depend more than it has upon its own resources. It should have more facilities, and should not be cramped as it has been in some respects.

Southern California is a missionary field, a large part of which has received but little missionary effort. Henceforth it should receive more attention. The various lines of work that can be carried on should be diligently studied, and the advantages of such cities as Redlands and Riverside, and the need of putting forth decided effort for them, faithfully investigated.

Los Angeles demands constant labor because of its changing population. San Bernardino calls for earnest missionary effort. The work for all these places needs to be done by those who can adapt themselves to the needs of the field. In our work we miss the labors of Elder _____; but we must not leave the work undone because some of the faithful workers fall by the way. —*December 1907. (p. 579, pars. 1-3)*

We have been indolent in regard to our duty to Southern California. The many tourists who visit the cities in this conference should be given opportunity to hear the truth for this time. Let us do all in our power to enlighten the people in this large field. It is the privilege of every believer to let the light shine forth. We are drawing near to the close of this earth's history; we have not one hour to devote to needless matters. Our ministers in the Southern California Conference should now devote their best efforts to proclaiming the message of truth in all these large resorts. The Lord will impart His grace to all who will work in Christ's lines. And hope and faith will strengthen as the workers for God put their trust in Him. —*December 1907. (p. 580, par. 2)*

The workers in the Southern California Conference need to be minute men. No one is to exalt his own judgment or entertain the thought that he can carry the work in his own way. My brethren, when difficulties arise, do not leave the Lord out of your councils. Self-ruling will bring no strength to the church. A worker may magnify self to large proportions, but in doing so he will bring embarrassment to the work, and give an example to the church that God never designed it should have. —*January 13, 1908. (p. 591, par. 3)*

Work for Southern California

God has a work of special importance to be done in Southern California, and I know from the light given me that this work must now be perfected. —*June 20, 1908. (p. 695, par. 2)*

The enemy has worked in Southen California, and has tried to thwart the purposes of God. Messages of reproof have been sent to leading men whose work was not done in righteousness. Reformations have been called for. What is now needed is that the leaders in the Lord's work shall be fully converted. It is time that the Lord's voice was heeded, and that men should put away the spirit of self-confidence and self-sufficiency. Should the ideas of some who are wise in their own estimation be carried out, there would result a condition of things that would demand a most thorough reformation. —*October 11, 1909. (p. 790, par. 2)*

For several years there have been leading men in the Northern California Conference who exercised an authority which they supposed was theirs by virtue of their office, to control the work according to their own disposition and judgment. The work was becoming confused, and the Lord gave me a message regarding the movements that should be made. Because of the strange conditions in the Conference, Elder _____ was to be called to take the presidency. —*December 6, 1909. (p. 816, par. 3)*

Elder _____ and his wife have been engaged in the work for years, and their faith in the truth and in the Testimonies given by the Holy Spirit is strong. They have unitedly served according to the Lord's appointment, and we have sought to sustain them in their work. Conditions in the churches have changed decidedly, but the Lord has shown me that some in responsible positions are not yet converted, and without thorough conversion, they cannot conduct the work in right lines. Some who have been reproved and warned are not established and settled, and fully yielded to the guiding power of the Holy Spirit. Satan is not yet fully cast out of the minds of some, and it would take very little to produce again the conditions that existed ten years ago. —*December 6, 1909. (p. 817, par. 1)*

"I have a decided message for our people in Southern California. For months I have carried on my soul the burden of the medical missionary work in Southern California. Recently much light has been given me in regard to the manner in which God desires us to conduct sanitarium work. We are to encourage the patients to spend much of their time out of doors. I have been instructed to tell our brethren to keep on the look-out for cheap, desirable property in healthful places suitable for sanitarium purposes. Soon the reputation of the health resorts in Southern California will stand even higher than it stands at present. Now is our time to enter that field for the purpose of carrying forward medical missionary work. As soon as possible, sanitariums are to be established in different places in Southern California. Let a beginning be made in several places. If possible, let land be purchased on which buildings are already erected. Then, as the prosperity of the work demands, let appropriate enlargements be made. —*Early in 1902. (p. 832, par. 3)*

In Southern California there are many properties for sale on which buildings suitable for sanitarium work are already erected. Some of these properties should be purchased, and medical missionary work carried forward on sensible, rational lines. Several small sanitariums are to be established in Southern California for the benefit of the multitudes drawn there in hope of finding health. Instruction has been given me that now is our opportunity to reach the invalids flocking to the health resorts of Southern California, and that a work may be done also in behalf of the attendants. —*Early in 1902. (p. 833, par. 1)*

In a communication dated March 17, 1902, I read: "I am unable to sleep. My mind is much burdened in regard to the location of the sanitarium in Southern California. There is a great work to be done in California that has been strangely neglected. This work must now be done. Southern California is to be worked. Not half the energy has been brought into the management of the various lines of God's work that should be brought into them. The question of the location of the sanitarium in Southern California is of great importance, and is not to be settled by the judgment of man, or of several men who are all inclined to want the same thing.

"At the time when this matter was under consideration before, it was left unsettled because all did not agree. The delay has been long, but this abrupt haste does not show wisdom. Many are to have the privilege of considering the subject of the location of the sanitarium in Southern California. The Lord is interested in every line of His work. He understands when men are prepared to take hold of the work in the right spirit, when they are prepared to carry it forward wisely. His way is the best way." —*March 17, 1902. (p. 837, pars. 3, 4)*

During my stay in Southern California I was enabled to visit places that in the past had been presented to me by the Lord as suitable for the establishment of sanitariums and schools. I have been instructed that the work in Southern California should have advantages that it has not yet enjoyed. I have also been shown that in Southern California there were properties for sale on which buildings are already erected that could be utilized for our work, and that such properties will be offered to us at much less than their original cost. The work in Southern California is to advance more rapidly than it has advanced in the past. The means lying in banks or hidden in the earth is now called for to strengthen the work in Southern California. Every year many thousands of tourists visit Southern California, and by various methods we should seek to reach them with the truth. —*October 19, 1902. (p. 839, par. 1)*

"There are many other places in Southern California, besides Los Angeles and San Diego, in which sanitarium work could be started. To sanitariums in Southern California, people will come from far and near, because the fame of the climate is worldwide. It is the Lord's purpose that sanitariums shall be established in Southern California, and that from these institutions shall go forth the light of truth for this time.

Work for Southern California

By them the claims of the true Sabbath are to presented, and the third angel's message proclaimed. —*October 19, 1902. (p. 840, par. 4)*

"At San Diego we have made an advance move by purchasing the Potts' Sanitarium in Paradise Valley. Three years ago light was given me that our people in Southern California must watch for opportunities to purchase such properties. I told our brethren that they would find, all ready for use and for sale at reasonable prices, just the buildings they would need for their work. And thus it has proved. In a most remarkable way the Lord is preparing the way for the advancement of His work in Southern California. —*October 19, 1902. (p. 841, par. 2)*

"From the light which was given me when I was in Australia, and which has been renewed since I came to America, I know that our work in Southern California must advance. The people flocking there for health must hear the last message of mercy.

"God has not been pleased with the way in which this work has been neglected. From many places in Southern California, the light is to shine forth to the multitude. Present truth is to be as a city set on a hill which cannot be hid. —*October 19, 1902. (p. 842, pars. 4, 5)*

"More decided efforts are to be put forth in Southern California. There is a great work to be done in this field. We have done all in our power to advance the work there, and now that this sanitarium property in San Diego County has been purchased, we call to our brethren and sisters to aid us in properly equipping the institution that we may do successful work. I ask those who have been entrusted with the Lord's money to make gifts to the sanitarium, that it may be prepared to do the work that must be done for the sick and suffering. —*June 26, 1905. (p. 844, par. 4)*

"Brethren and sisters, I plead with you to help forward our sanitarium work. The Paradise Valley Sanitarium is in need of assistance. I ask you, my dear friends, to help us in this time of need, and I believe you will." —*June 26, 1905. (p. 845, par. 1)*

Earnest work should be done in Southern California in carrying the Fernando School forward successfully, and earnest work should be done in establishing a sanitarium near Los Angeles. Several buildings have already been offered for sale. If these are not suitable, or if they cannot be purchased for a reasonable sum, land should be purchased and buildings erected. —*June 30, 1904. (p. 69, par. 2)*

The purchase of the school buildings at Fernando was in the order of God. Valuable property was obtained at a price far below its original cost. The brethren did right to buy it, and the school can be sustained if the families of believers in Southern California will do their best to make it a success. The young men and women who expect to attend school should do all in their power, before entering the school, to earn money to meet their expenses. —*June 30, 1904. (p. 70, par. 4)*

"Jerusalem and all Judea, and all the region round about Jordan," went out to hear John the Baptist, "and were baptized of him in

Jordan, confessing their sins." Just such a work as this can be done today in Southern California. —*April 15, 1904. (p. 60, par. 1)*

My brother, we need means to advance the work of the Lord in many places. We must firmly establish the work at the captial of our nation. Do you not wish to have a part in the work that God has given us to do there? Will you not do your best to help us to secure the facilities that we must have in order to advance the work in Washington, D.C. and in Southern California? —*April 15, 1904. (p. 64, par. 3)*

I have passed a wakeful night; for there have been presented to me some things connected with the past, present, and future of the work in Southern California.

I have now no hesitation in speaking plainly, and in calling things by their right names. For three nights in succession, the message has been given to me that _____, as president of this conference, is out of his place. He should not occupy such a position in any of our conferences. He is leading some of his brethren to ignore the messages that the Lord is sending to His people. He has refused to accept the testimonies that have not harmonized with his own mind and judgment.

The results of his administration will be further developed in the future. Why should men be entrusted with such grave responsibilities before they have been sufficiently proved? _____ has made the work of _____ exceedingly difficult. He has worked in an underhand manner to thwart the efforts of _____ to do the work that should be done at Loma Linda. The influence of _____ has been counter to the messages of instruction that the Lord has given concerning this sanitarium. For two years this work of opposition has been carried forward.

The work of the Lord, in unmistakable language, is that _____ should not occupy the position of a conference president. He needs to learn some of the first lessons of what God requires of His people who are living amid the perils of the strong temptations of these last days. He needs to be converted—heart, soul, and mind to the truth. Self has borne rule in his plans, and he has endeavored to convert others to his own ideas. As yet there has been but a part development of his character; but if he continues in his present course it will not be long before there will be a more open opposition to the work that we have, under the direction of God, endeavored to accomplish in Southern California.

The authoritative utterances of our brother, in their commands and their forbiddings, hear not the heavenly impress. They are not inspired by the Holy Spirit of God. Unless he becomes thoroughly convinced that his mind is not infallible, his future life will be characterized by a spirit of exalting whomsoever he will, and of hindering those who are not in harmony with him. In his present state of mind, he should not be entrusted with responsibilites that would give him the power to dictate to any church.

Work for Southern California

I have borne the testimony that _____ should have no control over _____. I have borne a testimony, even in the meeting that has just been held here, that the Lord's servants are to seek their counsel from God. It is contrary to God's plan that men shall exercise arbitrary authority over their brethren. God would convince those who have felt called upon to exercise a wrong authority over their brethren, that He has not authorized them to take upon themselves such responsibilities. He has not appointed a man to take the place of God in this conference.

The Saviour bids us pray, "Lead us not into temptation." Our heavenly Father will lead His people in the paths of righteousness. The word of the Lord to the churches in this conference is: "Watch and pray, lest ye enter into temptation. Be on your guard against the efforts of the powers of darkness to resist the testimonies of God's Spirit, that are to be understood." Actions spring form desires and purposes. God alone can discern the thoughts and intents of the heart. He weighs with unerring accuracy the very motives of the mind.

The President of the Southern California Conference needs the power to see himself as he is in the sight of God. He is as a man lost in the woods, blinded by a dangerous confidence in himself. A humbling of the soul, with earnest prayer, and a diligent study and reception of the Word of God, are the means by which to overcome these peculiar temptations. The armor of truth is to be found in the Word of God. Clothed in this armor, a man will be humble, not dictatorial, but a learner from the Great Teacher.

The Lord has witnessed the unnecessary hardships that have been brought upon _____. Avenues of assistance have been hedged up, and it has been made well nigh impossible to raise the money that has been needed at Loma Linda for the addition of bathrooms and other needed facilities. There must be a change in these conditions. Relief must be given to this institution, which, by the working of God in our behalf, has been brought within our reach.

Influences have been brought to bear upon minds and hearts to lead men away from God, that they should obey men, and show to men the honor that belongs alone to God. He alone is to be honored and glorified. Men placed in positions of trust may be a help to the churches, but they are not to lord it over God's heritage. Neither are they to show favors to certain ones, with the expectation that they will in return receive certain favors from these persons.

During the past night there has passed before me scene after scene, where men in positions of trust were bearing rule over their fellow men. There seemed to be with them but little burden for the sacred truth for this time, that would sanctify the heart, the thoughts, the speech, and the actions.

One stood by my side, and said, "These men are becoming too wise to follow a plain 'Thus saith the Lord.' They are departing from God."

A Bible lay upon the stand, and the heavenly messenger held it to view, saying in solemn tones: "The Holy Scriptures of the Old and the New Testament! Together they are to act a more important part in presenting before the people God's saving truth. The Word is to be carefully studied, but not to present theories that will lead away the minds of the people, diverting them from the warnings sent to prepare a people to stand in the day of the Lord.

God has a message to be proclaimed in all the world. By every teacher in our schools, every minister, every medical missionary, the only true God is to be uplifted. But some of the watchmen are asleep. They are as the blind leading the blind. The time to labor is fast passing away, and Satan is leading some to stand as the accusers of their brethren who are bearing heavy burdens.

Who of our ministers are awake, giving the trumpet a certain sound? The trumpet of some in official positions has been sounding their own exploits. The spirit that has characterized their work has borne the disapproval of God. Who of those that have been appointed to office in the work of God understand what that office embraces? Where are the faithful watchmen?

Some who should be watchmen are seeking to gain advantages for themselves in commercial lines. For the sake of financial profits they are becoming tainted with the spirit of commercialism. This spirit has so blinded the eyes of their understanding that they have not a clear scriptural understanding of Bible principles. At times when they have not been guided by the Spirit of God, they have dictated to their brethren, and have considered that any proposition that they might make should be accepted without question. Their position has been such that many of their brethren have been deceived and deluded.

The Word of the living God is to be our lesson-book. Here, in both the Old and New Testaments, is a statement of the mistakes made by ancient Israel. Shall we, as did they, fail to improve the most precious opportunities for doing the work of God? If, during the three years past, the opportunites had been truly improved to meet the requirements of this time, some who are now lost to the cause of God would stand ready to serve as genuine missionaries.

Awake, awake from your stupor, you who have been under the control of other human minds. No longer allow yourselves to treat with indifference subjects that need to be presented to the people with clearness. Your president does not realize where he stands in the sight of God. Influences have been brought in that have turned his mind away from the preparation that is essential for these last days. And as he has turned away from Christ, the spirit of commercialism has absorbed his mind. The Light of the World has been eclipsed. There is a profession to know God, but there is often a denial of Him in words and in action.

God permitted Christ, the Sun of Righteousness, to come to our world to seek and to save perishing souls. But today some who have been entrusted with the care of these blood-bought souls are denying Him in word, in method, in action. Darkness covers the earth and gross darkness the people.

Where are the earnest calls that should be given to arouse the people to that preparation of heart that will purify, refine, and ennoble characters to shine as lights amid the moral darkness? The soul is never safe, save under divine guidance. The Word of God coming from sanctified hearts and lips will soften and break hard hearts. And if ever there was a period of time when the words of Christ should be heard, it is now.

None but He who created man can effect a change in the human heart. Every teacher is to realize that he must be moved by divine agencies. The mind and judgment must be submitted to the Holy Spirit. Through the sanctification of the truth we may bear a decided testimony for righteousness both before believers and before unbelievers.

We are far behind what we should be in our experience. We are backward in pronouncing the testimony that should flow from sanctified lips. Even when sitting at the table, Christ taught truths that brought comfort and courage to the hearts of His hearers. Whenever it is possible, we are to present the words of Christ. If His love is in the soul, abiding there as a living principle, there will come forth from the treasure-house of the heart, words suitable to the occasion—not light, trifling words, but uplifting words—words of truth and spirituality.

Let teachers and students watch their opportunities whenever possible to confess Christ in their conversation, speaking of their experiences in following Christ, praying with their brethren for the Holy Spirit. Confessing Christ openly and bravely, exhibiting in the choice of words the simplicity of true godliness, will be more effective than many sermons. There are but few who give a true representation of the meekness of Christ. Oh, we need, and we must have, His meekness! Christ is to be formed within, the hope of glory.

We are preparing for translation to the heavenly world. Our conversation should be in heaven, from whence we look for the Lord Jesus. He is to be acknowledged as the Giver of every good and perfect gift, the Author of all our blessings, in Whom is centered our hope of eternal life.

Angels of heaven are taking note of all our works, and watching to see how they can minister to our needs. With intensity of spirit, all heaven stands ready to lend aid to us in our divine progress. Shall we improve our present opportunities and receive the impress of the divine image?

I am instructed that those who believe in the present truth, and who are set as guides to the people of God, are not to become engaged in commercial pursuits. Their minds must not become so absorbed that they cannot distinguish between the sacred and the common. A strife for victory in business deals will develop a pugilistic spirit, a spirit that is spoiling the record of some of our brethren in Los Angeles. Such a course will develop in these brethren characters that may not now be clearly discerned. We are to educate the mind in pleasant considerations of divine things. But those who suppose that they are to guide other minds must in a most earnest manner seek the Lord.

The only way that temptation may be overcome is through watchfulness and prayer. The trial of the faith must come. Satanic agencies are busy, endeavoring to spoil the record of many souls. Those who are neglectful of Bible study are in danger of disregarding the Testimonies. Those who seem to feel that position and influence place them above temptation are under a strong delusion of the enemy. In this conference there is a strong temptation to consider that position makes the man. Men placed in positions of responsibility are to honor that position by a most earnest determination to be like Christ, as He gave us example in His earthly life. His life testifies that the strongest of temptations are no excuse for yielding to sin.

"In the last day, that great day of the feast, Jesus stood and cried, saying, If any man thirst, let him come unto Me, and drink. He that believeth on Me, as the scripture hath said, out of his belly shall flow rivers of living water. (But this spake He of the Spirit, which they that believe on Him should receive.)" "Come unto Me, all ye that labor and are heavy laden, and I will give you rest. Take My yoke upon you, and learn of Me; for I am meek and lowly in heart: and ye shall find rest unto your souls. For My yoke is easy and My burden is light." —*November 3, 1907. (pp. 549-556)*

Work for Redlands, Riverside, and San Bernardino

Redlands and Riverside have been presented to me as places that should be worked. These two places should not longer be neglected. I hope soon to see an earnest effort put forth in their behalf. Will you please consider the advisability of establishing a sanitarium in the vicinity of these towns, with treatment rooms in each place to act as feeders to the institution?

We cannot afford to allow these places to go unwarned. Instead of _____ going somewhere else to work, would it not be better to let a determined effort be put forth to make a success of the work in these places? There are other cities in Southern California in which a work similar to that carried on by _____ in Los Angeles should be conducted. The Lord would have His ministers working zealously for these who have never heard the truth. But _____ should have someone connected with him to help him in the work. —*April 12, 1905. (p. 142, pars. 2, 3)*

Your letter has just been read. I had no sooner finished reading it than I said, "I will consult no one; for I have no question at all about the matter." I advised Willie to send you a telegram without spending time to ask the advice of the brethren. Secure the property by all means, so that it can be held, and then obtain all the money you can and make sufficient payments to hold the place. This is the very property that we ought to have. Do not delay; for it is just what is needed. As soon as it is secured, a working force can begin operations in it. I think that sufficient help can be secured to carry this matter through. I want you to be sure to lose no time in securing the right to purchase the property. We will do our utmost to help you raise the money. I know that Redlands and Riverside are to be worked, and I pray that the Lord may be gracious and not allow anyone else to get this property instead of us. —*May 14, 1905. (p. 150, par. 1)*

Here is the word of the Lord. Open up every place possible. We are to labor in faith, taking hold of a power that is pledged to do large things for us. We are to reach out in faith in Los Angeles and in Redlands and Riverside. —*May 14, 1905. (p. 152, par. 3)*

Redlands and Riverside must be worked, and they could be worked from the place about which you have written us. If Brother and Sister _____ can possibly get away from Nashville, I should like them to spend a little time in Southern California. —*May 23, 1905. (p. 153, par. 2)*

I could not but weep for joy as I saw how plainly the providence of God had been revealed in our selection of places for sanitarium work in San Diego, Los Angeles, and Redlands and Riverside districts. —*July 1905. (p. 184, par. 2)*

For a long time we have desired to see a work begun in Redlands. Now, in the providence of God, we have come into possession of Loma Linda. This will give us an influence in Redlands and Riverside, enabling us to find openings for the proclamation of present truth. This beautiful property was offered to us at a very low price. It is completely furnished. We have only to take possession. We trust that our people will rally to the support of this institution, that it may not be burdened with a large interest-bearing debt. —*September 9, 1905. (p. 213, par. 3)*

The Lord has signified that the time has come for us to work Redlands, San Bernardino, Riverside, and the neighboring towns. I am filled with a solemn joy at the thought that these places are soon to be entered by our workers. —*September 15, 1905. (p. 219, par. 2)*

Dr. _____, I write you to come and see Loma Linda. It is a grand place for sanitarium work. It is the Lord's doing that this place has come into our possession, and we praise His holy name. We realize that we are highly favored in having been able to obtain possession of this property. We are greatly pleased with it.

Right around the Loma Linda Sanitarium there is a wide field for missionary effort. Redlands is only five miles from the institution, San Bernardino about the same distance, and Riverside a little further away. These cities are all important places. Elder _____ has done some work in Redlands and Riverside and in each a neat little meeting house has been erected. But the Lord has a larger work to be done in these places. In the future I expect to spend a portion of my time at Loma Linda. 1905. —*(p. 238, pars. 5, 6)*

By placing Loma Linda in our hands, the Lord has opened the way for us to work these places. We are to regard the district in which these towns are situated as our special field of missionary work. We are anxious to become known to the people living in these places, and especially to those whom we can help in spiritual and physical lines. Through the power of Jesus Christ our Lord, we may lift them out of suffering, and bring them to health of body and soul. You know what joy there is in taking the weak and suffering by the hand and raising them up. You have rejoiced in this work in the past, and there is much for you to do in the future. It will bring you lasting joy and satisfaction.

A great battle must be fought. Time is short. Let us keep step with Christ. Let us by faith clasp His hand and hold it fast. He will never repulse us. —*1905. (p. 239, pars. 1, 2)*

We thank the Lord that we have a good sanitarium at Paradise Valley, seven miles from San Diego; a sanitarium at Glendale, eight miles from Los Angeles; and a large and beautiful place at Loma Linda, sixty-two miles east from Los Angeles, and close to Redlands, Riverside and San Bernardino. The Loma Linda property is one of the most beautiful sanitarium sites I have ever seen. —*1905. (p. 241, par. 3—portion)*

Redlands and Riverside are places which the Lord has shown me should be thoroughly worked. _____ has done some evangelical work in these places, and in each of them a company of believers has been raised up, and a meeting house built. But more work must be done there, and a work must be done in San Bernardino.

By the securing of Loma Linda, the Lord has opened the way for a work to be done in the neighboring cities and towns. The securing of this property at such a price as we paid for it, is a miracle that should open the eyes of our understanding. If such manifest workings of God do not give us a new experience, what will? If we cannot read the evidence that the time has come to work in the surrounding cities, what could be done to arouse us to action? —*1905. (p. 242, pars. 1, 3)*

I am so thankful to our heavenly Father that for a long time He has kept before me that there were buildings that we could obtain at a greatly reduced price. This instruction kept me from trying to purchase land on which to erect buildings at large cost. The Lord has certainly prepared the way for us, and He wants us to work interestedly in securing sanitariums.

I feel thankful for the school property at Fernando. And I do thank the Lord for the property at Paradise Valley. And now you can see that the Lord designs that these places should be worked. It may be that there will have to be another building secured at a distance from Los Angeles; for thus it has been presented to me. But we cannot yet reach out for more, unless the Lord should make it known that the time has come. If we consecrate our individual service to the Lord, we shall have that wisdom which will enable us to move intelligently.

I thank the Lord with heart and soul and voice that He has brought Loma Linda to our notice, that we might obtain it.

I thank the Lord that He has sent you to help me carry out in determined effort that which He designed should be a great blessing to us. Redlands will be a center, and so also will Loma Linda. A school will be established as soon as possible, and the Lord will open the way. I could not but think, as I read the notice of the people flocking into Los Angeles, if Loma Linda had not been sold to us, there would now be a ready sale for it. With all the buildings in connection with the main building, we have large advantages. If we will walk humbly with God, and do according to that which He has prospered us, we will have Christ as our Friend and our Helper. "If any man will come after Me, let him deny himself, and take up his cross, and follow Me." These are the terms of our discipleship. Will we comply with them? —*November 1, 1905. (p. 234, pars. 2-4)*

Work for Los Angeles and San Diego

I wish to write you a few lines regarding the work in San Diego. We have long desired to see sanitarium work established in this place, not that we ourselves may be benefited; but that those who have never heard the truth may have an opportunity of hearing the last message of mercy to be given to the world. If you have known and enjoyed the comfort of the Holy Spirit, the assurance of the grace of God, the hope of the gospel of Christ, your heart must be drawn out in earnest longing that this work may extend rapidly, while Mercy's sweet voice is still heard inviting perishing souls to come to the Saviour.

I have always looked with great interest upon the work in Los Angeles and in San Diego, hoping that right moves would be made, and that the sanitarium work might be established in these important places. Every year large numbers of tourists visit these places, and I have longed to see men moved by the Holy Spirit, meeting these people with the message borne by John the Baptist: "Repent ye; for the kingdom of heaven is at hand." —*April 15, 1904. (p. 59, pars. 1, 2)*

At San Diego we have made an advance move by purchasing the Potts' Sanitarium in Paradise Valley, near National City, and about six miles from San Diego. We hope soon to be able to furnish a part of the building, and to open its doors to those for whom it was purchased. —*April 15, 1904. (p. 64, par. 4)*

Three years ago light was given me that our people in Southern California must watch for opportunities to purchase such properties. I told our brethren that they would find all ready for use, and for sale at reasonable prices, just the buildings they would need for their work. And thus it has proved. In a most remarkable way the Lord is preparing the way for the advancement of His work in Southern California.

For two years I have been interested in the Potts' Sanitarium property, and have advised and urged our people to secure it. Two years ago we thought it could be secured for twelve thousand dollars. One year ago it was offered for eight thousand, and this spring it was offered for still less. I advised those having in charge the medical work in Southern California, to purchase the building, and when they hesitated, because of lack of funds, I persuaded _____ and _____ to join me, and we have purchased the Potts' Sanitarium, and eight acres adjoining for five thousand dollars. —*April 15, 1904. (p. 65, pars. 2, 3)*

Something similar can be done in the neighborhood of Los Angeles, if wise plans are adopted for the carrying forward of the work, and if the men to whom the Lord has entrusted His talent of means will put their money into use for the honor of God and the blessing of humanity.

We have not purchased the Potts' Sanitarium to gain advantage for ourselves, but to help in carrying forward the work that Christ has given us to do—the work outlined in the following scripture:

"Go ye therefore, and teach all nations, baptizing them in the name of the Father, and of the Son, and of the Holy Ghost: teaching them to observe all things whatsoever I have commanded you." "These signs shall follow them that believe; In My name they shall cast out devils; they shall speak with new tongues; they shall take up serpents; and if they drink any deadly thing, it shall not hurt them; they shall lay hands on the sick, and they shall recover." "Ye shall be witnesses unto Me both in Jerusalem, and in all Judea, and in Samaria, and unto the uttermost part of the earth." "And, lo, I am with you alway, even unto the end." —*April 15, 1904. (p. 66, pars. 1-3)*

To Our Brethren and Sisters in Southern California

I am instructed to bear a message to you: You have a great work to do in soul-saving, but you cannot accomplish this work by following man-made plans and human devisings.

Special light has been given me regarding the character and magnitude of the work to be done in Los Angeles. Several times messages have been given regarding the duty that rests upon us of proclaiming the third angel's message with power in that city.

And now, as we see that the Lord has blessed the labor of _____ and his faithful helpers, and that large additions have been made to the Los Angeles church, it is our duty to be wide-awake to the privileges and opportunity of the hour. Wherever such an interest is awakened as that which is now manifested in Los Angeles, men of the best ability should be called in to help with the work. They should enter heartily into the work of visiting and holding Bible readings with those newly come to the faith, and with those interested, laboring to establish them in the faith. The new believers are to be carefully instructed, that they may have an intelligent knowledge of the various lines of work committed to the church of Christ. One or two men should not be left alone with the burden of such a work.

For a long time our people in Southern California have had messages from the Lord that there should be sanitariums near Los Angeles. For want of means the work has been delayed. But not long ago a building at Glendale, eight miles from Los Angeles, was purchased, and is now being fitted up for the work. I have visited the building and can say that it is beautifully situated and is well adapted for sanitarium work. —*December 12, 1905. (p. 127 all)*

We hope that our people in Southern California will come quickly and heartily to the support of this sanitarium, so providentially placed in our hands, and that it may begin without delay its work.

The Lord has not been honored or glorified by the past showing of the sanitarium work in Southern California. This work has been placed upon human wisdom, and failure has been the result. But we now see a united force of workers anxious to push the enterprise forward along right lines; and we are confident that if they will follow the Lord's instruction and rely upon His guidance, He will cooperate with them. —*December 12, 1904. (p. 128, pars. 1, 2)*

One night we seemed to be in a council meeting, and the question being considered was, how can the sanitarium work in Southern California be best advanced? One present proposed one thing and still another proposed something entirely opposite. —*December 12, 1904. (p. 129, par. 5)*. One of dignity and authority arose and said, "I have words of counsel for you. Never, never repeat the mistakes of the past."

Men have placed too much confidence in themselves, and have allowed cultivated and hereditary tendencies to wrong, which ought

[41]

to have been overcome, to control and to bear away the victory. Various lines of work are to be earnestly carried forward, for the enlightening of those who are in spiritual darkness. Evangelical work must receive first attention, and is to be intelligently carried forward, in all lines of your medical work.

"You have," said our Instructor, "come to an important place in the history of your work. Who shall be chosen to carry responsibilities in the sanitarium at the beginning of its work? No mistake must be made in this matter. Men are not to be placed in positions of trust who have not been tested and tried. Men and women who understand the will of the Lord are to be chosen—men who can discern the work that needs to be done, and prayerfully do it, that the mistakes and errors of the past need not be repeated."

"The one who is placed in the position of business manager," He said, "must daily be managed by the Lord. He occupies a very important place, and he must posses the necessary qualifications for the work. He should have dignity and knowledge, blended with a clear sense of how to use his authority. Christ must be revealed in his life. He must be a man who can give religious instruction and exert a spiritual influence. He must know how to deal with minds, and he must allow his own mind to be controlled by the Spirit. Wisdom is to come forth from his lips in words of encouragement to all with whom he is connected. He must know how to discern and correct mistakes. He must be a man who will harmonize with his fellow-workers, a man who possesses adaptability. He should be able to speak of the different points of our faith, as occasion requires. His words and acts should reveal justice." —*December 12, 1904. (p. 130 all)*

By unmistakable representations the Lord has given evidence that a great work is to be done in Southern California.

Elder _____ has been holding tent-meetings in Los Angeles with good results. Many souls have been converted to the truth. We thank the Lord that we have a good sanitarium at Paradise Valley, seven miles from San Diego; a sanitarium at Glendale, eight miles from Los Angeles; and a large and beautiful place at Loma Linda, sixty-two miles east from Los Angeles, and close to Redlands, Riverside, and San Bernardino. The Loma Linda property is one of the most beautiful sanitarium sites I have ever seen. —*H. 277, 1905. (p. 241, pars. 2, 3)*

In a place like Los Angeles, where the population is constantly changing, a wonderful opportunity is presented for the sale of our books. A great loss has been sustained because our people have not more fully embraced this opportunity. Why should not teachers and students from the San Fernando School make Los Angeles a special field for the sale of "Object Lessons"? If with earnestness and faith they will work out the plan that has been given us for the use of this book, angels of God will attend their steps and the blessing of heaven will be upon their efforts. —*September 12, 1907. (p. 473, par. 3)*

There are many church members who need to feel the converting power of God upon mind and heart and character. There are many in Los Angeles who, if they would move out of the city and find homes in more retired places, would have an experience of a higher character. There is a great work to be done for the city of Los Angeles. —*January 12, 1908. (p. 590, par. 3)*

Our medical work in Los Angeles should be in a much more favorable condition than it is. The Lord designs that much more shall be done in this city than has been done there. But I cannot speak freely about this at present, for fear that men will take advantage of what I say, and will endeavor by my words to vindicate wrong plans. Some of the brethren in Los Angeles have at times lacked spiritual discernment. They have not always been able to see what could be done by proper efforts on their part. A large work has been done in some lines, but the methods followed have not been such as to bring glory to God in the saving of souls. —*October 19, 1902. (p. 839, par. 2)*

"There are many other places in Southern California besides Los Angeles and San Diego, in which sanitarium work could be started. To sanitariums in Southern California people will come from far and near because the fame of the climate is worldwide. It is the Lord's purpose that sanitariums shall be established in Southern California, and that from these institutions shall go forth the light of truth for this time. By them the claims of the true Sabbath are to be presented, and the third angel's message proclaimed." —*October 19, 1902. (p. 840, par. 4)*

For years the Lord has instructed us that we should have a sanitarium in the vicinity of San Diego, where many thousands of tourists come every year. A valuable property was secured at National City at a very small part of its original cost. There an important work is to be done in caring for the sick, and in reaching many with the light of truth. At the Paradise Valley Sanitarium also it was found necessary to add to the original building, and obligations have been made that must soon be met. The Lord has blessed this institution, and some have been converted to the truth as the result of the work already done. —*May 19, 1907. (p. 356, par. 1)*

"During the spring of 1902, the attention of several of our brethren was called to the Paradise Valley Sanitarium building, which was erected for a sanitarium by Mrs. Mary L. Potts about twenty years ago.

"In September, 1902, after the Los Angeles camp-meeting, we spent a week in San Diego and visited several places that were offered us for sanitarium work. In the building offered us by Mrs. Potts, it seemed to me we found about all that could be asked.

"A year before, light had been given me that our people in Southern California must watch their opportunity to purchase such properties, and it seemed plain to me and to those who were with me that the opportunity for securing this place was a fulfillment of the encouragement given us.

"In December we learned that this place could be purchased, and I encouraged _____ to take steps to secure it. But our leading brethren in the Southern California conference were not ready to cooperate in the matter, and nothing was done. In the summer of 1903 the property was offered us for eight thousand dollars, and again we found that our brethren were not in a position to act. In January, 1904, _____ wrote me that the mortgage could be bought for six thousand dollars, and perhaps less. Again I advised our brethren connected with the medical work in Southern California to secure the place. But I learned that they were not prepared to act. Then I laid the matter before _____, and she consented to join me in securing the place. We then telegraphed an offer of four thousand dollars for the mortgage. Two days later a telegram was returned accepting the offer. Meanwhile a letter from other parties in San Diego was on its way to New York, offering five thousand dollars for the mortgage." —*March 16, 1906. (p. 843 all)*

Glendale Sanitarium

We are glad that notwithstanding some delay the property at Glendale has been secured for a sanitarium. Years ago the Lord gave me instruction that there should be a sanitarium near the city of Los Angeles. Instruction was also given that we should find properties for sale on which there would be buildings suitable for sanitarium purposes, and that we might secure such properties at a very low cost. The location of the Glendale Sanitarium meets the representation given me of places God has reserved for us. The electric cars running close by the institution make access to it very convenient.

Let all connected with this sanitarium keep in mind the purpose for which this property has been secured. The institution is to act a special part in bringing souls to Christ, leading them to love God and keep His commandments. Unless the workers have a living connection with God, unless there is seen in the institution a spirit of kindness and compassion which will recommend Bible truth and win souls to Christ, the establishment of the sanitarium will have been in vain. Spiritual as well as physical healing is to be brought to those who come for healing. —*March 14, 1905. (p. 137, pars. 1, 2)*

Brother and Sister _____, I am glad that you have a part in the work of the Glendale Sanitarium. May the Lord increase your wisdom and courage and faith. I am glad that Dr. _____ and her husband can unite with you. You and Dr. _____ and the other workers may do a precious work in letting the light of present truth shine forth in clear rays. Remember that you are doing a work for time and for eternity. You should have an ever-increasing faith in the promises of God's word. It is your privilege to seek wisdom and help from God. Come to the Saviour in humility, confessing your sins, and asking for strength and grace.

The Holy Spirit enlightens the mind of the one who depends on the merits of a crucified and risen Saviour, and indites a prayer of confession and repentance that is acceptable to the Lord. "We know not what we should pray for as we ought: but the Spirit itself maketh intercession for us, with groanings that cannot be uttered." "He that searcheth the heart knoweth what is the mind of the Spirit, because He maketh intercession for the saints according to the will of God."

Let no man boast that he does not confess the sins that the Lord has pointed out to him. If he makes no confession, he receives no forgiveness and pardon from God. He must go forth in sorrow, to work in his own strength. The enemy finds him in this position, a subject to be deceived.

There are many, many of this class. May the Lord open their eyes, that they may see the danger of their self-sufficiency. A superficial work is always a snare to every professed Christian. Satan finds easy access to the heart of the one who is careless and slack in his experience, and beguiles him with seducing theories that will destroy his faith in God. "He that cometh to God must believe that He is, (as He has declared Himself personal) and that He is a rewarder of those who diligently seek Him." —*March 14, 1905. (p. 137, par. 3 to p. 138 all)*

In every sanitarium there must be kept before all in the institution the principles of true service. From the institution is to go forth light and knowledge. All connected with it are to act their part intelligently, as representatives of the truth for this time. It is that they may be trained to do true missionary work, that young people are brought to our sanitariums. —*March 14, 1905. (p. 139, par. 1)*

All the promises of God's word are made on gospel terms. If we on our part will fulfill the conditions, if we will seek the Lord while He may be found, we may claim the promise:

"For ye shall go out with joy, and be led forth with peace: the mountains and the hills shall break forth before you into singing, and all the trees of the field shall clap their hands. Instead of the thorn shall come up the fir tree, and instead of the brier shall come up the myrtle tree: and it shall be to the Lord for a name, for an everlasting sign that shall not be cut off."

Let this message be sounded to all people: Seek the Lord while He may be found. Seek Him against Whom you have been in rebellion. Let us make every effort to check the seducing sentiments that would come into our ranks. Let every soul be wide-awake to close every avenue of the soul to the sophistry of Satan, as revealed in heaven and in Eden. Let us be armed with that vigilance that shall resist his enchantments. —*March 14, 1905. (p. 141, par. 1)*

Still the light kept coming to me that the work should be conducted after a different order; that many plans and devisings of men needed to be changed. Of late some moves have been made. The Lord has wrought in the securing of properties at Fernando, at Paradise Valley, and at Glendale. —*August 19, 1906. (p. 317, par. 5)*

At Glendale, a few miles from Los Angeles, we purchased a sanitarium at about one fourth its real value. This institution is at the present time full of patients. It is well equipped for work, and is in a position of influence. Its need is not so pressing as that of the sanitariums at Loma Linda and National City. —*May 19, 1907. (p. 356, par. 2)*

Work for Cities

Those who have crowded into Battle Creek, and are being held there, see and hear many things that tend to weaken their faith, and engender unbelief. They would gain a more practical knowledge in an effort to impart to others that which they receive of the Word of God. They should scatter out, and be working in all our cities under the training of men who are sound in the faith. If those who teach these workers are true and loyal, a great work will be accomplished. —*H. 277, 1905. (p. 244, par. 6)*

There is to be a working of our cities as they never have been worked. That which should have been done twenty, yes, more than twenty years ago, is now to be done speedily. The work will be more difficult to do now than it would have been years ago; but it will be done.

Our work is made exceedingly hard because of many false theories that have to be met, and because of the dearth of efficient teachers and willing helpers.

The Lord is to do a strange work very soon. A representation has been given me that I have not yet had strength to trace upon paper. I must know when to speak and when to keep silent. When the Lord bids me speak, I cannot keep silent. —*1905. (p. 245, pars. 1, 2, 4)*

When the New England Sanitarium was removed from South Lancaster to Melrose, the Lord instructed me that this was in the order of His opening Providence. The buildings and grounds at Melrose are of a character to recommend our medical missionary work, which is to be carried forward not only in Boston, but in many other unworked cities in New England. The Melrose property is such that conveniences can be provided that will draw to that sanitarium persons not of our faith. The aristocratic as well as the common people will visit that institution to avail themselves of the advantages offered for restoration of health.

Boston has been pointed out to me repeatedly as a place that must be faithfully worked. The light must shine in the outskirts and in the inmost parts. The Melrose Sanitarium is one of the greatest agencies that can be employed to reach Boston with the truth. The city and its suburbs must hear the last message of mercy to be given to our world. Tent-meetings must be held in many places. The workers must put to the very best use the abilities God has given them. The gifts of grace will increase by wise use. But there must be no self-exaltation. No precise lines are to be laid down. Let the Holy Spirit direct the workers. They are to keep looking unto

Work for Cities

Jesus, the Author and Finisher of their faith. The work for this great city will be signalled by the revelation of the Holy Spirit, if all will walk humbly with God. —*May 14, 1906. (p. 289, pars. 1, 2)*

The terrible disasters that are befalling great cities ought to arouse us to intense activity in giving the warning message to the people in these congested centers of population, while we still have opportunity. The most favorable time for the presentatin of our message in the cities has passed by. Sin and wickedness are rapidly increasing; and now we shall have to redeem the time by laboring all the more earnestly.

The medical missionary work is a door through which the truth is to find entrance to many homes in the cities. In every city will be found those who will appreciate the truths of the third angel's message. The judgments of God are impending. Why do we not awaken to the peril of threatening the men and women living in the cities of America? Our people do not realize as keenly as they should the responsibility resting upon them to proclaim the truth to the millions dwelling in these unwarned cities. —*May 14, 1906. (p. 299, pars. 1, 2)*

There are many souls to be saved. Our own souls are to be firmly grounded in a knowledge of the truth, that we may win others from error to the truth. We need now to search the Scriptures diligently, and as we become acquainted with unbelievers, we are to hold up Christ as the anointed, the crucified, the risen Saviour, witnessed to by prophets, testified of by believers, and through whose name we receive the forgiveness of our sins.

We need now a firm belief in the truth. Let us understand what is truth. Time is very short. Whole cities are being swept away. Are we doing our part to give the message that will prepare a people for the coming of their Lord? May the Lord help us to improve the opportunities that are ours. —*May 14, 1906. (p. 299, par. 3; p. 300, par. 1)*

We had thought that the work would have been accomplished before this. But the light came from the Lord regarding the extension of the work. "Jesus came and spake unto them, saying, All power is given unto Me in heaven and in earth." This power we needed then, in the early history of our work. "Go ye therefore, and teach all nations, baptizing them in the name of the Father, and of the Son, and of the Holy Ghost." Then we understood that there was a world to be warned. "Teaching them to observe all things whatsoever I have commanded you: and, lo, I am with you alway, even unto the end of the world." Here is our work, our commission. The truth was to go to every city in America, and we were to gather up our forces to proclaim the message in the regions beyond. —*January 19, 1908. (p. 598, par. 2)*

Had the work been done that God designed should be done, the condition of things in our world now would be very different. But the professing followers of Christ are asleep; the churches have not fulfilled the solemn charge laid upon them. Men placed as watchmen have been asleep at their post, and many refuse to wake up. They are not fulfilling the Gospel Commission. —*January 19, 1908. (p. 599, par. 1)*

Again and again I have been instructed to present to our churches the work that should be done for the cities. Let us encourage a spirit of consecration and earnest seeking after God in our schools and sanitariums. We need to feel the deep movings of the Spirit of God in our midst. Then humble workers will be encouraged to offer themselves in faith to the service of God. They will do this, not for the wages they receive, but out of sincere love for sin-sick, suffering souls. —*February 23, 1908. (p. 643, par. 1)*

Let the Lord's work go forward. Let the medical missionary and the educational work go forward. I am sure that this is our great lack—earnest, devoted, intelligent, capable workers. In every large city there should be a representation of true medical missionary work. Let many now ask: "Lord, what wilt Thou have me to do?" It is the Lord's purpose that His method of healing without drugs shall be brought into prominence in every large city through our medical institutions. God invests with holy dignity those who go forth, farther and still farther, in every place to which it is possible to obtain entrance. Satan will make the work as difficult as possible; but divine power will attend all true-hearted workers. Guided by our heavenly Father's hand, let us go forward, improving every opportunity to extend the work of God. —*No date. (p. 689, par. 3)*

There is another line of work to be carried forward, the work in the large cities. There should be companies of earnest laborers working in the cities. Men should study what needs to be done in the places that have been neglected. The Lord has been calling our attention to the neglected multitudes in the large cities, yet little regard has been given to the matter. —*May 7, 1909. (p. 726, par. 3)*

We are not willing enough to trouble the Lord, and to ask Him for the gifts of the Holy Spirit. And the Lord wants us to trouble Him in this matter. He wants us to press our petitions to the throne. The converting power of God needs to be felt in our ranks. The most valuable education that can be obtained will be found in going out with the message of truth to the places that are in darkness, just as the first disciples went out in obedience to the commission of Christ. The Saviour gave the disciples their directions in a few words. He told them what they might expect. "I send you forth," He said, "as sheep in the midst of wolves. Be ye therefore wise as serpents and harmless as doves." These workers were to go forth as the representatives of Him Who gave His life for the life of the world. —*March 7, 1909. (p. 727, par. 1)*

In the night season I seemed to be conversing with you, and encouraging you to go forward in the name of the Lord, preparing your school to give the education most needed at this time. The education that is to be given by our people in the large cities of

Work for Cities

Southern California is set before me day and night. The people in these cities are to be made to understand what constitutes "higher education." Higher education means conformity to the plan of salvation. —*June 9, 1909. (p. 737, par. 1)*

In the night seasons I seem to be repeating the messages of warning and the encouragement that I bore at the General Conference; and I am instructed to urge upon our people that we, as the people of God, are not to follow the customs and fashions of the world. The world is following their leader, the great apostate; and we are to follow the great Teacher, Jesus Christ.

I have endeavored to arouse our people to labor for the unworked portions of the great missionary field, yet but few seem to respond to the appeals of the Spirit of God. We do not realize the extent to which Satanic agencies are at work in these large cities. The work of bringing the message of present truth before the people is becoming more and more difficult. It is essential that new and varied talents unite in intelligent labor for the people. If the burden of these unworked cities rested upon the hearts of our people as it should, they would arouse to labor as they have not yet done for the souls that are perishing in sin.

The message that I am bidden to bear to our people at this time is, "Work the cities without delay, for time is short." The Lord has kept this work before us for the last twenty years or more. A little has been done in a few places, but much more might be done. I am carrying a burden day and night because so little is being accomplished to warn the inhabitants of our great centers of population of the judgments that will fall upon the transgressors of God's law.

It will be a great advantage to have our buildings in retired locations so far as possible. The healthfulness of the surroundings should be fully considered. Locations should be selected a little out from the noisy cities. Those who labor in the large cities need special advantages, that they may not be called to sacrifice life or health unnecessarily. —*December 1, 1909. (p. 808, pars. 1-3)*

I write these things because it has been presented to me as a matter of importance that our workers should so far as possible avoid everything that would imperil their health. We need to exercise the best of judgment in these matters. Feeble or aged men and women should not be sent to labor in unhealthful, crowded cities. Let them labor where their lives will not be needlessly sacrificed. Our brethren who bring the truth to the cities must not be obliged to imperil their health in the noise and bustle and confusion, if retired places can be secured.

Those who are engaged in the difficult and trying work in the cities should receive every encouragement possible. Let them not be subjected to unkind criticism from their brethren. We must have a care for the Lord's workers who are opening the light of truth to those who are in the darkness of error. We have a high standard presented before us.

Now is the opportune time to work the cities for we must reach the people there. As a people, we have been in danger of centering too many important interests in a few places. This is not good judgment nor wisdom. An interest is now to be created in the principal cities. Many small centers must be established, rather than a few large centers.

Let missionaries be laboring two and two in different parts of all our large cities. The workers in each city should frequently meet together for prayer and counsel that they may have wisdom and grace to work together effectively and harmoniously. Let all be wide awake to make the most of every advantage. Our people must gird the armor on and establish centers in all the large cities. The agencies of Satan are active in the field, putting forth efforts to confuse the minds of men, and to fill them with vain imaginations, that they may not become interested in the truth. —*December 1, 1909. (p. 809, pars. 1-3)*

The cause of God in Oakland, San Francisco, and the surrounding places needs men of solid, Christian character, who fear God and take counsel of God, or believers will be misled by those who attach themselves to the work, and who desire to guide and control according to human judgment and plans. The Lord desires to work through men of clean purposes and decided experiences, men who will learn from the Testimonies of His Spirit where they have not been in harmony with the Lord's will, and who will be converted. Then decided changes will be made. The perils threatening the work will be seen, conversions will be experienced, and our people will be preparing to stand firmly and united with God to build up His kingdom in the earth. —*December 6, 1909. (p. 817, par. 2)*

"The time will come when God's people will have to move away from the cities, and live in small companies, by themselves. If our people regard God's instruction as of value, they will move out of the cities, so that they will not be pained by its revolting sights, and so that their children will not be corrupted by its vices. Those who chose to remain in the cities must share the disaster that will come upon them." —*March 14, 1902. (p. 836, par. 3)*

Again in a council meeting, dated April 18, 1902, "Our sanitariums should not be established in the large cities. According to the light that the Lord has given me, in a little while from now, these cities will be terribly shaken. No matter how large or how strong the buildings may be, no matter how many safeguards against fire have been provided, if God touches it, in a few moments or in a few hours it is in ruins." —*April 18, 1902. (p. 838, par. 2)*

We are not half awake.... I was so astonished when I came back the first time after we had been gone nearly ten years in Australia, to see nothing being done scarcely at all in San Francisco and Oakland. There was so little being done! Well, I tried to inquire into it—what it meant. "Oh, well," they said, "they had men out." "How many have you? How many will it take in the manner you are doing the work?" "Well," they said, "they had other duties to do," but they did not tell me what they were, and there the very work they ought to be doing, there was only one man going round visiting, and he was not competent. He did not have the experience he needed and was a man of incompetency. But what right had that minister to do as he did, unless he would take a company and with them get out and hold meetings in different sections?

God wants active men. He wants men that will work. He wants men that will understand that there is work for them to do. They can go in and give Bible readings. We know because we have seen that accomplished. We have advised it and they have done it and the Spirit of the Lord has blessed their labors but not one thousandth part has been done in these cities that ought to have been done. That is what is presented to me. —*April 5, 1910. (p. 888, par. 1)*

Now, I want to tell our brethren that there is a work we are to do and that work is—to be interested in the cases of others. There are cities all around us and when I was in Australia how glad I would have been if we could have gone right around where the people were (as you can here). —*April 15, 1910. (p. 889, par. 1 to 5th line)*

Those who stand here are to be an example in humility, in steadfastness, in high standing, showing to the world what is the higher education, showing what it means to be linked up with Christ. If your will is united with Jesus Christ, we shall see the work of God advance steadily in this place. It will reach to Riverside; it will reach to other places that are all around. There is a work to be done in many little settlements round about here. There is no virtue in settling down in one place, and spending all your time and energies there. There are many towns and settlements where earnest work needs to be done for the saving of souls. You are to have an arm of strength in all these places. The work comes to you: "Be wise; be vigilant." —*No date. (p. 932, par. 3)*

In every large city there should be a representation of true medical missionary work. The principles of genuine health reform are to be brought out in clear lines, in our health publications, and in lectures delivered to the patients in our sanitariums. In every city there are men and women who would go to a sanitarium were it near at hand, who would not be able to go to one a long way off. There are many who will be convicted and converted, who now appear indifferent. I look at this matter in a very decided light.

Let many now ask, "Lord, what wilt Thou have me to do?" It is the Lord's purpose that His method of healing without drugs shall be brought into prominence in every large city through our medical institutions. God invests with holy dignity those who go forth farther and still farther in every place to which it is possible to obtain entrance. Satan will make the work as difficult as possible, but divine power will attend all true-hearted workers. Guided by our heavenly Father's hand, let us go forward, improving every opportunity to extend the work of God. —*July 18, 1905. (p. 83, pars. 1, 2)*

All around us are doors open for service. We should become acquainted with our neighbors, and seek to draw them to Christ. As we do this, He will approve and cooperate with us.

Often the inhabitants of a city where Christ labored, wished Him to stay with them and continue to work among them. But He would tell them that He must go to cities that had not heard the truths that He had to present. After He had given the truth to those in one place, He left them to build upon what He had given them, while He went to another place. His methods of labor are to be followed today by those to whom He has left His work. We are to go from place to place carrying the message. As soon as the truth has been proclaimed in one place, we are to go to warn others. —*June 16, 1903. (p. 103, pars. 1, 2)*

The cities in the San Bernardino Valley were presented before me as places where the truth should go with power. The small printing press that Brother _____ has furnished should prove a blessing to the work in that part of the field, by printing publications that will be needed for the furtherance of the work in the Southern California cities. Our publications must now be greatly multiplied. Papers and leaflets containing the best discourses preached by our ministers are to be published and scattered widely throughout the regions where meetings are being held. —*December 1907. (p. 597, par. 5)*

Melrose and Loma Linda are both very beautiful places. Each has excellent advantages, and these two places near the cities will open the way for the truth to find access to many people who have never heard it.

Elder _____ and wife have begun work at San Bernardino, and they are sparing no pains. They are doing their best. They labor earnestly to keep the workers all alive and interested to sell the literature, and the work is certainly taking hold. Some souls have already taken their stand.

We feel deeply interested to see our cities worked. We hope that our workers in Boston will have courage in the Lord. The Lord is soon to come, and there is need that every talent shall be improved. I have seen the city of San Francisco, and what a scene of devastation it presents! We were an hour and a half riding through the ruins. As we looked at such complete destruction, we could hardly realize that the largest city in California was in ruins. We shall do all we possibly can to get the truth before the people now. The special number of the "Signs" is a medium through which much good will be accomplished. If I were twenty-five years younger, I would certainly take up labor in the cities. But I must reach them with the pen.

Looking at the tall buildings in San Francisco, some of them having one side still standing, it seemed to say, The touch of the Lord's finger will lay in ruins the most costly and the highest of buildings. One of the standing walls of these high structures came down with a crash as we were looking at it. The completeness of the ruin cannot be described.

We know not what may come next to arouse the people to investigate Bible truth. The day of the Lord will come unlooked for, as a thief in the night. If these awful calamities do not make an impression on our minds, what will?

"Be ye also ready, for in such a day as ye think not the Son of man cometh." —*May 28, 1906. (pp. 305, 306)*

Medical Missionary Work

Christ gives to all the invitation, "Come unto Me, all ye that labor and are heavy laden, and I will give you rest. Take My yoke upon you, and learn of Me; for I am meek and lowly in heart: and ye shall find rest unto your souls. For My yoke is easy, and My burden is light." If God's people will wear Christ's yoke, if they will learn in His school the lessons that He teaches, there will be sufficient means to establish gospel medical missionary work in many places. —*April 15, 1904. (p. 63, par. 1)*

The Lord has given me these words to speak and write over and over again, until a decided adherence to the principles of truth shows that men have been called to repentance. A grand side of the work of God is revealed by the words, "medical missionary." To be a medical missionary means to be a laborer together with God. Medical missionary work, a work that is to be a great help and strength to the cause, is to be carried forward in all carefulness and wisdom. Into this work not one thread is to be drawn that will spoil the beautiful pattern that God designs shall be worked out.

The medical missionary work is God's own work, and it is to be controlled by no human power. Human agencies are to act as the Lord's helping hand, guided and controlled by the power of the Holy Spirit. Not one act is to be done that will dishonor the work. —*September 15, 1902. (p. 86, pars. 1, 2)*

Our churches who have a deep interest in the children and youth, and in the work of training workers to carry forward the work essential for this time, need not blunder; for God will open ways before all who are perfecting Christian characters. He will have places ready for them in which to begin to do true missionary work. It was to prepare workers for this work, that our schools and sanitariums were established. —*August 27, 1903. (p. 92, par. 3)*

Oh, how I long to see those who claim to be medical missionaries honoring the great Examplar, whose life declares what is comprehended in the claim to be a medical missionary! I would that they were learning the Saviour's meekness and lowliness. My heart aches to think that Christ is so greatly disappointed in His followers. They bear a name that their daily life does not give them the right to bear.

We must be sanctified, soul and body, through the truth; then we shall honor the name, Medical Missionary. Oh, this name means so much! It calls for a representation altogether different from the representation given by many who bear it. Soon these will understand how far they have departed from the principles of heaven, and how greatly they have grieved the heart of Christ. —*June 24, 1903. (p. 95, pars. 4, 5)*

The real end of the gospel is to develop in human beings supreme sanctified love for God and unselfish love for one another. This love is not a fitful impulse; it is not merely the exercise of benevolence, or philanthropy; it is the fruit of a heart purified from all defilement.

The gospel was made known by God to raise human beings from sin to righteousness. He who receives the gospel constantly reaches out for the divine, perseveringly taking hold of the strength of the Saviour. His heart is an abiding place for the Holy Spirit. Day by day he shows forth the praises of Him Who has called him out of darkness into His marvelous light.

Does not this help you to see the full significance of being a gospel medical missionary? Every one who bears the name of medical missionary is to work as Christ worked. The love of Christ in his heart is to make him an example to others. He is to serve the Lord with all humility of mind, doing his appointed work, to accomplish, not his own ends, but *God's purposes.* —*September 2, 1903. (p. 96, pars. 1-3)*

The very same reasons that were given for the removal of the old Battle Creek College from Battle Creek, should now lead our brethren to decide to train in other places the youth who now expect to prepare themselves for medical missionary work. Those who expect to become medical missionary workers must be thoroughly educated in Bible lines. They should have the very best spiritual advantages, in order that they may be fitted to teach and to train others. —*August 2, 1903. (p. 96, par. 4)*

My brother, I am surprised that you are found asleep on this point. I declare unto you, in the name of the Lord, that the arrangements being made for the training of medical missionaries in Battle Creek are not right. A great work is to be done in a short time, and God forbids that we should encourage so many of our youth to bind themselves up for three, or four, or six years of training, before engaging in active work. Men and women should gain an education by working along practical lines in different places, in accordance with the light that God has given, and under the instruction of experienced leaders. —*August 2, 1903. (p. 97, par. 1)*

May the Lord increase our faith, and help us to see that He desires us all to become acquainted with His ministry of healing and with the mercy seat. He desires the light of His grace to shine forth from many places. We are living in the last days. Troublous times

Medical Missionary Work

are before us. He Who understands the necessities of the situation arranges that advantages should be brought to the workers in various places, to enable them more effectually to arouse the attention of the people. He knows the needs and the necessities of the feeblest of His flock, and He sends His own message into the highways and byways. He loves us with an everlasting love.

There are souls in many places who have not yet heard the message. Henceforth medical missionary work is to be carried forward with an earnestness with which it has never yet been done. This work is the door through which the truth is to find entrance to the large cities, and sanitariums are to be established in many places. —*August 9, 1905. (p. 97, pars. 2, 3)*

The Lord speaks to all medical missionaries, saying, "Go work today in My vineyard to save souls." God hears the prayers of all who seek Him in truth. He has the power that we all need. He fills the heart with love, and joy, and peace, and holiness. Character is constantly being developed. We cannot afford to spend time working at cross purposes with God.

There are physicians who because of a past connection with our sanitariums find it profitable to locate close to them; and they close their eyes to the great fields neglected and unworked in which unselfish labor would be a blessing to many. Missionary physicians can exert an uplifting, refining, sanctifying influence. Physicians who do not do this, abuse their power, and do a work that the Lord repudiates. —*August 9, 1905. (p. 98, pars. 1, 2)*

Sanitarium work is one of the most successful means of reaching all classes of people. Our sanitariums are the right hand of the gospel, opening ways whereby suffering humanity may be reached with the glad tidings of healing through Christ. In these institutions the sick may be taught to commit their cases to the great Physician, Who will co-operate with their earnest efforts to regain health, bringing to them healing of soul as well as healing of body.

Christ is no longer in this world in person to go through our cities and towns and villages healing the sick. He has commissioned us to carry forward the medical missionary work that He began and in this work we are to do our very best. Institutions for the care of the sick are to be established, where men and women suffering from disease may be placed under the care of God-fearing physicians and nurses, and be treated without drugs. —*October 27, 1905. (p. 98, pars. 3, 4)*

And the needed knowledge will be given to all who come to Christ, receiving and practicing His teachings, making His words a part of their lives. Those who place themselves under the instruction of the great Medical Missionary, to be workers together with Him, will have a knowledge that the world, with all its traditionary lore, cannot supply. —*October 17, 1903. (p. 101, par. 3)*

Christ, the great Medical Missionary, is our example. Of Him it is written, that He "went about all Galilee, teaching in their synagogues, and preaching the gospel of the kingdom, and healing the sick. In His service, healing and teaching were linked closely together. Today they are not to be separated.

The nurses in this institution (St. Helena Sanitarium) are to be fitted up to go out as medical missionary evangelists, uniting the ministry of the Word with their ministry of physical healing.

We must let our light shine amid the moral darkness. Many who are now in darkness, as they see a reflection of the light of the world, will realize that they have a hope of salvation. Your light may be small, but remember that it is what God has given you, and that He holds you responsible to let it shine forth. Someone may light his taper from yours, and his light may be the means of leading others out from darkness. —*June 16, 1903. (p. 102, pars. 3-5)*

In the gospel medical missionary work there are noble men who bear aloft the banner upon which is inscribed, "The commandments of God and the faith of Jesus." Consideration should be given to these faithful missionaries. They are not to be left to the caprice of men who are neither cold nor hot, and who because of their lukewarm condition are an offense to God.

Young men who have a practical knowledge of how to treat the sick are now to be sent out to do gospel medical missionary work in connection with more experienced gospel workers. If these young men will give themselves to the study of the Word, they will become successful evangelists. The ministers with whom these young men labor are to give them the same opportunity to learn that Elijah gave Elisha. They are to show them how to teach the truth to others. Where it is possible, these young men should visit the hospitals, and in some cases they may connect with them for a while, laboring disinterestedly. —*October 16, 1903. (p. 106, pars. 1, 2)*

Medical missionary work is yet in its infancy. The meaning of genuine medical missionary work is known by but few. Why?—Because God's money has been misapplied. Practical evangelistic work is being done in many places; but the workers who go forth as did the disciples are collected in one place, as they have been in the past, notwithstanding God's warning that this should not be.

The men and women who should be in the field as medical missionaries, helping those engaged in the gospel ministry, are collected in Battle Creek, acting over the same program that has been acted over in the past, confining the forces, binding them up in one place. God has spoken against this by sending His judgments on the institutions in Battle Creek. But every movement on the part of these heeding the warnings, to change the order of things, has been made very hard by the misconception of some regarding the way in which the medical missionary work should be carried forward. —*August 17, 1903. (p. 109, pars. 3, 4)*

From the light that has been given me, the medical missionary work and the gospel ministry are never to be divorced. They are to be bound together as one work. Christ is the Head of the body—the Church, and we are to work unitedly with Him. Referring to our relation to Him, the apostle says, "We are laborers together with God."

In the days of Christ there were no sanitariums in the Holy Land. But wherever He went, He Himself was a sanitarium. The Great Physician carried with Him the healing efficacy that was a cure for every disease, spiritual and physical. This He imparted to those who were under the afflicting power of the enemy, healing their diseases and infirmities....

In doing medical missionary work we shall meet the same opposition that Christ met. He declares: "Ye shall be hated of all men for My name's sake: but he that endureth to the end shall be saved. But when they persecute you in this city, flee ye into another: for verily I say unto you, 'Ye shall not have gone over the cities of Israel till the Son of man be come.'"

We are to teach others how to obtain eternal life. And we should ever remember that the efficiency of the medical missionary work is in pointing sin-sick men and women to Jesus. We are to call upon them to "behold the Lamb of God, which taketh away the sin of the world." —*July 8, 1902. (p. 112, pars. 1-4)*

The life of Christ and His ministry to the afflicted are inseparably connected. And today He is the same compassionate Physician. We should let all the afflicted understand that in Him there is healing balm for every disease, restoring power for every infirmity.

The world has departed far from true principles of restoration and health. Perverted appetite and base passion have taken control of the minds of many. Too often inclination to be irritable is strengthened by cultivation. Ill temper, cherished, destroys the delicate, pure, holy perceptions of the soul. Satan desires to cause us to be worried and harassed over mere trifles, so that we shall lose sight of the weighty matters pertaining to our eternal welfare.

The Lord desires every one to do his best. You may think that you can do very little; but remember that in the parable of the talents, Christ did not represent all the servants as receiving the same amount. To one servant was given five talents; to another, two; and to still another, one. If you have but one talent use it wisely, increasing it by putting it out to the exchangers. Do what you can to roll back the wave of disease and suffering that is sweeping over the world. Come up to the help of the Lord, to the help of the Lord against the mighty powers of darkness.

This medical dispensary work that _____ has outlined to us is similar to the work that we did in Australia. While we were in Cooranbong, there was no physician within many miles of us; and my nurse, a woman of experience in treating the sick, took the place of a physician in our community.

She responded to the many calls made, traveling from place to place and doing the work that God wants many others to do. In this line of work, some cannot do as much as others, but every one is to do what he can to relieve suffering. God desires every one of His children to have intelligence and knowledge, so that with unmistakable clearness and power His glory shall be revealed in our world. —*July 8, 1902. (p. 113, pars. 1-4)*

Into the medical missionary work there must be brought more of a yearning for souls. It was this yearning that filled the hearts of those who established our first medical institution. Christ is to be present in the sick-room, filling the heart of the physician with the fragrance of His love. When his life is such that Christ can go with him to the bedside of the sick, there will come to them the conviction that He, the compassionate Saviour, is present, and this conviction will do much to restore them to health.

In word and deed the physicians and nurses in our medical institutions are to say, so plainly that it cannot be misunderstood, "God is in this place," to save, not to destroy. Christ invites our physicians to become acquainted with Him. When they respond to His invitation, they will know that they receive the things they ask for. Their minds will be enlightened by wisdom from above. Constantly beholding the Saviour, they will become more and more like Him, till at last it can be said of them in the heavenly courts, "Ye are complete in Him." Christ has pledged Himself to give His disciples what they ask for in His name. As they labor in harmony with Him, they can ask Him to aid them in every time of need. —*February 3, 1904. (p. 114, pars. 1, 2)*

Our people in the churches of Southern California need to arouse to do a work that is necessary within their own borders. Let them awake to prayer and labor. They need more spiritual vitality. They need to be converted that they may labor for souls. Wherever there is spiritual life, there will be an imparting as well as a receiving of light and blessing. The nourishment from God's Word will be received and earnest work will be done. The act of imparting keeps open the channel for receiving this truth our Saviour ever sought to keep before the people.

I have a message to bear to the church members in Southern California. "Arouse and avail yourselves of the opportunities open to you. While Christ pleads in your behalf, plead for yourselves, that you may be purified from every unrighteous thought, every unholy action. Make an entire surrender to God of body, soul, and spirit. Be determined to do all in your power to learn the true science of soul-saving. While the light of God's mercy still shines, gather up every divine ray."

Are you prepared to sell all that you may purchase the field that contains the treasure? Said the apostle Paul, "I count all things loss for the excellency of the knowledge of Christ Jesus, my Lord,... that I may win Christ, and be found in Him."

Give up the self-righteousness that you have been cherishing. If the Lord permits you to behold such work as has been done in Los Angeles, seek with all humility, to act your part. Not in your strength, but in the strength of Christ, you are to ascend the ladder heavenward, round by round. Make diligent, thorough work in humbling yourselves, that the old habits and practices and all evil speaking may be put away. Draw nigh to God, and He will draw nigh to you. Die to self; live to God.

Brother _____, say to the church that the Lord will manifest Himself to all who seek Him with humble hearts. The end of all things is at hand. Let your eyes be fixed upon Christ. As the called and chosen of God, we must represent truth in its purity. Our lives are to be such that the world will take knowledge of us that we have been with Christ, and that truth may seem to them more desirable than error.

If rightly conducted, our sanitariums may exert a refining, ennobling influence, and lead many souls to Christ. The religious principles maintained in these institutions will demonstrate that there is relief for the soul, weary and sick with sin. Many are weak and sick because of disease of the soul. Let Christ be held up before them as the great Healer, Who invites them to come to Him and find rest. Tell them that the heart of Christ is drawn out in compassion and love for His blood-bought heritage. He will heal the troubled heart that looks to Him in faith.

To the poor, sin-sick soul repeat the Saviour's invitation: "Come unto Me, all ye that labor and are heavy laden, and I will give you rest. Take My yoke upon you, and learn of Me; for I am meek and lowly in heart: and ye shall find rest unto your souls. For My yoke is easy, and My burden is light." There is true joy in learning of Christ.

Tell the suffering ones of a compassionate Saviour. He is the only Physician Who can heal both body and soul. He has given His life for the world, that men should not perish, but have everlasting life. He looks with compassion upon those who regard their cases as hopeless. —*April 12, 1905. (pp. 143, 144)*

While the soul is filled with fear and terror, the mind cannot see the tender compassion of Christ. Our sanitariums are to be an agency for bringing peace and rest to the troubled minds. If you can inspire the despondent with hopeful, saving faith, contentment and cheerfulness will take the place of discouragement and unrest. Wonderful changes can then be wrought in their physical condition. Christ will restore both body and soul, and, realizing His compassion and love, they will rest in Him. He is the bright and morning star, shining amid the moral darkness of this sinful, corrupt world, and all who give their hearts to Him will find peace and rest and joy.

The world is filled with sickness. Sin is increasing, especially in the large cities. Death is taking away large numbers. But the great Medical Missionary invites men to come to Him. "Come unto Me," He says, "and I will give you rest." "Ask, and ye shall receive; seek, and ye shall find; knock, and it shall be opened unto you."

Our part is, by believing His word, to find rest in Christ Jesus. His words are spirit and life. In believing them there is rest and peace. "Knock, and it shall be opened unto you."

Our prayers will reach the ear of Christ, and He will open unto us the rich treasures of His grace. Through prayer we are brought into communion with the high and holy One Who inhabiteth eternity. He opens the door to every one who will knock.

As I think of how the skillful physician longs to heal every sin-sick soul, I feel so anxious that those who are drawn to our sanitariums may there find what they need for the cure of their physical and spiritual maladies. —*April 12, 1905. (p. 145, pars. 1-5)*

"Come out from among them, and be ye separate, saith the Lord, and touch not the unclean thing; and I will receive you, and will be a Father unto you, and ye shall be My sons and daughters, saith the Lord Almighty." This invitation will be accepted by those who are burdened for souls. They will become members of the royal family, children of the heavenly King.

The law of God is to be obeyed. Obedience is the life of the soul. It brings health and peace and assurance. Seek the Lord in every necessity, and know that you have a friend in Jesus, One Who loves you with an everlasting love. He will be as an anchor to the soul, both sure and steadfast. When men and women come just as they are, He cleanses them from their sins, and they become His sons and daughters. —*April 12, 1905. (p. 146, pars. 1, 2)*

Forty years ago the Lord began to give us instruction in regard to the establishment of sanitariums, as one of His chosen ways for proclaiming the third angel's message. Men and women bring disease upon themselves by transgressing the laws of God. The laws of nature, as truly as the precepts of the Decalogue, are divine, and only in obedience to them can health be recovered or preserved. Many are suffering as the result of hurtful practices, who might be restored to health if they would do what they might for their own restoration. They need to be taught that every practice which destroys the physical, mental or moral energies is sin, and that health is to be secured through obedience to the laws that God has established for the good of all mankind. —*July 1905. (p. 182, par. 3)*

Our sanitariums are to be schools in which people of all classes shall be taught the way of salvation. In them the sick are to be taught to overcome the appetite for tea, coffee, flesh meat, tobacco, and intoxicating liquor of all kinds.

In every one of our medical institutions the sick and suffering are to be pointed to the Saviour as their only hope. In the Christian life there is strength and joy and courage. Turning away from the injurious fashions of this degenerate age brings peace of mind and the assurance of the love and friendship of the heavenly Father. Receiving the Lord in simplicity places men and women where they know the meaning of the words, "As many as received Him, to them gave He power to become the sons of God." —*July 1905. (p. 183, pars. 1, 2)*

There are souls in many places who have not yet heard the message. Henceforth medical missionary work is to be carried forward with an earnestness with which it has never yet been done. This work is the door through which the truth is to find entrance to the large cities, and sanitariums are to be established in many places. —*August 9, 1905. (p. 187, par. 1)*

Sanitarium work is one of the most successful means of reaching all classes of people. Our sanitariums are the right hand of the gospel, opening ways whereby suffering humanity may be reached with the glad tidings of healing through Christ. In these institutions the sick may be taught to commit their cases to the great Physician, Who will co-operate with their earnest efforts to regain health, bringing to them healing of soul as well as healing of body. —*October 27, 1905. (p. 233, par. 1)*

But more important than magnificent scenery and beautiful buildings and spacious grounds, is the close proximity of these institutions to densely populated districts, and the opportunity thus afforded of communicating to many, many people a knowledge of the third angel's message. We are to have clear spiritual discernment; else we shall fail of understanding the opening providence of God that are preparing the way for us to enlighten the world. The great crisis is just before us. Now is the time for us to sound the warning message, by the agencies that God has given us for this purpose. Let us remember that one most important agency is our medical missionary work. Never are we to lose sight of the great object for which our sanitariums are established,— the advancement of God's closing work in the earth.

Loma Linda is in the midst of a very rich district, including three important cities—Redlands, Riverside, and San Bernardino. This field must be worked from Loma Linda, as Boston must be worked from Melrose. —*May 14, 1906. (p. 297, pars. 2, 3)*

Our sanitariums were instituted for a special work, and God cannot prosper them unless they maintain a high standard in religious matters. The truth for these times is to be revealed in every department of the sanitarium work. —*August 8, 1907. (p. 399, par. 2 last part)*

Our sanitariums should all be in running order, so that they may act their part in influencing that class of people who can be reached in no other way than by the work of the sanitarium. Our physicians are to rebuke in decided terms the sins which are the cause of sickness and disease. We have need of men who, under the inspiration of the Holy Spirit, will rebuke gambling and liquor drinking, which are such prevalent evils in these last days. We need men who will bear their message against the selfishness that is eating out the very vitals of godliness. God calls for men of faith and prayer. "Pray ye therefore the Lord of the harvest, that He will send forth laborers into His harvest." —*October 11, 1907. (p. 533, par. 4)*

Let Seventh-Day Adventist medical workers remember that the Lord God omnipotent reigneth. Christ was the greatest Physicain that ever trod the sin-cursed earth. The Lord would have His people come to Him for their power of healing. He will baptize them with His Holy Spirit, and fit them for a service that will make them a blessing in restoring the spiritual and physical health of those who need healing. —*November 3, 1907. (p. 561, par. 3)*

The truth for this time, the third angel's message, is to be proclaimed with a loud voice, (meaning with increased power), as we approach the great final test. *This test must come to the churches in connection with true medical missionary work,* a work that has the great Physician to dictate and preside in all it comprehends.... The present truth for this time comprises the messages, the third angel's message succeeding the first and second. The presentation of this message, with all it embraces, *is our work....* The third angel's message, in its clear, definite terms, is to be made the prominent warning; all that it comprehends is to be made intelligible to the reasoning minds of today. —*Unpub. MS. H. 121, 1900. (p. 602, par. 1)*

To Every Man His Work

The Lord has need of all kinds of skillful workmen. "He gave some, apostles; and some, prophets; and some, evangelists; and some, pastors and teachers; for the perfecting of the saints, for the work of the ministry, for the edifying of the body of Christ: till we all come in the unity of the faith, and of the knowledge of the Son of God, unto the perfect man, unto the measure of the stature of the fullness of Christ."

Every child of God should have sanctified judgment to consider the cause as a whole and the relation of each part to every other part, that none may lack. The field is large and there is a great work of reform to be carried forward, not in one or two lines, but in every line. The medical missionary work is a part of this work of reform; but it should never become the means of separating the workers in the ministry from their field of labor. The education of students in medical missionary lines is not complete unless they are trained to work in connection with the church and the ministry, and the usefulness of those who are preparing for the ministry would be greatly increased if they would become intelligent on the great and important subject of health. The influence of the Holy Spirit is needed that the work may be properly balanced, and that it may prove forward solidly in every line. —*1905. (p. 602, pars. 2, 3) Vol. 6, p. 291, pars. 2, 3.*

Let those who are laboring in the ministry or in the medical missionary work wear the yoke of Christ, walking in humility of mind before God, and using their varied gifts to bless humanity. Then God will use them as His helping hand. All are to be united in one body under Christ. All parts of the work are to be controlled and guided by the wisdom which God gives. There is to be harmony in every action. There is to be no jealousy or Paul or Apollos or Cephas. All are to draw in even cords, without a sign of friction. —*1901. Unpub. MS. B107, 1901. (p. 603, par. 1)*

Satan often finds a powerful agency for evil in the power which one human mind is capable of exerting on another human mind. This influence is so seductive that the person who is being molded by it is often unconscious of its power. God has bidden me speak warning against this evil, that His servants may not come under the deceptive power of Satan. The enemy is a master worker, and if God's people are not constantly led by the Spirit of God, they will be snared and taken.

For thousands of years Satan has been experimenting upon the properties of the human mind, and he has learned to know it well. By his subtle workings, in these last days, he is linking the human mind with his own, imbuing it with his thoughts, and he is doing this work in so deceptive a manner that those who accept this guidance know not that they are being led by him at his will. The great deceiver hopes so to confuse the minds of men and women, that none but his voice will be heard.

When Christ revealed to Peter the time of trials and suffering that was just before Him, and Peter replied, "Be it far from thee, Lord; this shall not be unto Thee," the Saviour commanded, "Get thee behind Me, Satan." Satan was speaking through Peter, making him act the part of the tempter. Satan's presence was unsuspected by Peter, but Christ could detect the presence of the deceiver, and in His rebuke to Peter He addressed the real foe.

One occasion, speaking to the twelve, and referring to Judas, Christ declared, "One of you is a devil." Often in the days of His earthly ministry the Saviour met His adversary in human form, when Satan as an unclean spirit took possession of men. Satan takes possession of the minds of men today. In my labors in the cause of God, I have again and again met those who have been thus possessed, and in the name of the Lord I have rebuked the evil spirit.

It is not by force that Satan takes possession of the human

mind. While men sleep, the enemy sows tares in the church. While men are spiritually sleeping, the enemy accomplishes his work of iniquity. It is when his subject "understandeth it not" that he catcheth away the good seed sown in the heart. When men and women are in this condition, when their spiritual life is not being constantly fed by the Spirit of God, Satan can imbue them with his spirit, and lead them to work his works.

I will not write more on this subject at this time. But I entreat that there may be a putting away from the life every action which does not bear the approval of God. We are drawing near to the close of earth's history; the battle is growing daily more fierce. There is a day appointed when men who have bowed to the mandates of Satan will find themselves the subjects of the wrath of God, when the Judge of all the earth shall pronounce the sentence against Satan and his adherents, "Depart from Me, ye cursed, into everlasting fire, prepared for the devil and his angels." —*August 8, 1907. (pp. 400, 401)*

Medical Missionary Work a Part of the Gospel

The rich and wonderful provisions of the gospel embrace the medical missionary work. This work is to be to the third angel's message as the right arm is to the body. Some have endeavored to make it the head, but this is not right.

The Lord reproves those who do not watch unto prayer, those who forget that they are wholly dependent upon Him and amenable to Him. He reproves those who misrepresent the great Medical Missionary, those who do not keep the way of the Lord, doing their utmost to prepare a people to become members of the family of the redeemed. He is dishonored by those whose course leads away from Christ and the truth for this time. The Lord desires that our medical workers shall proclaim the last warning message of the gospel. When they leave out the principles of present truth, skepticism runs through their work, and God cannot endorse it.

The principles of present truth are to be studied and practiced by our people, that the line of demarcation between him that serveth God and him that serveth Him not may be kept unmistakably distinct. A close examination of God's Word will reveal the riches of the grace of Christ, which are to be received by God's people, and by them imparted to those in need. —*1903.*

Christ, the great Medical Missionary, is our example. Of Him it is written, that "He went about all Galilee, teaching in their synagogues, and preaching the gospel of the kingdom, and healing all manner of sickness and diseases among the people." He healed the sick and preached the gospel. In His service, healing and teaching were linked closely together. Today they are not to be separated.

We are to teach others how to obtain eternal life. And we should ever remember that the efficiency of the medical missionary work is in pointing sin-sick men and women to Jesus. We are to call upon them to "behold the Lamb of God, Which taketh away the sin of the world."

Christ understood the work that needed to be done for suffering humanity. As He was sending out the twelve disciples on their first missionary tour, He said to them, "As ye go, preach, saying, The kingdom of heaven is at hand. Heal the sick, cleanse the lepers, raise the dead, cast out devils: freely ye have received, freely give." The fulfillment of this commission by the disciples made their message the power of God unto salvation.

It is the divine plan that we shall work as the disciples worked. Connected with the divine Healer, we may do great good in the world. The gospel is the only antidote for sin. As Christ's witnesses we are to bear testimony to its power. We are to bring the afflicted ones to the Saviour. His transforming grace and miracle-working power will win many souls to the truth. His healing power, united with the gospel message will bring us success in emergencies. The Holy Spirit will work upon hearts, and we shall see the salvation of God.

In a special sense the healing of the sick is our work. But in order to do this work we must have faith,—that faith which works by love and purifies the soul.

In ministry to the sick, we have before us the work that Christ would have us do in behalf of our fellow men in every place where we can teach and practice the true principles of healing for both soul and body. Our time for work is short, and we must be more in earnest. There is a great work to be done, and we need means with which to do this work; said Christ, "If any man came after Me, let him deny himself, and take up his cross, and follow Me." Shall we not follow Him in self-denial and sacrifice, laboring with all our power to prepare men and women, physically and spiritually, for the coming of Christ? For the Son of man is coming in His glory, with all the holy angels, and then will He fulfil the promise made to His disciples: "And if I go and prepare a place for you, I will come again, and receive you unto Myself; that where I am, there ye may be also." —*1905.*

Medical Missionary Work
to Prepare the Way for Gospel Ministry

Our Saviour never used His power to make His own life less taxing. He went about doing good, healing the sick and preaching the gospel. In our work today the ministry of the Word and medical missionary work are to be combined.

Luke is called the "beloved physician." Paul heard of his skill as a physician, and he sought him out as one to whom the Lord had entrusted a special work. He secured his co-operation in his work. After a time he left him at Philippi. Here Luke continued to labor for several years, doing double service as a physician and a gospel minister. He was indeed a medical missionary. He did his part, and then besought the Lord to let His healing power rest upon the afflicted ones. His medical skill opened the way for the gospel message to find access to hearts. It opened many doors for Him, giving Him opportunity to preach the gospel among the heathen.

Our sanitariums are established to break down the prejudice which exists in the world against the truth for this time. How important, then, that those connected with such institutions be free from reproach in any line. —*1901.*

The purest example of unselfishness is now to be shown by our medical missionary workers. With the knowledge and experience gained by practical work, they are to go out to give treatment to the sick. As they go from house to house, they will find access to many hearts. Many will be reached who otherwise would never have heard the gospel message.

Union of Medical Missionary and Gospel Work

Both home and foreign missions should be conducted in connection with the ministry of the Word. The medical missionary work is not to be carried forward as something apart from the work of the gospel ministry. The Lord's people are to be one. There is to be no separation in His work. Time and means are being absorbed in a work which is carried forward too earnestly in one direction. The Lord has not appointed this. He sent out His twelve disciples and afterward the seventy to preach the Word to the people, and He gave them power to heal the sick and to cast out devils in His name. The two lines of work must not be separated. Satan will invent every possible scheme to separate those whom God is seeking to make one. We must not be misled by his devices. The medical missionary work is to be connected with the body; and the education of students in medical missionary lines is not complete unless they are trained to work in connection with the church and the ministry....

The medical missionary work is not to take men from the ministry but to place them in the field. Wherever camp-meetings are held young men who have received an education in medical missionary lines should feel it their duty to act a part. They should be encouraged to speak, not only on these special lines, but also upon the points of present truth, giving the reasons why we are Seventh-Day Adventists. These young men, given an opportunity to work with older ministers, will receive much help and blessing. —*1899.*

To our physicians and ministers I send the message, "Lay hold of the Lord's work as if you believed the truth for this time. Medical missionary workers and workers in the gospel ministry are to be bound together by indissoluble ties. Their work is to be done with freshness and power. Throughout our churches there is to be a reconversion, and a reconsecration to service. Shall we not, in our work in the future and in the gatherings that we hold, be of one accord?"

Let us now consecrate ourselves to the proclamation of the message, "Prepare ye the way of the Lord, make straight in the desert a highway for our God."

The nurses in our sanitariums are to be fitted up to go out as medical missionary evangelists, uniting the ministry of the Word with their ministry of physical healing.

No line is to be drawn between the genuine medical missionary work and the gospel ministry. These two must blend. They are not to stand apart as separate lines of work. They are to be joined in an inseparable union, even as the hand is joined to the body. Those in our institutions are to give evidence that they understand their part in the genuine gospel medical missionary work. A solemn dignity is to characterize genuine missionaries.

Many are asking me how I regard the ministry of the gospel with reference to medical missionary work. These two lines of work should blend. They should both help to compose the body. The genuine medical missionary work should not be exalted above the gospel ministry. Some are in danger of regarding the medical missionary work as the body when it is only the arm and the hand.

To those who go out to do medical missionary work I would say, "Serve the Lord Jesus Christ with sanctified understanding, in connection with the ministers of the gospel and the Great Teacher. He who has given you your commission will give you skill and understanding as you consecrate yourselves to His service, engaging diligently in labor and study, doing your best to bring relief to the sick and suffering."

To those who are tired of a life of sinfulness, but who know not where to turn to obtain relief, present the compassionate Saviour, full of love and tenderness, longing to receive those who come to Him with broken hearts and contrite spirits. Take them by the hand, lift them up, speak to them words of hope and courage. Help them to grasp the hand of Him Who has said, "Let him take hold of My strength, that he may make peace with Me; and he shall make peace with Me." —*1903*.

In the gospel medical missionary work there are noble men who bear aloft the banner upon which is inscribed, "The commandments of God, and the faith of Jesus."

Young men who have a practical knowledge of how to treat the sick, are now to be sent out to do gospel medical missionary work, in connection with more experienced gospel workers. If these young men will give themselves to the study of the Word, they will become successful evangelists. The ministers with whom these young men labor are to give them the same opportunity to learn, that which Elijah gave Elisha. They are to show them how to teach the truth to others. Where it is possible, these young men should visit the hospitals, and in some cases they may connect with them for a while, laboring disinterestedly.

Many will go out to labor for the Master who have not been able to take regular courses of study in school. God will help these workers. They will obtain knowledge from the higher school, and will be fitted to take their position in the rank and file of workers as nurses. The great Medical Missionary sees every effort that is made to find access to souls by presenting the principles of health reform. —*1903.*

Christ came to this world as the great Medical Missionary. When His example is followed, medical missionary work will be carried forward on a much higher plane than it is at the present time. God calls for a reconversion among gospel teachers, and especially among physicians and other medical missionary workers, that Christ may not be misrepresented and put to shame. The cleansing must begin in the heart and mind, and flow forth in the actions. The characters of our medical missionary workers need to be refined and ennobled. This result can be brought about only as these are made partakers of the divine nature, having escaped the corruption that is in the world through lust.

Should we not see in the world today medical missionaries who in all the features of their work are worthy of the name they bear? Who will aspire to the doing of deeds worthy of valiant soldiers of Christ? We are living near the close of the great conflict, when many souls are to be rescued from the slavery of sin. We are living in a time when to Christ's followers the promise especially belongs, "Lo, I am with you alway, even unto the end of the world." He Who commanded the light to shine out of darkness, He Who has called us out of darkness into His marvelous light, bids us let our light shine brightly before men, that they may see our good works, and glorify our Father Who is in heaven. In such rich measure has light been given to God's people that Christ is justified in telling them that they are to be the light of the world.

True sympathy between man and his fellow man is to be the sign distinguishing those who love and fear God from those who are unmindful of His law. How great the sympathy that Christ expressed in coming to this world to give His life a sacrifice for a dying world. His religion led to the doing of genuine medical missionary work. He was a healing power. "I will have mercy and not sacrifice," He said. This is the test that the great Author of truth used to distinguish between true religion and false. God wants His medical missionaries to act with the tenderness and compassion that Christ would show were He in our world. Is it not time that we understood that not a sparrow falls to the ground without the notice of our heavenly Father? —*1903. (pp. 603-610)*

We have come to a time when every member of the church should take hold of medical missionary work. The world is a lazar-house filled with victims of both physical and spiritual disease. Everywhere people are perishing for lack of a knowledge of the truths that have been committed to us. The members of the church are in need of an awakening, that they may realize their responsibility to impart these truths. Those who have been enlightened by the truth are to be light-bearers to the world. To hide our light at this time is to make a terrible mistake. The message to God's people today is, "Arise, shine; for thy light is come, and the glory of the Lord is risen upon thee."

The medical missionary work should be a part of the work of every church in our land. Disconnected from the church, it would soon become a strange medley of disorganized atoms. —*No date. (p. 611, pars. 1, 2)*

Through the first disciples a divine gift was proffered to Israel; the faithful evangelist today will do a similar work in every city where our missionaries enter. It is a work which to some extent we have tried to do in connection with some of our sanitariums, but a much wider experience in these lines is to be gained. Cannot our conference presidents open the way for the students in our schools to engage in this line of labor? Again and again it has been presented to me that "there should be companies organized, and educated most thoroughly to work as nurses, as evangelists, as ministers, as canvassers, as gospel students to perfect a character after the divine similitude." There is a grand work to be done in relieving suffering humanity, and through the labors of students who are receiving an education and training to become efficient medical missionaries, the people living in many cities may become acquainted with the truths of the third angel's message. Consecrated leaders and teachers of experience should go out with these young workers, at first, giving them instruction how to labor. When favors of food or of lodging are offered by those who fear and honor God, these favors may be accepted. Thus opportunity will be found for conversation, for explaining the Scriptures, for singing Bible songs, and praying with the family. There are many to whom such labor as this would prove a blessing. —*February 23, 1908. (p. 641, par. 1)*

And each worker, as he goes forth to labor, should realize that he is as surely sent of God as were the first disciples. God's eye follows them; His Spirit goes with them. To those who accept His great commission He gives the assurance, "Lo, I am with you alway, even unto the end of the world." "He that dwelleth in the secret place of the Most High shall abide under the shadow of the Almighty." The psalmist declares, "I will say of the Lord, He is my refuge and my fortress: my God; in Him will I trust. Surely He shall deliver thee from the snare of the fowler, and from the noisome pestilence. He shall cover thee with His feathers, and under His wings shalt thou trust: His truth shall be thy shield and buckler." Servants of God, you have great advantages, which you should appreciate.

A Plea for Medical Missionary Evangelists

The end of all things is at hand. The signs foretold by Christ are fast fulfilling. The nations are angry, and the time of the dead has come that they should be judged. There are stormy times before us, but let us not utter one word of unbelief or discouragement. Let us remember that we bear a message of healing to a world filled with sin-sick souls. May the Lord increase our faith and help us to see that He desires us all to become acquainted with His ministry of healing and with the mercy seat. He desires the light of His grace to shine forth from many places.

We are living in the last days. Troublous times are before us. He Who understands the necessities of the situation arranges that advantages should be brought to the workers in various places, to enable them more effectually to arouse the attention of the people. He knows the needs and the necessities of the feeblest of His flock, and He sends His own message into the highways and the byways.

There are souls in many places who have not yet heard the message. Henceforth medical missionary work is to be carried forward with an earnestness with which it has never yet been done. This work is the door through which the truth is to find entrance to the large cities, and sanitariums are to be established in many places.

Sanitarium work is one of the most successful means of reaching all classes of people. Our sanitariums are the right hand of the gospel, opening ways whereby suffering humanity may be reached with the glad tidings of healing through Christ. In these institutions the sick may be taught to commit their cases to the great Physician, Who will co-operate with their earnest efforts to regain health, bringing to them healing of soul as well as healing of body. No date given. —(p. 688, pars. 1-4)

I have been instructed that we are not to delay to do the work that needs to be done in health reform lines. Through this work we are to reach souls in all the walks of life. I have been given special light that in our sanitariums many souls will receive and obey present truth. In these institutions men and women are to be taught how to care for their own bodies, and at the same time how to become sound in the faith. They are to be taught what is meant by eating the flesh and drinking the blood of the Son of God. Said Christ, "The words that I speak unto you, they are spirit, and they are life."

Our sanitariums are to be schools in which instruction shall be given in medical missionary lines. They are to bring to sin-sick souls the leaves of the tree of life, which will restore to them peace and hope and faith in Christ Jesus.

Let the Lord's work go forward. Let the medical missionary and the educational work go forward. I am sure that this is our great lack—earnest, devoted, intelligent, capable workers. In every large city there should be a representation of true medical missionary work. Let many now ask, "Lord, what wilt Thou have me to do?" It is the Lord's purpose that His method of healing without drugs shall be brought into prominence in every large city through our medical institutions. God invests with holy dignity those who go forth farther and still farther, in every place to which it is possible to obtain entrance. Satan will make the work as difficult as possible, but

Medical Missionary Work

divine power will attend all true-hearted workers. Guided by our heavenly Father's hand, let us go forward improving every opportunity to extend the work of God. —*No date. (p. 689, pars. 1-3)*

The Lord speaks to all medical missionaries, saying, "Go, work today in My vineyard to save souls." God hears the prayers of all who seek Him in truth. He has the power that we all need. He fills the heart with love, and joy, and peace, and holiness. Character is constantly being developed. We cannot afford to spend the time working at cross purposes with God. —*No date. (p. 690, par. 1)*

The Lord calls upon our young people to enter our schools, and quickly fit themselves for service. In various places, outside of cities, schools are to be established, where our youth can receive an education that will prepare them to go forth to do evangelical work and medical missionary work.

The Lord must be given an opportunity to show men their duty, and to work upon their minds. No one is to bind himself to serve for a term of years under the direction of one group of men or in one specified branch of the Master's work; for the Lord Himself will call men, as of old He called the humble fishermen, and will Himself give them instruction regarding their field of labor and the methods they should follow. He will call men from the plow and from other occupations, to give the last note of warning to perishing souls. There are many ways in which to work for the Master, and the great Teacher will open the understanding of these workers, enabling them to see wondrous things in His Word.

Medical missionary work is yet in its infancy. The meaning of genuine medical missionary work is known by but few. Why?— Because the Saviour's plan of work has not been followed. God's money has been misapplied. In many places practical, evangelistic medical missionary work is being done; but many of the workers who should go forth as did the disciples are being collected together and held in a few places, as they have been in the past, notwithstanding the Lord's warning that this should not be.

Many of the men and women who should be out in the field, working as medical missionary evangelists, helping those engaged in the gospel ministry, are collecting in a favored locality, acting over the same program that has been acted ever in the past, confining the forces, binding them up in one place. —*No date. (p. 691, pars. 1-4)*

Christ stands before us as a pattern Man, the great Medical Missionary—an example for all who should come after. His love, pure and holy, blessed all who came within the sphere of its influence. His character was absolutely perfect, free from the slightest stain of sin. He came as an expression of the perfect love of God, not to crush, not to judge and condemn, but to heal every weak defective character, to save men and women from Satan's power.

He is the Creator, Redeemer, and Sustainer of the human race. He gives to all the invitation, "Come unto Me, all ye that labor and are heavy laden, and I will give you rest. Take My yoke upon you, and learn of Me; for I am meek and lowly in heart: and ye shall find rest unto your souls. For My yoke is easy, and My burden is light."

What, then, is the example that we are to set to the world? We are to do the same work that the great Medical Missionary undertook in our behalf. We are to follow the path of self-sacrifice trodden by Christ. —*No date. (p. 694, pars. 1, 2)*

The light that God has given in medical missionary lines will not cause His people to be regarded as inferior in scientific medical knowledge, but will fit them to stand upon the highest eminence. God would have them stand as a wise and understanding people because of His presence with them. In the strength of Him Who is the source of all wisdom, all grace, defects and ignorance may be overcome. —*October 1, 1909. (p. 782, par. 2)*

On the night of October 10, 1901, I was unable to sleep after half past eleven at night. Many things regarding the sanitarium work were presented to me in figures and symbols. I was shown a sanitarium near Los Angeles in running order. At one place I saw sanitarium work being carried on in a beautiful building. On the grounds surrounding the building there were many fruit trees.

"As in the visions of the night I saw this place, I said to our brethren: 'O, ye of little faith. You have lost much time.' On the lawn were the sick in wheelchairs. On the grounds of this beautiful place that I saw in the visions of the night, there were many shade trees, the boughs of which hung down in such a way as to form leafy canopies somewhat in the shape of tents. Underneath these canopies patients were resting. The sick were delighted in their surroundings. While some worked, others were singing. There was no sign of dissatisfaction.

"I awoke and for some time could not sleep. Many vivid scenes had passed before me, and I could not forget the words I had spoken to the helpers and patients. Again I lost consciousness, and other scenes passed before me. I was in another locality surrounded by different scenery. Again it seemed as if I were pleading with those who were sick to look unto Jesus, The Great Healer. I then awoke, and began writing out some cautions that had been given me. —*Early 1902. (p. 833, pars. 2-4)*

"Last night the same scenes passed before me that passed before me thirty-five years ago, when the light was given to establish a sanitarium that would be the means of educating many souls in regard to right principles of living, and of bringing them to a knowledge of the truth. We must establish sanitariums for this purpose, and they must be so conducted that God can co-operate with the efforts made in them to relieve physical and spiritual suffering. God wants the sick and suffering to understand what it means to have the advantage of living in a sanitarium conducted in accordance with the principles of the gospel. Every worker connected with these institutions is to follow on to know the Lord, that he may know that His going forth is prepared as the morning. If our missionary spirit were stronger, if the love of Jesus filled the hearts of those in service for Him, many of the sick and suffering would be drawn to Jesus, led to the tree of life, to take of its health-restoring, life-sustaining power." —*Early in 1902. (p. 838, par. 1)*

I wish to express to you some thoughts that should be kept before the sanitarium workers. That which will make them a power for good is the knowledge that the great Medical Missionary has chosen them to this work, that He is their chief Instructor, and that it is ever their duty to recognize Him as their Teacher. —*April 27, 1910. (p. 899, par. 1)*

God's true commandment-keeping people will be instructed by Him. The true medical missionary will be wise in the treatment of the sick, using the remedies that nature provides. And then he will look to Christ as the true Healer of disease. The principles of health reform brought into the life of the patient, the use of nature's remedies, and the co-operation of divine agencies in behalf of the suffering, will bring success. —*April 27, 1910. (p. 902, par. 3)*

I have written to you the instruction that has been given me regarding the special work to be done by the lady physicians in our sanitariums. It is the Lord's plan that men shall be trained to treat men; and the women to treat women. In the confinement of women, midwives should take the responsibility of the case. In Bible times it was not considered a proper thing for men to act in this capacity; and it is not the will of God that men should do this work today. Very much evil has resulted from the practice of men treating women, and women treating men. It is a practice according to human devising, and not according to God's plan. Long has the evil been left to grow, but now we lift our voice in protest against that which is displeasing to God. —*June 7, 1911. (p. 948, par. 3)*

Publications containing the precious truths of the gospel should be in the rooms of the patients, or where they can have easy access to them. There should be a library in every sanitarium, and it should be supplied with books containing the light of the gospel. Judicious plans should be laid that the patients may have conant access to reading matter that contains the light of present truth.

The work of the true medical missionary is largely a spiritual work. It includes prayer and laying on of hands; he therefore should be as sacredly set apart for his work as is the minister of the gospel. Those who are selected to act the part of missionary physicians, are to be set apart as such. This will strengthen them against the temptations to withdraw from the sanitarium work to engage in private practice. No selfish motive should be allowed to draw the worker from his post of duty. We are living in a time of solemn responsibility; a time when consecrated work is to be done. Let us seek the Lord diligently and understandingly. If we will let the Lord work on human hearts, we shall see a great and grand work accomplished.

The medical missionary work done in connection with the giving of the third angel's message, is to accomplish wonderful results. It is to be a sanctifying, unifying work, corresponding to the work which the great Head of the church sent forth the first disciples to do. Calling these disciples together, Christ gave them their commission, "Go not into the way of the Gentiles, and into any city of the Samaritans enter ye not: But go rather to the lost sheep of the house of Israel. And as ye go, preach, saying, The kingdom of heaven is at hand. Heal the sick, cleanse the lepers, raise the dead, cast out devils: freely ye have received, freely give." —*February 23, 1908. (p. 639, pars. 1-3)*

"Provide neither gold, nor silver, nor brass in your purses, nor scrip for your journey, neither two coats, neither shoes, nor yet staves: for the workman is worthy of his meat. And into whatsoever city or town ye shall enter, inquire who in it is worthy; and there abide till ye go thence.... Behold, I send you forth as sheep in the midst of wolves: be ye therefore wise as serpents, and harmless as doves."

It is well for us to read this chapter, and let its instruction prepare us for our labors. The early disciples were going forth upon Christ's errands, under His commission. His spirit was to prepare the way before them. They were to feel that with such a message to give, such blessings to impart, they should receive a welcome in the homes of the people.

Some restraint was placed upon them in this, their first experience. They were not to go in the way of the Gentiles, nor enter into any city of the Samaritans; for this would bring upon them trial and perplexity. This first offer of salvation was to be made to the lost sheep of the house of Israel. Their deeds of mercy and love, their message of truth, was first to be given to the Jewish nation. In the blessings that they were thus carrying to the people, they were to proclaim, "The kingdom of God is come nigh unto you." —*(p. 640, pars. 1-3)*

A time will come when medical missionaries of other denominations will become jealous and envious of the influence exerted by Seventh-Day Adventists who are working in these lines. They will feel that influence is being secured by our workers which they ought to have. We should have in various places, men of extraordinary ability who have obtained their diplomas in medical schools of the best reputation, who can stand before the world as fully qualified and legally recognized physicians. Let God-fearing men be wisely chosen to go through the training essential in order to obtain such qualifications. They should be prudent men who will remain true to the principles of the message. These should obtain the qualifications, and the authority to conduct an educational work for our young men and our young women who desire to be trained for medical missionary work. Now while the world is favorable toward the teaching of the health reform principles, moves should be made to secure for our own physicians the privilege of imparting medical instruction to our young people who would otherwise be led to attend the worldly medical colleges. The time will come when it will be more difficult than it is now, to arrange for the training of our young people in medical missionary lines. —*April 27, 1910. (p. 903 all)*

Satan will try to place barriers in the way of the true medical missionary. He will seek to bring discouragement upon those who recognize the commandments of God, and are determined to obey them. We must be careful not to carry our views of health reform to extremes, thus making it "health deform."

Our food should be plain and free from all objectionable elements, but let us be careful that it is always palatable and good. —*(p. 902, par. 4)*

Perils of Last Days

I have had much to write in regard to the shortness of time. Our work is soon to close, and we are now to place ourselves in working order in God's way. We are not to link ourselves up with those who are not wise to discern what is the will of God. We are to come out from among them and be separate. The end of all things is at hand, and the message of warning must be given. A spirit of anger is stirring the nations, and it will soon be too late to work for the Lord. Every conceivable deception will be brought in, and the enemy will work with masterly power. Stronger and stronger will be his efforts, until in heaven it is said, "It is finished." —*July 1905. (p. 185, par. 1)*

Let none think that they can pass safely through the perils of these last days, while puffed up with self-sufficiency. Some would unsettle minds by urging the carrying out of false plans. False theories are taught as truth, and I am charged to meet these errors decidedly. We should heed the instruction found in the third and fourth chapters of second Timothy, especially the solemn charge given by Paul to Timothy. —*October 11, 1909. (p. 790, par. 3)*

"I charge thee therefore before God, and the Lord Jesus Christ, Who shall judge the quick and the dead at His appearing... Preach the Word; be instant in season, out of season; reprove, rebuke, exhort with all longsuffering and doctrine. For the time will come when they will not endure sound doctrine; but after their own lusts shall they heap to themselves teachers, having itching ears; and they shall turn away their ears from the truth, and shall be turned unto fables. But watch thou in all things, endure affliction, do the work of an evangelist, make full proof of thy ministry."

"I am now ready to be offered, and the time of my departure is at hand. I have fought a good fight, I have finished my course, I have kept the faith: henceforth there is laid up for me a crown of righteousness, which the Lord, the righteous Judge, shall give me at that day: and not to me only, but unto all them also that love His appearing." —(p. 790, par. 4; p. 791, par. 1)

I see a crisis before us, and the Lord calls for His workmen to come into line. Every soul should now stand in a position of deeper, truer consecration to God, than during the years that are past. —December 6, 1909. (p. 818, par. 2)

Cultivate Both Mental and Physical Powers

The students are to unite faithfully in the medical work, keeping their physical powers in the most perfect condition possible, and laboring under the instruction of the great Medical Missionary. The healing of the sick and the ministry of the Word are to go hand in hand. —August 19, 1906. (p. 316, par. 1)

We are to educate the youth to exercise equally the mental and the physical powers. The healthful exercise of the whole being will give an education that is broad and comprehensive. We had stern work to do in Australia in educating parents and youth along these lines; but we persevered in our efforts until the lesson was learned that in order to have education that was complete, the time of study must be divided between the gaining of book knowledge and the securing of a knowledge of practical work. Part of each day was spent in useful work; thus students learned how to clear the land, how to cultivate the soil, and to build houses, in time that would otherwise have been spent in playing games and seeking amusement. And the Lord blessed the students who thus devoted their time to learning lessons on usefulness. —May 7, 1909. (p. 728, par. 2)

You may say, the world will not acknowledge us. What if the world will not acknowledge you? It is the power of God that makes the impress on the human mind. Let it be more and more deeply impressed upon every student that every one of us should have an intelligent understanding of how to treat the physical system. And there are many who would have greater intelligence in these matters if they would not confine themselves to years of study without a practical experience under the instruction of learned physicians and surgeons. The more fully you put yourself under the direction of God, the greater knowledge you will receive from God. As you keep yourself in connection with the Source of all power, and as you minister to the sick, suggestions will come to your mind how you can apply to the case in hand the principles learned in your student days. "Ye are laborers together with God." He is to be your Chief Instructor. —May 7, 1909. (p. 729, par. 1)

Exercise the mental powers, and in no case neglect the physical. Let not intellectual slothfulness close up your path to greater knowledge. Learn to reflect as well as to study, that your minds may expand, strengthen and develop. Never think that you have learned enough, and that you may now relax your efforts. The cultivated mind is the measure of the man. Your education should continue during your lifetime; every day you should be learning, and putting to practical use the knowledge gained.
—*October 1, 1909. (p. 761, par. 1)*

Economy To Be Used

For several days I have thought of writing you, but could not because so many things demanding immediate attention have come in. I may have written to you regarding the equipment of your treatment rooms, but fearing that I have not, I will come right to the point.

When we were at the Paradise Valley Sanitarium, we were conducted through the new treatment rooms. One room was elaborately fitted up with electrical appliances for giving the patients treatments. That night I was instructed that some connected with the institution were introducing things for the treatment of the sick that were not safe. The application of some of these electrical treatments would involve the patient in serious difficulties, imperiling life.

One was conversing with the doctors, and with great earnestness was saying, "Never, never carry out your wonderful plans. There have been various mechanical devices brought into the treatment rooms that are expensive and the men who make a specialty of treating certain cases are liable to make grave mistakes."

There are men who make a specialty of treating the rectum, and some feel that they have been greatly benefited. But I have been instructed that this treatment, as well as many surgical operations, leaves with many a serious weakness.

Several things were mentioned that have been brought into the Paradise Valley Sanitarium, which were not necessary, and which should not have been purchased without consultation with other physicians. The amount of money which some of these machines cost, and the salary which must be paid to the one who operates them, should be taken into consideration. I felt impelled to talk with _____ in reference to these matters, although we were driving with a number of people, and it was not a favorable place to converse about such matters.

Now I am certain that great care should be taken in purchasing electrical instruments and costly mechanical fixtures. Move slowly _____, and do not trust to men who suppose that they understand what is essential, and who launch out in spending money for many things that require experts to handle them.

Several times I have been instructed that much of the elaborate, costly machinery used in giving treatments, did not help in the work as much as is supposed. With it we do not get so good results as with the simple appliances we used in our earlier experiences. The application of water in the various simple ways is a great blessing.

I have been instructed that the x-ray is not the great blessing that some suppose it to be. If used unwisely, it may do much harm.

The results of some of the electrical treatments are similar to the results of using stimulants. There is a weakness that follows...

Keep the patients out of doors as much as possible, and give them cheering, happy talks in the parlor, with simple reading and Bible lessons easy to be understood which will be an encouragement to the soul. Talk on health reform, and do not you, my brother, become burden-bearer in so many lines that you cannot teach the simple lessons of health reform. Those who go from the sanitarium should go so well instructed that they can teach others the methods of treating their families.

There is danger of spending far too much money on machinery and appliances which the patients can never use in their home lessons. They should rather be taught how to regulate the diet, so that the living machinery of the whole being will work in harmony. Let them become intelligent in regard to the importance of laying aside corsets and shortening their skirts. Such lessons will be to the women more valuable than they can estimate. —*June 2, 1906. (pp. 307-309)*

Simplicity Without Display

In the establishment and carrying forward of sanitarium work, the strictest economy is ever to be shown. Workers are to be employed who will be producers as well as consumers. In no case is money to be invested for display. Gospel medical missionary work is today to be carried forward in simplicity, even as it was carried forward by the Majesty of heaven, who, seeing the necessities of a lost, sinful world, laid aside His royal robe and Kingly crown, and clothed His divinity with humanity, that He might stand at the head of humanity. In His way of working, He has left us a perfect example. "If any man will come after Me," He declared, "let him deny himself, and take up his cross, and follow Me." The true medical missionary will obey these words. He will not strain every nerve to make a display, thinking thus to win souls to the Saviour. The Son of God left His heavenly home to come to a world all seared and marred by the curse, that He might seek and save the lost. Ought we not, His followers, to show the same self-denial and self-sacrifice that His life revealed? For us He endured the privations

Simplicity Without Display

of poverty. Shall we refuse to deny ourselves for His sake? —*April 15, 1904. (p. 62, par. 1)*

Christ gives to all the invitation, "Come unto Me, all ye that labor and are heavy laden, and I will give you rest. Take My yoke upon you, and learn of Me; for I am meek and lowly in heart: and ye shall find rest unto your soul. For My yoke is easy, and My burden is light." If God's people will wear Christ's yoke, if they will learn in His school the lessons that He teaches, there will be sufficient means to establish gospel medical missionary work in many places.

Christ might have come to this world with a retinue of angels; but instead, He came as a babe, and lived a life of lowliness and poverty. His glory was in His simplicity. Shall we refuse to engage in medical missionary work unless we can follow the customs of the world, making a display such as worldings make? To one who asked if he might follow Him, Christ said, "Foxes have holes, and the birds of the air have nests; but the Son of man hath not where to lay His head." Shall those who profess to be His followers refuse to engage in the work of helping their suffering fellow-beings unless they can be placed where their dignity will not be lessened?

In no other way can we do the work of God successfully, than by following in the footsteps of the One Who gave up His high command to come to our world, that through His humiliation and suffering, human beings might become partakers of the divine nature. For our sake He became poor, that through His poverty we might come into possession of the eternal riches. —*April 15, 1904. (p. 63, pars. 1-3)*

I call upon the presidents of our conferences to exert their God-given influence to open the fields that have never yet been worked. These fields stand as a reproach to our people. Organize your work intelligently, and then proceed to action. Let your simplicity of speech, and your simplicity and neatness of dress speak of your work as missionaries. Educational advantages will be provided, and the Lord will go before those who will take up the work in the spirit of self-sacrifice. —*August 27, 1903. (p. 93, par. 2)*

In order that our institutions shall teach right lessons there must be connected with them men of such simplicity that they are willing to learn of the great Teacher. "To you it is given," Christ said, "to the people who keep My commandments and do these things that I have presented in My word, to know the mysteries of the kingdom of heaven." —*June 2, 1905. (p. 161, par. 4)*

In the work of the school maintain simplicity. No argument is so powerful as is success founded upon simplicity. And you may attain success in the education of students as medical missionaries without a medical school that can qualify physicians to compete with the physicians of the world. —*November 3, 1907. (p. 559, par. 1)*

The work of educating our youth, as outlined for us in the instruction given of God, is to be sacredly maintained. For this reason we must select as teachers those who will educate in right lines. Said my Instructor: Let not teachers be chosen to educate and train the youth who will not maintain the simplicity of Christ's methods. His teachings contained the very essence of sanctified simplicity.

Those teachers who present matters to the students in an uncertain light are not fitted for the work of educating the youth. No man is qualified for this work unless he is daily learning to speak the words of the Teacher sent from God. Now is the time to sow the gospel seed. The seed we sow must be clean and pure, and that which will produce the choicest fruit. We have no time to lose.

The work of our schools is to become more and more in character like the work of Christ. Only the power of the grace of God working on human hearts and minds will make and keep the atmosphere of our schools and churches clean. —*May 17, 1908. (p. 677, pars. 2, 3)*

There have been teachers in our schools who could pass well in a worldly institution of learning, but were unfitted for the training of our youth because they were ignorant of the truths of the gospel of Christ. They were unable to bring the simplicity of Christ into their labors. It should be the work of every teacher to present these truths, that have called us out to stand as a peculiar people, before the world, and which are able to keep us in harmony with heaven's laws. In the messages that have been sent to us from time to time, we have truths that will accomplish a wonderful work of reform in our characters. If we will give them a place, they will prepare us for entrance into the Holy City of God. It is our privilege to make continual advancement to a higher grade of Christian living.

One night I was awakened and instructed to write a straight testimony regarding the work of our school at Loma Linda. By that school a solemn and sacred work was to be done. The teachings of health reform were to stand out clearly and brightly that all the youth in attendance might learn to practice them. All our educators should be strict health reformers. The Lord desires that genuine missionaries shall go out as pioneers from our schools. They are to be fully consecrated to the work, as laborers together with God, daily enlarging their sphere of usefulness, and becoming more fully sanctified through the truth. The influence of a consecrated medical missionary teacher in our schools is invaluable.

I have been instructed to present these things before our teachers. We need to be converted from our faulty lives to the faith of the gospel. Christ's followers have no need to try to shine. —*May 17, 1908. (p. 678, pars. 1-3)*

If they will behold constantly the life of Christ, they will be changed in mind and heart into the same image. Then they will shine without any superficial attempt. The Lord asks for no display of goodness. In the gift of His Son He has made provision that our

Simplicity Without Display

inward lives may be imbued with the principles of heaven. It is the appropriation of this provision that will lead to a manifestation of Christ to the world. When the people of God experience the new birth, their honesty, their uprightness, their fidelity, their steadfast principles, will unfailingly reveal it. O, what words were spoken to me. What gentleness was recommended through the grace abundantly given. The greatest manifestation that men and women can make of the grace and power of Christ, is when the natural man becomes partaker of the divine nature, and through the power that the grace of Christ imparts, overcomes the corruptions that are in the world through lust.

"In the work of the school, maintain simplicity. No argument is so powerful as is success, founded upon simplicity. And you may attain success in the education of students as medical missionaries, without a medical school that can qualify physicians to compete with the physicians of the world. Let the students be given a practical education. And the less dependent you are upon worldly methods of education, the better it will be for the student. Special instruction should be given in the art of treating the sick without the use of poisonous drugs, and in harmony with the light that God has given. Students should come forth from the school without having sacrificed the principles of health reform." —*April 23, 1908. (p. 735, par. 3)*

The Lord has instructed us that in our institution of education, we should ever be striving for the perfection of character to be found in the life of Christ, and in His instruction to His disciples. Having received our commission from the highest Authority, we are to educate, educate, educate, in the simplicity of Christ. Our aim must be to reach the highest standard in every feature of our work. He Who healed thousands with a touch and a word is our Physician. The precious truths contained in His teachings are to be our front guard and our rearward.

The standard set for our sanitariums and schools is a high one, and a great responsibility rests upon the physicians and teachers connected with these institutions. Efforts should be made to secure teachers who will instruct after Christ's manner of teaching, regarding this of more value than any human methods. Let them honor the educational standards established by Christ, and following His instruction give their students lessons in faith and in holiness. —*April 7, 1910. (p. 900, pars. 1, 2)*

The Lord has blessed _____, and He will continue to bless him, as he continues to move in the fear of God, and plans wisely and economically with his associates for the fitting up and management of the institution. If any of his brethren act arbitrarily in an effort to restrain him in this, they would be found hindering the very work that the Lord has signified should be done. He is not to be forced to turn aside from his convictions as to the way in which the work under his charge shall be carried on. —*August 19, 1906. (p. 316, par. 3)*

I have words to speak to you. The Lord has laid upon you the responsibilities of no ordinary nature. At the time of the meeting held before you were settled at Loma Linda, when I was so sick, the Lord showed me what was to be your work as director of the sanitarium, and that if you would connect yourself with divine wisdom, you would be taught of God. You need a clear mind in order to settle wisely the many questions that come to you for decision. The Lord would have you taught of Him.

My brother, do not allow men of limited experience to come in, as _____ has done, and assume a controlling power. _____ has placed himself as teacher and adviser and ruler in many matters, and unless you work and watch carefully, such an influence will retard the work. _____ should learn that he is not qualified to do the work he supposes he is to do.

_____ supposes that if it were not for his watching of the finances, there would be serious losses; whereas if he had nothing to do and say in these matters, it would save many perplexities. He has taken upon himself burdens that the Lord has not laid upon him. He has learned some of his lessons of _____ who has done much to retard the work in the South. If he would attend to his work of ministry, and keep his hands off the work of directing, he would save himself and others many burdens. From the light that has been given me, I know that it is a mistake for him to be connected with our sanitariums; he should not be a manager. —*November 2, 1906. (p. 330, pars. 1-3)*

Obtain facilities for your school work. Let the means that shall come to you be used very economically. Do not spend one dollar unnecessarily. —*June 8, 1909. (p. 737, par. 2)*

There are many inventions which cost large sums of money which it is just as well should not come into our work. They are not what our students need. Let the education given be simple in its nature. In giving us His Son, the Father gave the most costly gift that heaven could bestow. This gift it is our privilege to use in our ministration to the sick. Let Christ be your dependence. Commit every case to the great Healer; let Him guide in every operation. The prayer offered in sincerity and in faith will be heard. This will give confidence to the physicians and courage to the sufferer. —*February 20, 1908. (p. 636, par. 3)*

I have been instructed that we should lead the sick in our institutions to expect large things because of the faith of the physician in the great Healer, Who, in the years of His earthly ministry, went through the towns and villages of the land and healed all who came to Him. None were turned empty away; He healed them all. Let the sick realize that, although unseen, Christ is present to bring relief and healing. —*February 20, 1908. (p. 637, par. 1)*

Section II

Individual Responsibility

Many workers who are bearing responsibilities are embracing too much authority; and they will certainly confuse the human judgment by their dictatorial authority. I must warn my brethren to be on their guard against this. The cause of God is imperiled when the workers become self-confident, and seek to embrace more than the Lord has laid upon them. Hindrance instead of advancement is the result of such a spirit. —*November 2, 1905. (p. 331, par. 4)*

Brother _____, carry your work intelligently, ever consulting the Word of God; for this Word is very precious to the worker in the cause. Study the messages that God has sent to His people for the last sixty years through the Spirit of Prophecy. Do not seek the counsel of men, but by the earnest prayer seek the wisdom of God. A mistake has been made in the past by leaning upon the guidance of men. Seek to correct this mistake. —*(p. 332, par. 1)*

Those who have considered themselves qualified to bear responsibilities in the churches, should seek to obtain light and a knowledge of how to prosecute their work at this time in the cities, north and south, east and west, that are calling for a knowledge of the truth for this time. Our camp-meetings should do a more thorough work in preparing the laborers for the work that is to be done in every place. —*November 2, 1906. (p. 332, par. 4)*

I have a message to bear to our church in every place. There is a matter that should be clearly understood by all. Every soul who claims to be a Christian is to bear the responsibility of keeping himself in harmony with the guidance of the Word of God. God holds each soul accountable for following for himself the pattern given in the life of Christ, and of having a character that is cleansed and sanctified.

I am bidden to say that the work of following the guidance and direction of men is a mistake, from the beginning to end. God now calls for genuine conversion on the part of those who have taken up the work of telling other men just where they shall go and how they shall labor. No man has been delegated by God to act as a dictator to his fellow-laborers, telling them what is their duty; for this is assuming by weak and erring men that which belongs to God alone. Our brethren should refuse to accept such responsibility; for by taking such a course they are teaching men to seek the direction and guidance of men instead of the control and guidance of God. Our Christian activity is to be greatly increased, and in this work the Lord is to be the Guide and Counselor of His servants.

One great object in the mission of Christ was to establish in every believer a sense of the guiding and controlling power of God.

This lesson is to be repeated again and again. No greater injury can be done to our churches than for members to be taught to look to their fellow-men for guidance. And there is no man so humble in heart and so respectful of his brethren that he can safely take upon himself this work.

The grace of humility is rare in these times; but he who possesses it will reveal the grace of Christ in word and spirit and action. We need individually to seek the Lord until we find Him, and then to follow on to know the beauty of His character. Christ invites His believing people: "Come unto Me, all ye that labor and are heavy laden, and I will give you rest. Take My yoke upon you, and learn of Me; for I am meek and lowly in heart: and ye shall find rest unto your souls. For My yoke is easy, and My burden is light." The worker who responds to this invitation will have a correct estimate of his individual duty. —*June 18, 1907. (pp. 370, 371)*

The Lord has given me a message for the laborers in the Southern California Conferences. The Lord Jesus wants us to believe that He is our Wisdom, and Sanctification, and Redemption. Influences are appearing among us that are decidedly opposed to the healthy development of the work which the Lord would have carried in straight lines.

God has instructed me to say to conference presidents and to ministers, "Teach every church in the Conference to look to God for an understanding of present truth and duty." The Lord has not placed upon presidents or ministers the responsibility of the position that He alone, as head of His church, can occupy. Church and conference organization do not give to man any such responsibility.

Listen to the words of the Saviour, "Come unto Me, all ye that labor and are heavy laden, and I will give you rest. Take My yoke upon you, and learn of Me; for I am meek and lowly in heart: and ye shall find rest unto your souls. For My yoke is easy, and My burden is light." "My sheep hear My voice, and I know them, and they follow Me: and I give unto them eternal life; and they shall never perish, neither shall any man pluck them out of My hand."

The exercise of authority has been carried to such extremes that it is now time to call a halt; for church members are receiving a false education. A mistake has been made that should be corrected before it is too late. Those who dare to accept responsibilities that are contrary to the gospel plan are in a dangerous place. They need to see its course of action in its true light. Their permissions and their forbiddings have fostered wrong ideas regarding the responsibility that individuals should carry, and have led believers to look to men instead of looking to God.

Brethren, the Lord will bless you in an effort to break up this wrong influence. Ministers will become weak and unchristlike if they continue to encourage this kind of work. God is to be the strength and wisdom of His people. Man power is not to rule the church of Christ.

A Change of Heart Needed

The men who have accepted kingly authority need to be converted; for the self-esteem and self-exaltation they have manifested is dishonoring to God. The Word of God is to be exalted as the rule of faith and practice; for this Word reveals the standard of character we are to reach and teaches us our duty to love as brethren. Its requirements are to be strictly obeyed. At this time, when God is calling every man to put away his natural and cultivated tendencies to wrong, and to rid himself of his preconceived opinions; at this time, when Satan's influences are coming into our ranks with such power, God's servants must understand the way of the Lord. The word of man is fallible, imperfect, unreliable; but the work of the Lord standeth sure, and is done in truth and uprightness.

The men bearing chief responsibility on our conference must not seek to embrace too much authority. I have been shown that men receive ideas from men, and follow their own judgment and the judgment of their fellows, and that the Lord is not always their Counselor. The work of setting up erring men to judge and dictate to their fellows is folly. When men suppose that they must watch God's laborers, and exercise over them their human judgment, the sure result must be confusion and dishonor to God.

The sweet psalmist of Israel said, "the Spirit of the Lord spake by me, and His word was in my tongue. The God of Israel said, the Rock of Israel spake to me, He that ruleth over men must be just, ruling in the fear of God. And He shall be as the light of the morning, when the sun riseth, even a morning without clouds; as the tender grass springing out of the earth by clear shining after rain."

The work of judgment has not been given to any minister or conference president. "Judge not," the Saviour says, "that ye be not judged. For with what judgment ye judge, ye shall be judged: and with what measure ye mete, it shall be measured to you again. And why beholdest thou the mote that is in thy brother's eye, and considerest not the beam that is in thine own eye? Or how wilt thou say to thy brother, Let me pull out the mote out of thine eye; and, behold, a beam is in thine own eye?"

The God of power and glory, the Strength of Israel, is being put out of sight by man's glorification of human capabilities. A change must be brought about. There is no need of so much of man's devising. We are nearing the close of this earth's history. God says I will overturn, overturn, until man stands in his appointed place. I am the true Shepherd of My flock. The voice and judgment of man is not to be the voice and judgment of My people. Church members are to be educated, line upon line, and precept upon precept, to look to God for wisdom and counsel.

"As every man hath received the gift, even so minister the same one to another," the apostle Paul exhorts "as good stewards of the manifold grace of God. If any man speak, let him speak as the oracles of God; if any man minister, let him do it as of the ability which God giveth: that God in all things may be glorified through Jesus Christ." When the principles of the Word of God are brought into the life practice of the workers we shall have men of God's appointment.

There are those who, had they placed themselves in a position where the Spirit of God could lead them, would have been a great help and blessing to God's people; but they have hindered the work that God purposed to do through them by taking upon themselves responsibilities which God never required them to carry. To all who have thus exalted themselves, I am bidden to say, "Let the principles of the Word of God find a place in your work. Let the strong traits of character, that would eclipse the attributes of mercy and love and compassion, be put away." Every principle of the Word of God is to stand magnified in the life of the servant of God. —*July 29, 1907. (pp. 387-390 all)*

"God desires to bring men into direct relation with Himself. In all His dealing with human beings, He recognizes the principles of personal responsibility. He seeks to encourage a sense of personal dependence, and to increase the need of personal guidance. His gifts are committed to men as individuals. Every man has been made a steward of sacred trusts; each is to discharge his trust, according to the direction of the Giver; and by each an account of his stewardship must be rendered to God.

"In all this, God is seeking to bring the human into association with the divine that through this connection man may become transformed into the divine likeness. Then the principle of love and goodness will be a part of his nature. Satan, seeking to thwart this purpose, constantly works to encourage dependence upon man, to make men the slaves of men. When he thus succeeds in turning minds away from God, he insinuates his own principles of selfishness, hatred and strife.

"In all our dealings with one another, God desires us carefully to guard the principles of personal responsibility to and dependence upon Him." —*September 2, 1907. (p. 452, pars. 1-3) Vol. 7, pp. 174-176.*

Tremendous responsibilities are ours; and men are called for who will not misinterpret their responsibilities, but will do their appointed work in a spirit of humility and in the fear of God. We should ever be afraid of a spirit that would lead us to place restrictions on the work of others, lest we hinder the advance of the message of truth. Those who have in the past allowed such a spirit to control them have sadly hurt the work. They need to repent and be converted; for the Holy Spirit cannot work with them as an oppressive power to close the lips that He has opened.

This age demands that the servants of God be men of faith and prayer, who realize the responsibilities that rest upon them as bearers of the last message of mercy to a perishing world. "Ye are the light of the world," Christ declared. "Let your light so shine before

Individual Responsibility

men, that they may see your good works, and glorify your Father which is in heaven." Many, many souls will be brought to a knowledge of the truth if intelligent labor is put forth in their behalf. —*October 11, 1907. (p. 534, pars. 1, 2)*

God's messengers are to sense their grave responsibility. They are to trust humbly in God. The Lord calls now for conscientious, humble minute-men. He invites them, "Take My yoke upon you, and learn of Me; for I am meek and lowly in heart: and ye shall find rest unto your souls." The Lord Jesus came to our world as its Redeemer. He came as an example to all men. The world was in need of a correct representation of the future inhabitants of the city of God.

Every one who has responsibilities to bear will reveal by his daily life whether or not he is fitted for the office that he holds. Ministers of the gospel will be tempted to strive for worldly and commercial advantages; but worldly interests must be laid aside. The glory of God must be kept in view. The saving of souls is to be their all-important burden.

Men who live in the atmosphere of Christ's presence will communicate the principles of heaven in conversation, in spirit, in tenderness, because they are learning of Christ. They will set a right example to their associates.

There are many who may be saved, if their prejudiced ideas can be removed, and if they consent to take upon them the yoke of Christ. All should bear in mind the words of Christ: "Ye are the salt of the earth: but if the salt have lost his savour, wherewith shall it be salted? It is thenceforth good for nothing, but to be cast out, and to be trodden under foot of men." —*November 11, 1907. (p. 570, pars. 1-3)*

A great many of the difficulties that have come into our work in California and elsewhere have come in through a misunderstanding on the part of men in official positions concerning their individual responsibility in the matter of controlling and ruling their fellow-laborers. Men entrusted with responsibilities have supposed that their official position embraced very much more than was ever thought of by those who place them in office, and serious difficulties arose as the result. —*December 6, 1909. (p. 815, par. 3)*

Simple organization and church order are set forth in the New Testament Scriptures, and the Lord has ordained these for the unity and perfection of the church. The man who holds office in the church should stand as a leader, as an adviser and a counselor and helper in carrying the burdens of the work. He should be a leader in offering thanksgiving to God. But he is not appointed to order and command the Lord's laborers. The Lord is over His heritage. He will lead His people if they will be led of the Lord in the place of assuming a power God has not given them. Let us study the twelfth and thirteenth chapters of first Corinthians, and the fifteenth chapter of Acts.

Let the men carrying responsibilities treat those who labor with them with the same consideration that they would wish to receive, were they the helpers, and others the leaders. "All ye are brethren," the Saviour declares. Position does not give a man kingly authority. The meekness of Christ is a wonderful lesson given to the fallen world. Learning this meekness from the great Teacher, the worker will become Christlike. —*December 6, 1909. (p. 816, pars. 1, 2)*

Many have refused to see and adopt the light, because they would not humble themselves before God, and be daily converted to Christ. Yet this must be the experience of all who overcome by the blood of the Lamb and the word of their testimony. When men humble their hearts, and are daily converted, following the example of the meek and lowly Jesus, then there is hope that they will become wise in their religious experience.

I see a crisis before us, and the Lord calls for His workmen to come into line. Every soul should now stand in a position of deeper, truer consecration to God, than during the years that are past.

God corrects His people when they are in danger of being corrupted by those who obey not the truth. I have been charged to stand faithfully in the position in which the Lord has placed me among His people, that they might be instructed and counseled.

I have been shown that there are men helping to form committees, and men filling important positions in the churches, who are self-righteous, men walking after the counsel of their own hearts. Neither these self-righteous men nor those who have been influenced to hurt the work of God, should now be put in places of large responsibility; for the work of God will be marred by such steps. There are some who will always be deceived. We are living amid the perils of the last days. Let the Word of God teach righteousness. Let the chaff be separated from the wheat. —*December 6, 1909. (p. 818, pars. 1-4)*

Those who have the responsibility of locating and keeping in operation our sanitariums and schools are ever to bear in mind that these institutions are to be regarded as divinely appointed agencies for the restoration of the entire man—physical, mental and spiritual. In planning for the establishment of sanitariums in places where God has designated we should do a special work, we are to allow no selfishness, no personal ambition, to mar the work. Over and over again I have repeated that the establishment and maintenance of sanitariums is ordained of God for the advancement of His cause in the earth. While Christ was on this earth, He ministered to the needs of suffering humanity. He is our example. We are to labor intelligently; and in planning for the extension of sanitarium work, we are to seek to secure the very places that God indicates are most suitable for carrying forward this line of our work. —*January 27, 1910. (p. 852, par. 4)*

Individually we should stand in freedom before God, serving Him intelligently. The Lord will work through every soul who is consecrated to Him. He will give them knowledge and spiritual understanding; and He will direct their steps. How shall we know that

Individual Responsibility

He is leading us? Because we act in accordance with the Holy Spirit, and are in harmony with Christ.

You know how hard the enemy worked that we should not get this place. Now it is in our possession, and you have been working to the point of occupying and using and improving the place for the benefit of the sick and the honor of Christ's name. The Lord is pleased with this. He wants you to work His vineyard faithfully; and your faithful service appeals to the understanding of the patients and visitors. If it were not for this faithfulness, you never would have secured the favor and gained the advantages that you enjoy today in regard to the educational work taken up here. You stand in favor before the people. This advantageous position you could not have gotten if there had been a laxness in the work and a leaving things at loose ends. "Wherefore, gird up the loins of your mind, be sober, and hope to the end for the grace that is to be brought unto you at the revelation of Jesus Christ." —*April 20, 1911. (p. 932, pars. 1, 2)*

Those who are bearing responsibilities in our institutions in various branches of the Lord's work, need to be constant learners in the school of Christ. We must understand and know that the Lord is at the head of the work, although we do not always discern His overruling power. At all times it is our privilege to know that He is there, and to have the assurance that He will work with us if we will work with Him. But if one plans one thing, and another plans another thing, and each endeavors to lead, we shall get things into confusion. We may avoid this if we will. We may carry the work intelligently, in the love and fear of God. If we will make up our minds to do this at any sacrifice, if we labor patiently, we shall not fail. —*March 28, 1912. (p. 991, par. 2)*

The Speaker said, "You can all be a blessing to one another, if you open your hearts to receive the precious love of Christ." Let all keep diligent guard over their own disposition, and then pleasant words will be spoken. Let not those who are connected with the sanitarium as helpers think that they have liberty to exercise authority over others. God will help the ones who are chosen to act a part in the duties connected with the sanitarium, to labor as workers together with God. Let them be sure to take charge of their own individual selves. Those who come to the sanitarium as patients are to see that Christian love and kindness are shown to all who are connected with the institution. Let every one stand in his lot and place, refusing to go out of his way to assume authority as a dictator. The Lord calls upon every man to be courteous and to discipline himself. He is not to exercise authority that is not given him. Let every one learn daily his lesson of preparing his own heart for the heavenly inspection, for the record is written in the books of heaven. Let souls be emptied of self. Then invite Christ to come in, and open the door of the heart to His knock. He says, "If any man hear My voice,... I will come in to him, and will sup with him, and he with Me." This divine companionship is what is needed in every home, in every church, in every sanitarium. There is need of strong spirited men, men who will be sure to do special honor to the Lord Jesus Christ. We must be preparing to become members of the royal family in the heavenly mansions Christ is preparing for every one who through the grace received will wear His yoke.

Christ invites us, "Learn of Me; for I am meek and lowly in heart: and ye shall find rest unto your souls. For My yoke is easy, and My burden is light." —*December 11, 1905. (p. 253 all)*

When a worker is selected for an office, that office of itself does not bring him any power of capability that he did not have before. A high position does not give to the character Christian virtues. The man who supposes that his individual mind is capable of planning and devising for all branches of the work, reveals a great lack of wisdom. Not one human mind is capable of carrying the many and varied responsibilities of a conference embracing thousands of people and many branches of work.

But a greater danger than this has been revealed to me in the feeling that has been growing among our workers that ministers and other laborers in the cause should depend upon the mind of certain leading workers to define their duties. One man's mind and judgment is not to be considered capable of controlling and molding a conference. The individual and the church have responsibilities of their own. God has given to every man some talent or talents to use and improve. In using these talents he increases his capability to serve. God has given to each individual judgment, and this gift He wants His workers to use and improve. The president of a conference must not consider that his individual judgment is to control the judgment of all.

In no conference should propositions be rushed through without time being taken by the brethren to carefully weigh all sides of the question. Because the president of a conference suggested certain plans, it has sometimes not been considered necessary to consult the Lord about them. Thus propositions have been accepted that were not for the spiritual benefit of believers, and which involved far more than was apparent at the first casual consideration. Such movements are not in the order of God. Many, very many matters have been taken up and carried by vote, that have involved far more than was anticipated and far more than those who voted would have been willing to assent to, had they taken time to consider the question from all sides. —*October 3, 1907. (p. 492, pars. 1-3)*

We cannot at this time afford to be careless or negligent in the work of God. We must seek the Lord earnestly every day if we would be prepared for the experiences that come to us. Our hearts are to be cleansed from every feeling of superiority, and the living principles of the truth are to be planted in the soul. Young and aged and middle-aged should now be practicing the virtues of Christ's character. They should daily be making spiritual development, that they may become vessels unto honor in the Master's service.

Individual Responsibility

"And it came to pass, that, as He was praying in a certain place, when He ceased, one of His disciples said unto Him, Lord, teach us to pray, as John also taught his disciples."

The prayer that Christ gave to His disciples in answer to this request is not made in highflown language, but expresses in simple words the necessities of the soul. It is short, and deals directly with the daily needs.

Every soul has the privilege of stating to the Lord his own special necessities, and to offer his individual thanksgiving for the blessings that he daily receives. But the many long and spiritless, faithless prayers that are offered to God, instead of being a joy to Him are a burden. We need, O so much clean, converted hearts! We need to have our faith strengthened. "Ask, and ye shall receive," the Saviour promised; "seek, and ye shall find; knock, and it shall be opened unto you." We need to educate ourselves to trust in this word, and to bring the light and grace of Christ into all our works. We need to take hold of Christ, and to retain our hold of Him until we know that the power of His transforming grace is manifested in us. We must have faith in Christ if we would reflect the divine character. —*October 3, 1907. (p. 493 all)*

Christ clothed His divinity with humanity, and lived a life of prayer and self-denial, and of daily battle with temptation. He is our efficiency and power. He desires that through the appropriation of His grace humanity shall become partakers of the divine nature, and thus escape the corruption that is in the world through lust. The Word of God in the Old and New Testaments if faithfully studied and received into the life will give spiritual wisdom and life. This word is to be sacredly cherished. Faith in the Word of God and in the power of Christ to transform the life will enable the believer to work His works, and to live a life of rejoicing in the Lord.

Again and again I have been instructed to say to our people, "Let your faith and trust be in God." Do not depend on any erring man to define your duty. It is your privilege to say, "I will declare Thy name unto my brethren: in the midst of the congregation will I praise Thee. Ye that fear the Lord, praise Him; all ye the seed of Jacob, glorify Him; and fear Him, all ye the seed of Israel. For He hath not despised nor abhorred the affliction of the afflicted; neither hath He hid His face from him; but when he cried unto Him, He heard. My praise shall be of Thee... I will pay my vows before them that fear Him. The meek shall eat and be satisfied: they shall praise the Lord that seek Him: your heart shall live for ever." —*October 3, 1907. (p. 494 all)*

These scriptures are right to the point. Every church member should understand that God is the One to Whom to look for an understanding of individual duty. It is right that brethren counsel together; but when men arrange just what their brethren shall do, let them answer that they have chosen the Lord as their Counselor.

Those who will humbly seek Him will find His grace sufficient. But when one man allows another to step in between him and the duty that God has pointed out to him, giving to man his confidence and accepting him as guide, then he steps from the true platform to a false and dangerous one. Such a man, instead of growing and developing, will lose his spirituality.

There is no power in any man to remedy the defective character. Individually our hope and trust must be in One Who is more than human. We need ever to remember that help has been laid on One Who is mighty. The Lord has provided the needed help for every soul who will accept it. —*October 3, 1907. (p. 495, pars. 1, 2)*

I have passed a wakeful night; for there have been presented to me some things connected with the past, present, and future of the work in Southern California.

I have now no hesitation in speaking plainly, and in calling things by their right names. For three nights in succession, the message has been given to me that _____, as president of this Conference, is out of his place. He should not occupy such a position in any of our conferences. He is leading some of his brethren to ignore the messages that the Lord is sending to His people. He has refused to accept the testimonies that have not harmonized with his own mind and judgment.

The results of his administration will be further developed in the future. Why should men be entrusted with such grave responsibilities before they have been sufficiently proved? _____ has made the work of _____ exceedingly difficult. He has worked in an underhanded manner to thwart the efforts of _____ to do that work that should be done at Loma Linda. The influence of _____ _____ has been counter to the messages of instruction that the Lord has given concerning this sanitarium. For two years this work of opposition has been carried forward.

The word of the Lord in unmistakable language is that Elder _____ should not occupy the position of a conference president. He needs to learn some of the first lessons of what God requires of His people who are living amid the perils of the strong temptations of these last days. He needs to be converted, heart, soul, and mind to the truth. Self has borne rule in his plans, and he has endeavored to convert others to his own ideas. As yet there has been but a part development of his character, but if he continues in his present course it will not be long before there will be a more open opposition to the work that we have, under the direction of God, endeavored to accomplish in Southern California.

The authoritative utterances of our brother, in their commands and their forbiddings, bear not the heavenly impress. They are not inspired by the Holy Spirit of God. Unless he becomes thoroughly convinced that his mind is not infallible, his future life will be characterized by a spirit of exalting whomsoever he will, and of hinder-

Individual Responsibility

ing those who are not in harmony with him. In his present state of mind, he should not be entrusted with responsibilities that would give him the power to dictate to any church.

I have borne the testimony that _____ should have no control over _____. I have borne a testimony, even in the meeting that has just been held here, that the Lord's servants are to seek their counsel from God. It is contrary to God's plan that men shall exercise arbitrary authority over their brethren. God would convince those who have felt called upon to exercise a wrong authority over their brethren, that He has not authorized them to take upon themselves such responsibilities. He has not appointed a man to take the place of God in this conference.

The Saviour bids us pray, "Lead us not into temptation." Our heavenly Father will lead His people in the paths of righteousness. The Word of the Lord to the churches in this conference is: "Watch and pray, lest ye enter into temptation." "Be on your guard against the efforts of the powers of darkness to resist the testimonies of God's Spirit that are to be understood." Actions spring from desires and purposes. God alone can discern the thoughts and intents of the heart. He weighs with unerring accuracy the very motives of the mind.

The president of the Southern California Conference needs the power to see himself as he is in the sight of God. He is as a man lost in the woods, blinded by a dangerous confidence in himself. A humbling of the soul, with earnest prayer, and a diligent study and reception of the Word of God, are the means by which to overcome these peculiar temptations. The armor of truth is to be found in the Word of God. Clothed in this armor, a man will be humble, not dictatorial, but a learner from the Great Teacher.

The Lord has witnessed the unnecessary hardships that have been brought upon _____. Avenues of assistance have been hedged up, and it has been made well nigh impossible to raise the money that has been needed at Loma Linda for the addition of bathrooms, and other needed facilities. There must be a change in these conditions. Relief must be given to this institution, which, by the working of God in our behalf, has been brought within our reach.

Influences have been brought to bear upon minds and hearts, to lead men away from God, that they should obey men, and show to men the honor that belongs alone to God. He alone is to be honored and glorified. Men placed in positions of trust may be a help to the churches, but they are not to lord it over God's heritage. Neither are they to show favors to certain ones, with the expectation that they will in return receive certain favors from those persons.

During the past night there has passed before me scene after scene, where men in positions of trust were bearing rule over their fellow men. There seemed to be with them but little burden for the sacred truth for this time, that would sanctify the heart, the thoughts, the speech, and the actions. One stood by my side, and said, "These men are becoming too wise to follow a plain, 'Thus saith the Lord.' They are departing from God."

A Bible lay upon the stand, and the heavenly messenger held it to view, saying in solemn tones: "The Holy Scriptures of the Old and the New Testament, together are to act a more important part in presenting before the people God's saving truth. The Word is to be carefully studied, but not to present theories that will lead away the minds of the people, diverting them from the warning sent to prepare a people to stand in the day of the Lord."

God has a message to be proclaimed in all the world. By every teacher in our schools, every minister, every medical missionary the only true God is to be uplifted. But some of the watchmen are asleep. They are as the blind leading the blind. The time to labor is fast passing away, and Satan is leading some to stand as the accuser of their brethren who are bearing heavy burdens.

Who of our ministers are awake, giving the trumpet a certain sound? The trumpet of some in official positions has been sounding their own exploits. The spirit that has characterized their work has borne the disapproval of God. Who of those that have been appointed to office in the work of God understand what that office embraces? Where are the faithful watchmen?

Some who should be watchmen, are seeking to gain advantages for themselves in commercial lines. For the sake of financial profits, they are becoming tainted with the spirit of commercialism. This spirit has so blinded the eyes of their understanding that they have not a clear scriptural understanding of Bible principles. At times when they have not been guided by the Spirit of God, they have dictated to their brethren and have considered that any proposition that they might make should be accepted without question. Their position has been such that many of their brethren have been deceived and deluded.

The Word of the living God is to be our lesson book. Here, in both the Old and New Testaments, is a statement of the mistakes made by ancient Israel. Shall we, as did they, fail to improve the most precious opportunities for doing the work of God? If, during the three years past, the opportunities had been truly improved to meet the requirements of this time, some who are now lost to the cause of God, would stand ready to serve as genuine missionaries.

Awake, awake from your stupor, you who have been under the control of other human minds. No longer allow yourselves to treat with indifference, subjects that need to be presented to the people with clearness. Your president does not realize where he stands in the sight of God. Influences have been brought in that have turned his mind away from the preparation that is essential for these last days.

And as he has turned away from Christ, the spirit of commercialism has absorbed his mind. The Light of the world has been

Individual Responsibility

eclipsed. There is a profession to know God, but there is often a denial of Him in words and in action.

God permitted Christ, the Sun of Righteousness, to come to our world to seek and to save perishing souls. But today some who have been entrusted with the care of these blood-bought souls are denying Him in word, in method, in action. Darkness covers the earth and gross darkness the people.

Where are the earnest calls that should be given to arouse the people to that preparation of heart that will purify, refine, and ennoble characters to shine as lights amid the moral darkness? The soul is never safe, save under divine guidance. The Word of God coming from sanctified hearts and lips will soften and break hard hearts. And if ever there was a period of time when the words of Christ should be heard, it is now.

None but He Who created man can effect a change in the human heart. Every teacher is to realize that he must be moved by divine agencies. The mind and judgment must be submitted to the Holy Spirit. Through the sanctification of the truth, we may bear a decided testimony for righteousness both before believers and before unbelievers.

We are far behind what we should be in our experience. We are backward in pronouncing the testimony that should flow from sanctified lips. Even when sitting at the table, Christ taught truths that brought comfort and courage to the hearts of His hearers. Whenever it is possible, we are to present the words of Christ. If His love is in the soul, abiding there as a living principle, there will come forth from the treasure-house of the heart, words suitable to the occasion, not light, trifling words, but uplifting words, words of truth and spirituality.

Let teachers and students watch their opportunities whenever possible to confess Christ in their conversation, speaking of their experiences in following Christ, praying with their brethren for the Holy Spirit. Confessing Christ openly and bravely, exhibiting in the choice of words the simplicity of true godliness will be more effective than many sermons. There are but few who give a true representation of the meekness of Christ. Oh, we need, and we must have, His meekness! Christ is to be formed within, the hope of glory.

We are preparing for translation to the heavenly world. Our conversation should be in heaven, from whence we look for the Lord Jesus. He is to be acknowledged as the Giver of every good and perfect gift, the Author of all our blessings, in whom is centered our hope of eternal life.

Angels of heaven are taking note of all our works, and watching to see how they can minister to our needs. With intensity of spirit, all heaven stands ready to lend aid to us in our divine progress. Shall we improve our present opportunities, and receive the impress of the divine image?

I am instructed that those who believe in the present truth, and who are set as guides to the people of God, are not to become engaged in commercial pursuits. Their minds must not become so absorbed that they cannot distinguish between the sacred and the common. A strife for victory in business deals will develop a pugilistic spirit, a spirit that is spoiling the record of some of our brethren in Los Angeles. Such a course will develop in these brethren characters that may not now be clearly discerned. We are to educate the mind in pleasant considerations of divine things. But those who suppose that they are to guide other minds, must in a most earnest manner seek the Lord.

The only way that temptation may be overcome is through watchfulness and prayer. The trial of the faith must come. Satanic agencies are busy, endeavoring to spoil the record of many souls. Those who are neglectful of Bible study, are in danger of disregarding the Testimonies. Those who seem to feel that position and influence places them above temptation, are under a strong delusion of the enemy. In this conference there is a strong temptation to consider that position makes the man. Men placed in positions of responsibility are to honor that position, by a most earnest determination to be like Christ, as He gave us example in His earthly life. His life testified that the strongest of temptations are no excuse for yielding to sin. "In the last day, that great day of the feast, Jesus stood and cried, saying, If any man thirst, let him come unto Me, and drink. He that believeth on Me, as the scripture hath said, out of His belly shall flow rivers of living water. (But this spake He of the Spirit, which they that believe on Him should receive....)"

"Come unto Me, all ye that labor and are heavy laden, and I will give you rest. Take My yoke upon you, and learn of Me; for I am meek and lowly in heart: and ye shall find rest unto your souls. For My yoke is easy, and My burden is light." —*November 3, 1907. (pp. 549-556)*

Great care should be exercised in regard to the influences that prevail in the institution. The influences under which the nurses are placed will mold their character for eternity. —*1903. (p. 612, par. 3)*

I am instructed that our only safety is in being joined to the Lord Jesus Christ. We can afford to lose the friendship of worldly men. Those who join themselves to worldly men, that they may carry out their unsanctified purposes, make a fearful mistake; for they forfeit the favor and blessing of God. I am to urge upon the attention of our people that the Lord Himself has placed a wall of separation between the world and that which He has established on the earth. God's people are to serve Him; for Christ has called them out of the world, and sanctified and refined them, that they may do His service. He has been given all power in heaven and in earth.

There is no such thing as maintaining concord between the profane and the holy. There can be no concord between Christ and

Belial. But "the Lord hath set apart him that is godly for Himself." And this consecration to the Lord, this separation from the world, is plainly declared and positively enjoined in both the Old and the New Testament. —*December 11, 1905. (p. 255, pars. 2, 3)*

The Speaker said, "You can all be a blessing to one another, if you open your hearts to receive the precious love of Christ." Let all keep diligent guard over their own disposition, and then pleasant words will be spoken. Let not those who are connected with the sanitarium as helpers think that they have the liberty to exercise authority over others. God will help the ones who are chosen to act a part in the duties connected with the sanitarium, to labor as workers together with God. Let them be sure to take charge of their own individual selves. Those who come to the sanitarium as patients are to see that Christian love and kindness are shown to all who are connected with the institution. Let everyone stand in his lot and place, refusing to go out of his way to assume authority as a dictator. The Lord calls upon every man to be courteous and to discipline himself. He is not to exercise authority that is not given him. Let everyone learn daily his lesson of preparing his own heart for the heavenly inspection, for the record is written in the books of heaven. Let souls be emptied of self. Then invite Christ to come in, and open the door of the heart to His knock. He says, "If any man hear My voice, and open the door, I will come in to him, and will sup with him, and he with Me." This divine companionship is what is needed in every home, in every church, in every sanitarium. There is need of strong spirited men, men who will be sure to do special honor to the Lord Jesus Christ. We must be preparing to become members of the royal family in the heavenly mansions Christ is preparing for every one who through the grace received will wear His yoke.

Christ invites us, "Learn of Me; for I am meek and lowly in heart: and ye shall find rest unto your souls. For My yoke is easy, and My burden is light." In our character-building give encouragement to every divine, sacred influence. —*December 11, 1905. (p. 253 all)*

The blessing from Jesus makes everything good and profitable. Have His praise in your heart, and in your voice, and in your words, and your hearts will become fit temples for the Holy Spirit of God. Your success depends upon constant watchfulness and earnest prayer. "Ye are My friends, if ye do whatsoever I command you." Depending upon the Lord, you can do the very things that are to be done, without murmuring and without disputing. —*(p. 254, par. 1)*

Satan is watching to secure every soul possible, to do him service by careless work and careless words. He desires to impress the minds of the converted and the unconverted that those connected with the sanitarium are lacking in piety and the meekness of Christ, and that they are not Christians. Jesus will help you to prevent this impression from being made.

Christ would have every one possess in abundance, the grace of heaven. He desires that His joy may be in you, and that your joy may be full. Every soul is to discipline himself in strict, faithful service, just as verily out of meeting as in meeting. You are in full view of the heavenly angels, and every faithful disciple may be, if he will, as was Ezra before the king. The hand of God is upon all those for good who seek Him, but His power and His wrath are against those who forsake Him and who trust in the help and friendship of the world, going to the god of Ekron to inquire, and heeding not the counsel of the living God. —*December 11, 1905. (p. 254, pars. 2, 3)*

Value of Counsel

I have no desire to hurt the soul of any one, but I must bear the straight testimony given me. Some of the ministers and leaders in the Southern California Conference need to realize the necessity of counseling with their brethren who have been long in the work, and who have thus gained a valuable exierience. Their disposition to shut themselves up to themselves, and to feel competent to plan and execute, according to their own judgment and preferences, brings them into financial embarrassment. Then, when the embarrassment bears heavily upon them, they are tempted to think that the Union Conference or the General Conference should help them out. This independent way of working is not right, and should not be followed. The ministers and teachers in our conferences are to work unitedly with their brethren of experience, asking them for advice, and paying heed to this advice. —*June 30, 1904. (p. 69, par. 1)*

No man's judgment is to be regarded as a safe and infallible guide. There is a certainty in sanctified submission to the will of God, and this is the only certainty that any man has the right to stand by. Any other position of certainty than this of humble submission to the will of God, is unsafe, and is liable to lead a man to lose his hold on God, and mar his religious experience.

Many trials come to all who are called to engage in the work of God. Those who have the responsibility of locating and fostering our sanitariums and training school, need the advice and counsel of men of sound judgment—men who trust not in their own supposed wisdom, but who stand ready to advance by faith in the opening providences of God, and who constantly look to the Lord for wisdom and guidance.

In this our age of the world, we claim to be, in a special sense, the Lord's chosen people, as did Israel of old. And we are, indeed, the Lord's covenant-keeping people, pledged by our baptismal vows to walk in newness of life, and in obedience to all the commandments of Holy Writ. The Lord God of Israel is our God, whom we serve. Throughout the ages, the Sabbath of Jehovah has lost none of its meaning. It is still a sign between God and His people, and will ever remain a sign. —*January 27, 1910. (p. 852, pars. 1-3)*

Unity in Work

Let us have faith that we shall have special help from God. Let us not talk unbelief, but be cheerful in the Lord. Let us be one in Christ. Unity is strength. Christ's last prayer with His disciples shows the importance of unity. —*July 15, 1904. (p. 76, par. 3)*

If the Lord has ever spoken by me, He speaks when I say that the workers engaged in educational lines, in ministerial lines, and in medical missionary lines must stand as a unit, all laboring under the supervision of God, one helping the other, each blessing each.

Those connected with them (our schools and sanitariums) are to labor with earnest alacrity. The work that is done under the ministration of the Holy Spirit, out of love for God and for humanity will bear the signature of God, and will make its impression on human minds. —*October 12, 1904. (p. 77, pars. 1, 2)*

May God help you, my brother, to be cheerful, to look on the bright side. Study the twelfth chapter of Romans. It points out the unity, the sympathy, the kindness, the unselfish love that is to exist amongst God's workers.

"As we have many members in one body, and all members have not the same office: so we, being many, are one body in Christ, and every one members one of another." "Let love be without dissimulation. Abhor that which is evil; cleave to that which is good. Be kindly affectioned one to another with brotherly love; in honor preferring one another; not slothful in business; fervent in spirit; serving the Lord; rejoicing in hope; patient in tribulation; continuing instant in prayer; distributing to the necessity of saints; given to hospitality. Bless them which persecute you: bless, and curse not. Rejoice with them that do rejoice, and weep with them that weep." "Be not overcome of evil, but overcome evil with good." —*October 12, 1904. (p. 79, pars. 2, 3)*

A Bible institute should be held in some place where medical missionary workers and ministers may meet together study the Scriptures. Let the Bible explain its own statements. Accept it just as it reads, without twisting the words to suit human ideas. "What is the chaff to the wheat?" —*December 1903. (p. 85, par. 3)*

I am glad that you see the evil influence of division. Had you put yourself where you should have been, there would long ago have been a united company, and a medical missionary work, in connection with the gospel ministry, would have had a far-reaching influence for good. This I know; for the truth has been represented to me too clearly for me to turn away from it. —*January 2, 1904. (p. 99, par. 1)*

If right principles had been followed, the relation existing between the physicians and their brethren would be exactly what the Lord designed it to be; but for years an effort has been put forth to make the medical missionary work the body. God designs that the medical missionary work shall be bound up with the gospel ministry. —*October 14, 1903. (p. 103, par. 3)*

I would not now speak so plainly, were it not for the intense desire I feel that our medical workers shall be molded and fashioned after the similitude of Christ, in order that all their work and their relation to God's cause may be in harmony with His purpose. God calls upon every physician and every other medical missionary worker to take his stand on the platform of truth, where he shall not be influenced by any man's false theories and wrong devising. The pure, living principles of the Gospel are to be respected. God has a people in His church who are laboring just as disinterestedly to save sinners, as the medical missionary workers have been laboring. He calls upon His medical missionary workers to labor unitedly with His church, and not to allow any physician to control their efforts by his authority. The Lord now calls upon His people to unify. Let all our medical missionaries unite with our ministers in soul-saving work.

Nothing should be allowed to stand in the way of perfect, complete unity between the medical missionary workers and the gospel ministry. God has not empowered Dr. _____ with spiritual grace to be a lord over all our physicians and other medical missionaries. It is time that the teachings of the great Medical Missionary should be brought into the life-practice of our medical missionary workers. It is time that God's voice should be heard; for His words, spoken in truth, are spirit and life. He never makes a mistake.

If Dr. _____ would unite with his ministering brethren and give them his confidence, believing that they will work as Christ works through them, then he himself could see that others should be granted the privilege of standing in their God-given lot and place, and that he should respect all whom God has called as gospel missionaries to work for His cause. Working as Christ worked, our brethren would not be divided at all. But so long as our brother determines to carry things in his own way, irrespective of the Lord's workers, as if he were the only man whom heaven could acknowledge as a leader, God is displeased.

If he were to occupy his proper place, he would be respected; but never is he to be regarded as he has regarded himself—as chief of all the medical missionary workers, as one who has the privilege of consulting only those who exalt him; and of ignoring, as not worthy of acting a part in the great medical missionary work, all the gospel ministers who disapprove of some of his ideas. —*October 14, 1903. (p. 104, pars. 1-3)*

To those who go out to do medical missionary work, I would say, Serve the Lord Jesus with sanctified understanding, in connection with the ministers of the gospel and the great Teacher. He Who has given you your commission will give you skill and understanding as you consecrate yourselves to His service, engaging diligently in labor and study, doing your best to bring relief to the sick and suffering. —*October 16, 1903. (p. 107, par. 5)*

Read the eighth chapter of Matthew, and learn from it how Christ united the ministry of the Word with medical missionary work. Study the methods of the great Healer, and labor as He labored.

Those who profess to be medical missionaries are to be consecrated, working for the best interests of the world, yet not ensnared with the wiles of the world. The Lord desires you to be a vessel unto honor. —*June 25, 1904; March 5, 1903. (p. 115, pars. 1, 2)*

Medical missionary workers are needed in the Southern field, who can engage in sanitarium work. Sanitariums are needed, in which successful medical and surgical work can be done. These institutions, conducted in accordance with the will of God, would remove prejudice, and call our work into favorable notice. The highest aim of the workers in these institutions is to be the spiritual health of the patients. Successful evangelistic work can be done in connection with medical missionary work. It is as these lines of work are united that we may expect to gather the most precious fruit for the Lord.

From the instruction that the Lord has given me from time to time, I know that there should be workers who make medical evangelistic tours among the towns and villages. Those who do this work will gather a rich harvest of souls, both from the higher and the lower classes. The way for this work is best prepared by the efforts of the faithful canvasser.

Many will be called into the field to labor from house to house, giving Bible readings, and praying with those who are interested.

It is of the utmost importance that harmony exist in our institutions. Better for the work to go crippled than for workers who are not fully devoted to be employed. It is unconsecrated, unconverted men who have been spoiling the work of God. The Lord has no use whatever for men who are not wholly consecrated to His service.

The hearts and interests of God's workers should be one. The workers should be bound up with Christ, and should esteem one another highly for their works' sake.... —*(pp. 116, 117, par. 1)*

The light that has been given at this time is only a repetition of the message that was sent in the past.

"Let every department of our work, every institution connected with our cause, be conducted on considerate, generous lines. Let every branch of the work, while maintaining its own distinctive character, seek to protect, strengthen and build up every other branch. Men of varied abilities and characteristics are employed for carrying forward the various branches of the work. This has always been the

Lord's plan. Each worker must give his own branch special efforts; but it is the privilege of each to study and labor for the health and welfare of the whole body of which he is a member.

Not consolidation, not rivalry or criticism, but cooperation is the Lord's plan for His insitutions, that "the whole body fitly joined together and compacted by that which every joint supplieth, according to the effectual working in the measure of every part," may make "increase of the body unto the edifying (building up) of itself in love." —*September 2, 1907. (p. 451, pars. 2-4)*

In order that the great work of sanctification that needs to be carried forward in the churches of Southern California may be accomplished, the minds and wills of our ministers, physicians, and teachers should be united, their hearts blending in one spirit to give the trumpet a certain sound. Let every voice proclaim distinctly the third angel's message. In word and act let those who are proclaiming the message reveal that they are numbered among those "that keep the commandments of God, and the faith of Jesus." —*November 3, 1907. (p. 564, par. 3)*

In our Los Angeles meeting there was a unity of sentiment in the councils that gives me great encouragement; and here at Loma Linda we must strive to see, not how much we can differ from one another, but how closely we can come into the perfect unity of which the word of God advises us. —*March 28, 1912. (p. 990, par. 1)*

The work to be carried on here at Loma Linda is a great work. To carry it forward successfully every one of us must stand in right relation to God, all striving to be learners in the school of Christ. We are not to stand in the position of persons looking for some opportunity to differ from one another. We are not to cherish differences of opinion and keep them to the front, but we are to seek to be of one mind, one heart, one spirit, because there is One Who stands at our head, and it is His character that we are to represent in our labors and association together.

When I was here last, representations were given to me showing what we as a people ought to be. We are to labor in perfect harmony, not trying to be as different as possible from our fellow-laborers, or to secure the leadership in some little matter, but striving to learn how to unify. The workers have come here from many different institutions, having different plans and methods of working, but no one is to put himself to the strain to bring in that which is new and odd, or something that nobody else has thought of or approves. Let us rather endeavor to come into harmony that the blessing of God may rest upon us. We should know and understand that the Lord Jesus is our Ruler; if we follow on to know the Lord, we shall know that His going forth is prepared as the morning. The righteousness and the peace of God will be given to all who will follow on to know the Lord.

My brethren and sisters, harmonize, harmonize. Bring your minds into the right relation to God, and as your minds are sanc-

Unity in Work

tified they will be refined. It cannot be otherwise because the refining influence of the Spirit of God is upon you. It is for us to understand and appreciate that God has done great things for us. He has manifested such an intense interest in us, and worked so wonderfully in our behalf, that it is impossible for us to fully comprehend His goodness and His grace. He "so loved the world that He gave His only begotten Son, that whosoever believeth in Him should not perish, but have everlasting life." —*March 28, 1912. (p. 992, pars. 1-3)*

Sometimes when I have seen brethren who do not appear to weigh carefully the influence of their words and actions upon those around them, I have felt an intense fear that they would miss the mark. We must walk humbly with God. We must learn to overcome difficulties through faith in the living God. "This is the victory that overcometh the world, even our faith."

We are here, a large company of workers, consecrated to the service of God. And when I have heard that this one wants to leave because something does not suit him, and another plans to go because he thinks something is going wrong, I have thought, Poor souls; it is you who must change. It is you who must come upon your knees to God, asking for the baptism of His Spirit. What we all need is a consecration and a faith that will stand the day of test and trial. We must have intelligence and confidence to look to God and say, We trust Thee, Our Saviour; and we will not be driven from our post of duty in order to gratify the enemy of the work.

What we need is a right hold on God; and if we have this, we shall come off victorious. Let us ask Him to bind us together in unity of mind, in an understanding of His guidance; and then He can work for us wonderfully. Then we shall see of the salvation of God.

I am thankful to see so many of my brethren here today—brethren whom I have not seen for a long time. The Lord will surely reveal Himself to His people in this place, that they may communicate the precious truth to all parts of the world. Let us bear in mind that it is faith that leads to perfection of character. I want to be in that position where I can hear the words of my Saviour to me. Let us each endeavor to keep our minds stayed upon God, and prove the Lord whether He will not give us wisdom and guidance at every step. —*March 28, 1912. (p. 993, pars. 1-3)*

No line is to be drawn between the genuine medical missionary work and the gospel ministry. These two must blend. They are not to stand apart as separate lines of work. They are to be joined in an inseparable union, even as the hand is joined to the body. Those in our institutions are to give evidence that they understand their part in the genuine gospel medical missionary work. A solemn dignity is to characterize genuine missionaries.

Many are asking me how I regard the ministry of the gospel with reference to medical missionary work. These two lines of work should blend. They should both help to compose the body. The genuine medical missionary work should not be exalted above the gospel ministry. Some are in danger of regarding the medical missionary work as the body when it is only the arm and the hand.

To those who go out to do medical missionary work I would say, "Serve the Lord Jesus Christ with sanctified understanding, in connection with the ministers of the gospel and the great Teacher." He Who has given you your commission will give you skill and understanding as you consecrate yourselves to His service, engaging diligently in labor and study, doing your best to bring relief to the sick and suffering.

To those who are tired of a life of sinfulness, but who know not where to turn to obtain relief, present the compassionate Saviour full of love and tenderness, longing to receive those who come to Him with broken hearts and contrite spirits. Take them by the hand, lift them up, speak to them words of hope and courage. Help them to grasp the hand of Him Who has said, "Let him take hold of My strength, that he may make peace with Me; and he shall make peace with Me." —*November 19, 1903. (p. 608, pars. 1-4)*

Do not let division come in to destroy the spirit of unity. We want unity; and when we pray together, let faith lay hold upon the Mighty One. Christ is looking upon us in love. If we will walk in His footsteps, following on to know the Lord, we shall know that His going forth is prepared as the morning.

The blessed Saviour did not refuse to die for men, but for their sakes submitted to abuse and mockery from His enemies. His life was taken away in cruelty. As He hung upon the cross, His enemies, standing at the foot, divided His garments among them. Consider how much Christ endured that we might believe that no experience can come to us that He does not fully understand. We are to be led by a spirit entirely opposite to that which inspired the enemies of Christ. It is our privilege to help one another and sustain one another, thus showing that the Spirit of God is working in heart and mind and character.

I am glad there are sensible men and women here. I am pleased that there is a strong force of physicians and teachers. —*No date. (p. 933, pars. 2-4)*

And I want to say to you all, Work in harmony. "I beseech you, brethren, by the name of our Lord Jesus Christ, that ye all speak the same thing, and that there be no divisions among you; but that ye be perfectly joined together in the same mind, and in the same judgment." The Lord wants you to do this, and I believe you will. If you cannot possibly do it here, just go away where you can. We need to draw steadily with Christ, and to labor to glorify His holy name. And the responsible men and women in this place should give thanks to God for His manifold mercies. But do not complain or indulge in criticism because this is all out of place. It will spoil the work. —*(p. 934, par. 1)*

Unity in Work

Let our ministers who have gained an experience in preaching the Word learn how to give simple treatments, and then labor intelligently as medical missionary evangelists. —*No date. (p. 693, par. 3)*

"Be very careful not to do anything that would restrict the work at Loma Linda. It is in the order of God that this property has been secured, and He has given instruction that a school should be connected with the sanitarium. A special work is to be done there in qualifying young men and young women to be efficient medical missionary workers. They are to be taught how to treat the sick without the use of drugs. Such an education requires an experience in practical work. The work at Loma Linda demands immediate consideration. Preparations must be made for the school to be opened as soon as possible. Our young men and young women are to find in Loma Linda a school where they can receive a medical missionary training, and where they will not be brought under the influence of some who are seeking to undermine the truth. The students are to unite faithfully in the medical work, keeping their physical powers in the most perfect condition possible, and laboring under the instruction of the Great Medical Missionary. The healing of the sick, and the ministry of the Word, are to go hand in hand.

"Much is involved in this work and it is very essential that a right beginning be made. The Lord has a special work to be done in this field. He instructed me to call on Elder and Mrs. _____, to help us in getting properly started, a work similar to that they had carried on at Avondale." —*October 1909. (p. 779, pars. 2, 4, 6)*

"There is a very precious work to be done in connection with the interest of the sanitarium and school at Loma Linda, and this will be done when all work to that end.... Ever bear in mind that heaven is interested in every question that agitates you in regard to your school and sanitarium. Both are to be strengthened. In our school at Loma Linda many can be educated to work as missionaries in the cause of Health and Temperance. The best teachers are to be employed in this educational work, not men who esteem highly their own capabilities, but men who will walk circumspectly, depending wholly upon the Lord."

Young men who have a practical knowledge of how to treat the sick are now to be sent out to do gospel medical missionary work, in connection with more experienced gospel workers. If these young men will give themselves to the study of the Word, they will become successful evangelists. The ministers with whom these young men labor are to give them the same opportunity to learn that Elijah gave Elisha. They are to show them how to teach the truth to others. Where it is possible, these young men should visit the hospitals, and in some cases they may connect with them for a while, laboring disinterestedly. —*October 16, 1903. (p. 106, par. 2)*

Then they will be able to see with anointed eyes how closely the medical missionary work is to be bound up with proclamation of the message for this time.

The Lord has presented before me the dangers that are threatening His people who have the sacred work of proclaiming the third angel's message with clearness and distinctness. God's people must beware lest they be ensnared by unsanctified propositions. Our young people must not be placed where they will be misled by wrong sentiments. The truth is not to be blanketed. The message for these last days is to be given in no indistinct utterance. —*October 23, 1903. (p. 109, pars. 1, 2)*

Hedging up Way for Others

Isaiah 55:6-13.

Let the instruction given in the fifty-eighth chapter of Isaiah be studied in connection with these scriptures. Wonderful would be the results if ministers and church members would be converted, and adopt Christ's manner of witnessing to the power of the Lord.

In many places, and especially in Southern California plans and methods of labor have been followed that have hindered the Lord's work, so that those upon whom the Lord has laid special burdens could not do the work to which they were appointed. In some cases watchers were set to restrict the work and to hedge up the way of some who were laboring most earnestly for advancement. Unsanctified plans were laid that worked counter to the plans of God. All this was greatly displeasing to the Lord, and it was work which He repudiated. There were cities that might have been entered and a good work begun, but through lack of faith there developed a counter-working influence. With unbelief, jealousies arose, and with sacred missionary enterprises were linked up men who themselves needed to experience the converting power of God, and to learn to walk humbly with Him.

To those who had kept the way hedged up, I wrote out the instruction given me, and trusted the the result with the Lord. The burden was heavy, and I feared I should not live to see the results of my efforts to break the yokes which men were placing upon their fellow-workers. The Lord presented before me in decided representations that it would take years to root out the evil resulting from placing in the hands of finite men the power to hinder and delay the work of God. Repeated messages of reproof and counsel were necessary that capable men whom the Lord had specified as the ones to do a special work might be set free to follow the light that God has given. —*December 6, 1909. (p. 814, pars. 1-3)*

There were strong men in Southern California who stood decidedly against the light the Lord was giving His messenger regarding the work to be done. They were following their own counsel and judgment, and were imperiling the cause of God. I was instructed that the only way to counterwork this evil was to have placed in positions of trust men who would be guided by the counsel of the Lord, and who would not be turned aside by those who were deficient in faith.

The Lord has wrought in a remarkable manner to uphold the messages sent to correct the strange work that was being done. The evil has been checked; but it has not yet been fully rooted out, and if there were not a continuation of the message from the Lord to His people, the will and ways of men would yet prevail to bring in strife and contention, and a deformed work would be the result. I was shown that human power is constantly working to weave itself into the work of God. This brings in disjointed and inharmonious action. The messages of pure and unadulterated truth are in danger of being trampled under feet by self-willed unconverted men who work to destroy confidence in the warnings that God would speak to the hearts of His people to correct error, and to encourage righteousness. —*December 6, 1909.*

A great many of the difficulties that have come into our work in California and elsewhere have come in through a misunderstanding on the part of men in official positions concerning their individual responsibility in the matter of controlling and ruling their fellow-laborers. Men entrusted with responsibilities have supposed that their official position embraced very much more than was ever thought of by those who placed them in office, and serious difficulties arose as the result. —*(p. 815, pars. 1-3)*

Elder _____ and his wife have been engaged in the work for years, and their faith in the truth and in the Testimonies given by the Holy Spirit is strong. They have unitedly served according to the Lord's appointment, and we have sought to sustain them in their work. Conditions in the churches have changed decidedly, but the Lord had shown me that some in responsible positions are not yet converted, and without thorough conversion they cannot conduct the work in right lines. Some who have been reproved and warned are not established and settled, and fully yielded to the guiding power of the Holy Spirit. Satan is not yet fully cast out of the minds of some, and it would take very little to produce again the conditions that existed ten years ago.

The cause of God in Oakland, San Francisco, and the surrounding places needs men of solid Christian character, who fear God and take counsel of God, or believers will be misled by those who attach themselves to the work, and who desire to guide and control according to human judgment and plans. The Lord desires to work through men of clean purposes and decided experiences, men who will learn from the Testimonies of His Spirit where they have not been in harmony with the Lord's will, and who will be converted. Then decided changes will be made. The perils threatening the work will be seen, conversions will be experienced, and our people will be preparing to stand firmly and unitedly with God to build up His kingdom in the earth.

Men who repudiate the teachings of the Spirit of God are not the proper persons to be placed in office as leaders in the church. There is danger that the teachings of men who are not soundly converted may lead others into by and forbidden paths. In our efforts to secure consecrated leadership, we may expect to encounter opposition, for the enemy is seeking through unconverted men in positions of trust to mold the work, and he has too much at stake lightly to lose their influence. —*December 6, 1909. (p. 817, pars. 1-3)*

Mistakes will be made. But let men be very careful how they bear down upon those who have made mistakes. Sometimes the one who treats the erring with little mercy has made mistakes far more grievous in the sight of God than those made by the one whom he so unsparingly condemns. Under the Lord's special guidance, some things have been done that are contrary to the specified directions laid down by men. Unseen agencies were guiding in another way than that marked out by human wisdom. Then let men be careful how they call their brethren to account, as though they were in God's place. The Lord has heard the humiliating censure that has been given to those who had not rebellion in their hearts, who thought they were doing just what they were told to do. The Lord saw that His work would be marred if the directions given by men were followed, and He guided the minds of the workers to do the work in the very way that He wished it done. The workers did not follow the plan laid out by men because God had a better plan for them. The divine guiding produced the right result. —*September 15, 1902. (p. 86, pars. 3-5)*

I am instructed to say to our ministers and medical missionary workers, "Be careful what spirit you manifest to one another." The Lord must be given an opportunity to show men their duty, and to work upon their minds. No one is to bind himself to serve for a term of years under the direction of one group of men or in one specified branch of the Master's work; for the Lord Himself will call men, as of old He called the humble fishermen, and will Himself give them instruction regarding their field of labor and the methods they should follow. He will call men from the plow and from other occupations, to give the last note of warning to perishing souls. There are many ways in which to work for the Master, and the great Teacher will open the understanding of these workers, enabling them to see wondrous things in His Word. I have repeatedly been instructed that no one should be advised to pledge himself to spend two, three, four, five, or six years under any one man's supervision. Let students stand where they can follow the will of God. Their service belongs to Him. Their capabilities and talents are to be refined, purified and ennobled. In this lower school—the school of earth—they are to be prepared for translation into the school of heaven, where their education will be continued under the personal supervision of Christ, the great Teacher, Who will lead them beside the living waters, and open to them the mysteries of the kingdom of God. —*September 21, 1903. (p. 87, pars. 1, 3, 4)*

General Instruction

Advantage should be taken of these opportunities to establish and extend gospel medical missionary work; for time is short, and we must sow the seeds of health reform principles....

I have been instructed that we are not to delay to do the work that needs to be done in health reform lines. Through this work we are to reach souls in the highways and byways. I have been given special light that in our sanitariums many souls will receive and obey present truth. In these institutions men and women are to be taught how to care for their own bodies, and at the same time how to become sound in the faith. They are to be taught what is meant by eating the flesh and drinking the blood of the Son of God. Said Christ, "The words that I speak unto you, they are spirit, and they are life." —*July 18, 1905. (p. 82, pars. 1, 2)*

We shall have to labor under difficulties, but because of this, let not our zeal flag. The Bible does not acknowledge a believer who is idle, however high his profession may be. There will be employment in heaven. The redeemed state is not one of idle repose. There remaineth, therefore, a rest to the people of God, but it is a rest found in loving service. Some among the redeemed will have laid hold of Christ in the last hours of life, and in heaven instruction will be given to these ones, who, when they died, did not understand perfectly the plan of salvation. Christ will lead the redeemed ones beside the river of life, and will open to them that which on this earth they could not understand. —*July 18, 1905. (p. 83, par. 3)*

"He showed me a pure river of water of life, clear as crystal, proceeding out of the throne of God and of the Lamb."

"In the midst of the street of it, and on either side of the river, was there the tree of life, which bare twelve manner of fruits, and yielded her fruit every month: and the leaves of the tree were for the healing of the nations. And there shall be no more curse: but the throne of God and of the Lamb shall be in it;... and they shall see His face; and His name shall be in their foreheads."

Thank God, thank God! Let us improve every opportunity to reach poor, suffering, sinsick souls with the message of salvation. Let the precious light of truth be shed abroad. —*July 18, 1905. (p. 84, par. to line)*

The Holy Spirit enlightens the mind of the one who depends on the merits of a crucified and risen Saviour, and indites a prayer of confession and repentance that is acceptable to the Lord. "We know not what we should pray for as we ought: but the Spirit Itself maketh intercession for us with groanings that cannot be uttered." "He that searcheth the hearts knoweth what is the mind of the Spirit, because he maketh intercession for the saints according to the will of God."

Let no man boast that he does not confess the sins that the Lord has pointed out to him. If he makes no confession, he receives not forgiveness and pardon from God. He must go forth in sorrow to work in his own strength. The enemy finds him in this position, a subject to be deceived.

There are many, many of this class. May the Lord open their eyes that they may see the danger of their self-sufficiency. A superficial work is always a snare to every professed Christian. Satan finds easy access to the heart of the one who is careless and slack in his experience, and beguiles him with seducing theories that will destroy his faith in God. "He that cometh to God must believe that He is, (as He has declared Himself personally) and that He is a rewarder of them that diligently seek Him." —*March 14, 1905. (p. 138, pars. 1-3)*

In every sanitarium there must be kept before all in the institution the principles of true service. From the institution is to go forth light and knowledge. All connected with it are to act their part intelligently, as representatives of the truth for this time. It is that they may be trained to do true missionary work that young people are brought to our sanitariums.

If you will co-operate with God, He will go before you and the glory of the Lord will be your rearward. Heavenly angels will break forth into singing as souls receive the great gift of God through Jesus Christ. You may assure the sick and afflicted that Christ is the great Healer. They may believe on Him and trust in His Word; for it will never fail.

"Thus saith the Lord, Keep ye judgment, and do justice: for My salvation is near to come, and My righteousness to be revealed. Blessed is the man that doeth this, and the son of man that layeth hold on it; that keepeth the Sabbath from polluting it, and keepeth his hand from doing any evil."

What a representation is here given! "My salvation is near to come"—that great salvation wrought out for each soul through Jesus Christ, the salvation for which the prophets have inquired and searched diligently. Our Lord is soon to come to us in mercy and compassion and love. We must go forth to receive Him as a welcome guest.

The Lord Jesus calls upon every one to become interestedly engaged in the work of becoming a channel of light through which the grace of Christ may flow. Jesus has said, "Ye are the light of the world.... Let your light so shine before men, that they may see your good works, and glorify your Father which is in heaven." In the great salvation wrought through Jesus Christ, the unbelieving world is to be helped through the work of believers. In the work you do in the sanitarium, many may become convinced that you are indeed the children of God. —*March 14, 1905. (p. 139, pars. 1-5)*

"Seek ye the Lord while He may be found, call ye upon Him while He is near: let the wicked forsake his way, and the unrighteous man his thoughts: and let him return unto the Lord, and He will have mercy upon him; and to our God, for He will abundantly pardon."

"For My thoughts are not your thoughts, neither are your ways My ways, saith the Lord. For as the heavens are higher than the earth, so are My ways higher than your ways, and My thoughts than your thoughts. For as the rain cometh down, and the snow from heaven, and returneth not thither, but watereth the earth, and maketh it bring forth and bud, that it may give seed to the sower, and bread to the eater: so shall My word be that goeth forth out of My mouth: it shall not return unto Me void, but it shall accomplish that which I please, and it shall prosper in the thing whereto I sent it."

All the promises of God's Word are made on gospel terms. If we on our part will fulfil the conditions, if we will seek the Lord, while He may be found, we may claim the promise.

"For ye shall go out with joy, and be led forth with peace: the mountains and the hills shall break forth before you into singing, and all the trees of the field shall clap their hands. Instead of the thorn shall come up the fir tree, and instead of the briar shall come up the myrtle tree: and it shall be to the Lord for a name, for an everlasting sign that shall not be cut off."
—*March 14, 1905. (p. 140, pars. 1-4)*

A word in season is to be spoken to every one in need. To the unbelievers, we must be as the light of the world, as a city set on a hill, which cannot be hid. Our time and our intelligence are to be spent in revealing the sanctification that comes through love and obedience. In this lower school the truth of the Word will prepare men for the heavenly school. All are to be learners, and in the humble walks of life are to exemplify the mighty power of God.

In humility all are to become living, eloquent commentaries on the words that God hath spoken: "God hath chosen the foolish things of the world to confound the wise; and God hath chosen the weak things of the world to confound the things which are mighty; and base things of the world, and things which are despised, hath God chosen, yea, and things which are not, to bring to naught things that are." There is power for all who will seek it. Let us yield our God-given faculties to Him Who is our Sanctification and our Redemption. We shall have faith, if we have strong confidence in God.

Our faith in eternal realities is to become stronger and firmer with exercise. In every sanitarium, in every school, an upward, spiritual influence needs to be exerted. I am instructed to say to all physicians, Awake, awake, and take hold of the real issues that are for the uplifting of men and the magnifying of present truth. Let not your sense of individual responsibility become feeble. Let not your mind grow weary, while there remain your talents of speech, your pen, and the privilege of service. Let the truth, eternal truth, be brought into action to impress, to convince, to convert minds. Let us proclaim that the day of the Lord is upon us.

Many are now perishing for want of knowledge. Shall we not give mind, soul and voice to proclaiming the truth as it is in Christ Jesus? To every worker I would say, Show to unbelievers that there is strength in God. Communicate your ideas in regard to what is required, by the words of warning, "Prepare to meet thy God." Sow the seeds of truth by all waters. Wake up the watchmen, and, with them, bear the message in words of power. "Cry aloud, spare not, lift up thy voice like a trumpet, and show My people their transgression, and the house of Jacob their sins." The increase of your own experience will be proportionate to your individual trust and confidence in God.

There are many, many to be converted through the instrumentality of men who will be taken from the plow and from the common vocations of life to engage in the great, grand work of giving soul-saving truth to the people.

There are all classes to be reached. Those who have been called to labor in hygienic restaurants where thousands are fed but are not given the bread of life, should inquire, What is the way of the Lord? There are some who are laboring in hygienic restaurants, who should be breaking away, and be giving themselves to the grand work of carrying the last gospel message to multitudes. They must make sure that the truth for this time is implanted within their own hearts by the Holy Spirit of God. Then with minds cleansed from all sin, they will be able to feed the flock of God with pure provender, thoroughly winnowed from all fanciful and fatal delusions. —*May 6, 1906.*

"Ye shall not surely die," the enemy declared in the beginning; "ye shall be as gods." Our first parents yielded to the sophistry of the tempter, and fell.

We are now to awaken the men who have known the truth, and have lost from their hearts the love of it. Let us not cease our warning, day nor night. With tenderness even unto tears and with prayers of faith, let us hold of souls for whom Christ has died. Let us not wait for some costly arrangement before we work out Christ's plan. Some will be reached by the provisions the Lord has made to reach souls in the highways as well as in the byways. He has furnished us with buildings in which a good work may be done. There are dangers of consuming and not producing; but the evidence is given us that buildings have been provided that will enable us to reach the higher classes and present to them the truths of the Word. —*May 6, 1906. (p. 292, par. 2 to p. 294, par. 2)*

There are some things that I desire to write to you. Do not be in haste about the health food business. There is a possibility of entering into a work that will bring gain of means but which would result in spiritual loss to the sanitarium.

Commercial enterprises often work to a large degree counter to the purpose for which our institutions are established. They detract from the influence which God desires shall attend the work. The condition brought about is sometimes the condition in which Christ found the barren fig tree. Searching for fruit with which to satisfy His need, the Saviour found nothing but a show of leaves. In visions of the night I have seen Christ searching in our institutions for fruit, for that virtue revealed in the lives of His workers that tells in the saving of the soul unto eternal life. You have a noble work to do in praying with the sick, and in feeding their souls with the bread of life. You are to be God's medical missionary, teaching souls what it means to eat the flesh and drink the blood of the Son of God. Christ explains the meaning of these words. "The flesh profiteth nothing," He said. "The words that I speak unto you, they are spirit and they are life." You have the ability to speak in a pleasant intelligent, interesting way to the sick. It is your privilege to inspire them with hope and courage, and lead them to a knowledge of the truth of the Word.

Many of the patients who come to the sanitarium are children in their understanding of the Word. If you will take hold of these cases, and seek to lead them to the truth, One Who is your righteousness will go before you, and the glory of the Lord will be your rearward.

Your mind must be a treasure house, full of good things. Keep the patients cheerful. Pleasant words of instruction may be given to them that will be a blessing to them while they are at the sanitarium; and when they return to their homes, the message of truth they have heard will be constantly repeating itself to them. We do not appreciate how far greater are the results for good when we bring cheerfulness and the joy of the Lord into our work.

I am very desirous that you shall feel as free as possible to do this gospel work. Your strength for it, and your success in it, will depend largely on the time and strength you reserve for this work. You should not allow yourself to be overwhelmed with responsibilities, so that you cannot have the realization in your own soul that you are in the right place.

It is necessary that you share your responsibilities with others. Those who are spiritually minded, and whom you can trust with the work should be employed to help carry out your plans. You will find that you accomplish much more in the end if you will allow others to bear burdens. Your perceptions are good, but, they must be worked in order to be improved. This is also true of your fellow workers.

In no place in the world can our influence tell on the Lord's side with such power as in the position to which He calls us. The most useful things we do in the service of God is to encourage the souls that are distressed, and lead them to Christ. Keep the lives of the patients constantly refreshed by the example of a Christlike example. You will have success if you will be a self-denying Christian. An earnest desire to be obedient to the will of your heavenly Father will bring you to the place where you will wear Christ's yoke. Those who are great in the sight of the Lord will, like John the Baptist, have humility of heart. Then good works will follow. Your example may be such that others will wish to emulate it. Your obedience and humbleness of mind will make obedience and humility a desirable thing to those who are associated with you.

The words of truth were so simple as Christ explained them that the disciples could comprehend them. The Word of God is our spirit and life. It is the weapon by which we are to resist the attacks of Satan. Those who are much with God in prayer and consent to wear the yoke of Christ, will be meek and lowly in heart. They will be one with Christ.

You and your wife can be a source of help and strength to each other, and a blessing to the sanitarium. Prayer is the key that will unlock the treasure of heaven to you. Let your faith increase. Increased faith and sanctification of the spirit will qualify you to be a wise counselor. Words spoken in season and in the spirit of tenderness, accompanied by the silent working of the Holy Spirit, will make the right impression. Do not think that you are accomplishing nothing because you cannot see definite results for your work. You are to sow the seed, knowing not which shall prosper, this or that. May the Lord help and strengthen and bless you in your work, is my prayer. —*April 3, 1907. (pp. 351-353 all)*

Special instruction has been given me for God's people, for perilous times are upon us. In the world, destruction and violence are increasing. In the church man power is gaining the ascendancy; those who have been chosen to occupy positions of trust think it their prerogative to rule.

Men whom the Lord calls to important positions in His work are to cultivate humble dependence upon Him. They are not to seek to embrace too much authority; for God has not called them to a work of ruling, but to plan and counsel with their fellow laborers. Every worker alike is to hold himself amenable to the requirements and instruction of God.

To our brethren in Southern California I bear this message: The president of your conference has the lesson to learn that he is not to endeavor to rule his fellow-laborers who have occupied positions of trust under God in the work; neither is he to consider himself capable of carrying all things after his own ideas. He has thought that it was his right to rule in every branch of the conference work, and this has led him to judge and criticize fellow-laborers who were better able than he to do the work. He must first rule himself before he can hope to rule others wisely, or to plan wisely for the advancement of the work. Position will not give to any man an all-round education.

Because of the importance of the work in Southern California, and the perplexities which now surround it, there should be selected no less than five men of wisdom and experience to consult with the presidents of the local and union conferences regarding general plans and policies. The Lord is not pleased with the disposition some have manifested to rule those of more experience than themselves. By this course of action, some have revealed that they are not qualified to fill the important positions which they occupy. Any human being who spreads himself out to large proportions, and who seeks to have the control of his fellows, proves himself to be a dangerous man to be entrusted with religious responsibilities. —*September 19, 1907. (p. 477 all)*

Often the Lord sees that His workers are in doubt as to what they should do. At such times, if they will put their confidence in Him, He will reveal to them His will. God's work is now to advance rapidly, and if His people will respond to His call, He will make the possessors of property willing to donate of their means, and thus make it possible for His work to be accomplished in the earth. "Faith is the substance of things hoped for, the evidence of things not seen." Faith in the Word of God will place His people in the possession of property which will enable them to work the large cities that are waiting for the message of truth.

The cold, formal, unbelieving way in which some of the laborers do their work is a deep offense to the Spirit of God. The apostle Paul says, "Do all things without murmurings and disputings: that ye may be blameless and harmless, the sons of God, without rebuke, in the midst of a crooked and perverse nation, among whom ye shine as lights in the world; holding forth the word of life; that I may rejoice in the day of Christ, that I have not run in vain, neither labored in vain. Yea, and if I be offered upon the sacrifice and service of your faith, I joy, and rejoice with you all."

We are to encourage in one another that living faith that Christ has made it possible for every believer to have. The work is to be carried forward as the Lord prepares the way. When He brings His people into strait places, then it is their privilege to assemble together for prayer, remembering that all things come of God. Those who have not yet shared in the trying experiences that attend the work in these last days, will soon have to pass through scenes that will severely test their confidence in God. It is at the time when His people see no way to advance, when the Red Sea is before them, and the pursuing army behind, that God bids them "Go forward." Thus He is working to test their faith. When such experiences come to you, go forward, trusting in Christ. Walk step by step in the path He marks out. Trials will come, but go forward. This will give you an experience that will strengthen your faith in God, and fit you for truest service.

A deeper and wider experience in religious things is to come to God's people. Christ is our example. If through living faith and sanctified obedience to God's Word, we reveal the love and grace of Christ, if we show that we have a true conception of

God's guiding providences in the work, we shall carry to the world a convincing power. A high position does not give us value in the sight of God. Man is measured by his consecration and faithfulness in working out the will of God. If the remnant people of God will walk before Him in humility of faith, He will carry out through them His eternal purpose, enabling them to work harmoniously in giving to the world the truth as it is in Jesus. He will use all men, women, and children, in making the light shine forth to the world, and calling out a people that will be true to His commandments. Through the faith that His people exercise in Him, God will make known to the world that He is the true God, the God of Israel.

"Let your conversation be as it becometh the gospel of Christ," the apostle Paul exhorts, "that whether I come and see you, or else be absent, I may hear of your affairs, that ye stand fast in one spirit, with one mind striving together for the faith of the gospel; and in nothing terrified by your adversaries: which is to them an evident token of perdition, but to you of salvation, and that of God. For unto you it is given in the behalf of Christ, not only to believe on Him, but also to suffer for His sake."

I have been instructed to present these words to our people in Southern California. They are needed in every place where a church is established, for a strange experience has been coming into our ranks. It is time now for men to humble their hearts before God, and to learn to work in His ways. Let those who have sought to rule their fellow-workers study to know what manner of spirit they are of. They should seek the Lord by fasting and prayer, and in humility of soul. Christ in His earthly life gave an example that all can safely follow. He appreciates His flock, and He wants no power set over them that will restrict their freedom in His service. He has never placed man as a ruler over His heritage. True Bible religion will lead to self-control, not to control of one another. As a people we need a larger measure of the Holy Spirit, that we may bear the solemn message that God has given us without exaltation.

Brethren, keep your words of censure for your individual selves. Teach the flock of God to look to Christ, not to erring man. Every soul who becomes a teacher of the truth must bear in his own life the fruit of holiness. Looking to Christ and following Him, he will present to the souls under his charge an example of what a living, learning Christian will be. Let God teach you His way. Inquire of Him daily to know His will. He will give unerring counsel to all who seek Him with a sincere heart. Walk worthy of the vocation wherewith you are called, praising God in your daily conversation as well as in your prayers. Thus, holding forth the Word of life, you will constrain other souls to become followers of Christ. —*September 19, 1907. (pp. 480-482)*

We shall have more decided opposition to meet from those who have departed from the faith. Those who were once strong teachers, but who have forsaken the way of the Lord, will be just as strong in their opposition of the truth. There is need now that our people be educated to put their trust in God alone. They must learn that their trust is not to be placed in any human voice or arm of flesh. We need ever to keep in mind the experiences of the children of Israel, and learn the lesson that the record of their failures is intended to teach us....

The Lord wants you to understand your individual responsibility for the salvation of your soul. With the Word of God as your guide and instructor, you are to personally work out your own salvation. You are to strive to secure eternal life, where you may dwell forever with the Lord. In studying how you may gain this, seek for that wisdom which God alone can impart. Accept the invitation, "If any of you lack wisdom, let him ask of God, that giveth to all men liberally, and upbraideth not; and it shall be given him." "My brethren," the apostle James writes, "count it all joy." —*James 1:2-8*.

There is an individual work for all to do before our labors can accomplish anything for others. Blessed is the man who endures temptation; who, when he is tried, takes the Word of life as his own, brings the promises to the Lord, and claims them as his. This man relies not on any human power, but on the strength of the Lord.

Faith in the Word of God will bring to us the fulfillment of His promises. "Whatsoever ye shall ask in My name, that will I do," the Saviour declares. "And all things, whatsoever ye shall ask in prayer, believing, ye shall receive." When we learn to place our reliance, not on the words of man, but in God, He will make that word yea and amen to us in Christ Jesus.

Brother and Sister _____, study the Word. You are not to go to any man to learn your duty. Take the Bible as your guide; live its teachings. "Ask, and ye shall receive." We all need a deeper spirituality; we should each seek God for ourselves. Let us ever remember that while we seek to follow one pattern Christ Jesus, we are to maintain our individuality. When the Word of God is received and obeyed, your light will shine forth in good works. —*James 1:22-27. October 2, 1907. (pp. 490, 491)*

"Ye are the light of the world. A city that is set on an hill cannot be hid. Neither do men light a candle, and put it under a bushel, but on a candlestick; and it giveth light unto all that are in the house. Let your light so shine before men, that they may see your good works, and glorify your Father Which is in heaven."

The special work of the leaders is to let the light so shine as to glorify God. As God's messengers, they must have a thorough knowledge of Bible truth. Through watchfulness and prayer they must maintain such a connection with God that they may be the light of the world, and that prejudice may be removed from those who behold their consistent walk, and hear their teachings, in regard to the Word of God. As a result of their influence and teachings, many will joyfully accept the present truth.

By kindness, by graceful behaviour, the messenger of the Lord is to give to the world an evidence of what the truth has done for his soul. The very grace of his words will be a convincing evidence; for the Lord will impress the human mind, and many will submit to the sweet influence of the Spirit of God. Angels of God will impress the minds with sacred truths.

If believers fall in love with the truth in its purity, if they become free from all worldliness and self-exaltation, if they are all agreed, the influence of their lives will make an impression on unbelievers. Their reward may not always come in this life, but even in this world they will possess a peace and quietude, a rest in God that passeth all understanding. Many will take knowledge of them that they have been with Jesus and have learned of Him.

In the future will come their exceeding great reward. In the heavenly courts they will hear the words, "Well done, thou good and faithful servant:... enter thou into the joy of thy Lord." In their purity, their humility, and their meekness, they have represented Christ, and they are now entering into their eternal riches. They are washed and made white in the blood of the Lamb. The joy of Christ is their exceeding great reward. —*November 11, 1907. (p. 571, pars. 1-4)*

I write these things to you, my brethren, although all of you may not fully comprehend them. If I did not believe that God's eye is over His people, I could not have the courage to write the same things over and over again. But I am bidden to say to the messengers, that no commercial spirit should be permitted to enter into their messages or into any part of their work. Said the angel, "Be ye clean that bear the vessels of the Lord." These words were twice repeated during the representation that was given me. —*November 11, 1907. (p. 572, par. 1)*

The people of God have received many admonitions and encouragements, to advance, and it is time that the purposes of God regarding His work shall be understood by them and carried out. By cherishing unbelief in the plans and directions that have been laid out for them to follow, and by exalting human judgment, much time and valuable experience have been lost. The Lord, He is God, and beside Him there is none else. Let all now search the Word of the Lord, and walk in His ways. Let the prophecies of Isaiah be studied and heeded, and the Lord will perform His part. "Search the Scriptures; for in them ye think ye have eternal life."

While no one should be presumptuous, there is need that wise efforts be put forth to reach many who by the ordinary methods of labor are not reached. Let the leading men and women, chosen of God, unite in carrying forward the work intelligently and in faith. I am pained when I see with some a desire for the highest position, and to be honored of men. This is not the leading of the Holy Spirit. Angels of God are commissioned to labor with every company that will work humbly and intelligently. Truth and righteousness must go forth as a lamp that burneth. —*December 1, 1909. (p. 810, pars. 1, 2)*

General Instruction 119

"And He went through the cities and villages, teaching, and journeying toward Jerusalem. Then said one unto Him, Lord, are there few that be saved? And He said unto them, Strive to enter in at the straight gate: for many, I say unto you, will seek to enter in, and shall not be able."

Why? Why, because they trust to uncertainties. They do not read the Bible. They do not understand what the Word says. When they read the Bible and understand what the Word says, let me tell you, there will be a hundredfold more accomplished by our churches, by the ministers, and by those that are teachers, and by all men in office, and they will then see of the salvation of our God. What is the matter with us? We haven't a love from above. We do not make a business of serving God. "And He went through the cities and villages, teaching, and journeying toward Jerusalem," teaching on the way. He did not go right straight along. He was teaching on the way, and when He saw persons who needed help He would take their cases and represent them in His teaching.

"Then said one unto Him, Lord, are there few that be saved? He said unto them, Strive to enter in at the straight gate: for many, I say unto you, will seek to enter in, and shall not be able." What is the matter? Why, they are not living their faith. They seek to enter in but are not able because it requires earnest effort for every one of us to walk in the narrow path that leads to eternal life. —*April 5, 1910. (p. 886, pars. 2-5)*

We see there is a great work to be done and we want everyone to be in the right position and do their part of the work. We are laborers together with God. Now, here God expects us to have a living experience as laborers together with God and He wants everyone of us to be in working order. We are careless; we are too indifferent; we do not seem to know the plan being worked out. Now, I see when I go on the cars, there is one that comes through with a great package of papers. We could read them, but what are they good for? We may find a little news in them, but what we need is the Word of life and to have a missionary spirit wherever we are. The world will never be warned if we take it so easy. We know how it was with the schools of the prophets. We know that they were learning out of the Scriptures and that they were praising God; because they understood the Scriptures, God was glorified. And as Saul was searching for David he came right up to the school of the prophets and behold the first thing they knew, he was prophesying right with the prophets. The school of the prophets was a special school to get the endowment of the Holy Spirit of God and then go forth into the dark places of the earth and seek for those who would listen to the testimony that they had to bring. —*April 5, 1910. (p. 887, par. 4)*

It is Satan's plan to talk about that which concerns himself. He is delighted to have human beings talk of his power, of his working through the children of men, but by indulgence in such conversation the mind becomes gloomy and sour and disagreeable.

We may become channels of communication for Satan through which words bring no sunshine to the heart. But let us decide that this shall not be. Let us decide not to be channels through which Satan shall send gloomy, disagreeable thoughts. Let our words be not a savor of death unto death, but of life unto life, in the words we speak to the people and in the prayers we offer. God desires us to give unmistakable evidences that we have a spiritual life. We do not enjoy the fullness of the blessing which the Lord has prepared for us because we do not ask in faith. If we could exercise faith in the Word of the living God, we should have the richest blessings. We dishonor God by our lack of faith; therefore we cannot impart life to others unless we ourselves bear a living, uplifting testimony. We cannot give that which we do not possess. If we will walk humbly with God, if we will walk in the spirit of Christ, none of us will carry heavy burdens. We shall lay them on the great burden bearer. Then we may expect triumphs in the presence of God, in the communion of His love.

Every camp-meeting may be a love feast from the beginning to the end because God's presence is with His people. All heaven is interested in our salvation. The angels of God, thousands upon thousands, and ten thousand times ten thousand are commissioned ministers to those who shall be heirs of salvation. They guard us against evil and press back the powers of darkness that are seeking our destruction. Have we not reason to be thankful every moment, thankful even when there are apparent difficulties in our pathway? The Lord Himself is our Helper. —*April 5, 1910. (p. 891, par. 1)*

"The Lord thy God in the midst of thee is mighty; He will save, He will rejoice over thee with joy; He will rest in His love, He will joy over thee with singing."

This is the testimony that the Lord desires to bear to the world. His praise should be continually in our hearts and upon our lips. Such testimonies will be an influence upon others as we seek to turn men from their self-indulgent efforts to secure happiness. We must show them that we have something better than that which they are seeking. When Jesus talked to the Samaritan woman He did not reprove her for coming to draw water from Jacob's well, but He presented something of far greater value. In comparison with Jacob's well, He presented the fountain of living waters. —*April 5, 1910. (p. 892, pars. 2, 3)*

If we prayed as much as we ought to pray, if we realized that there is an open communication between us and God, we should be in an altogether different position than we are. We should be cheerful and we shall see that there are a hundred blessings all around, no matter whether we belong to this institution or a different institution. You will see that you can speak a word for Christ in the different places. We have a work to do, everyone of us, and time is short. We have but a little time now. And we want that Satan shall not take the victory of the whole world. He is at work—the devil and the fallen angels. You remember that. They too, rebelled in heaven with Satan and were turned out of heaven. Now, they have the highest efficiency and power. They have the highest efficiency and they want to hinder every one of you from obeying the Lord. They want to hinder every one of you that they can, in building up coldness and indifference between you. Now, we have work to do every one of us, and I need not tell you of it. But men may be doing all they can, and still there are many on the lost side. In these books I have here:

"His praise should continually be in our hearts and upon our lips." Now, as I read, in comparison with Jacob's well, He presented the fountain of living waters, "If thou knewest the gift of God, and Who it is that saith to thee, Give Me to drink, thou wouldst have asked Him, and He would have given thee living water."

We had to work wonderfully hard before our institutions were established. We went from place to place giving treatments. There are a great many who cannot go to the sanitarium, but we may go right in where they are and see the sick and tell them how to treat themselves. That is the way my husband and I would do, and we took them right into our house. He would take the men and I would take the women and work that way. What is Satan doing? He links himself with every discordant spirit in the world. Satan and his vast, vast numbers who are disobedient to the heavenly commands, and they will represent these things that are of great importance and give all to understand that they know all about it and that they can do thus and so. We are not building up what we should outside of our churches, and this is the very work the Lord wants carried forward. We have every endowment and capability and every facility provided for discharging the duties that devolve upon us. We should be grateful to God for these advantages.

When we went to Australia I cannot begin to tell you and you can't understand how little were the advantages there, compared with the darkest places around here. It was hard to gain a foothold for the work there. Here you are better situated. Here are the sick and you can go into their houses and take the Bible in your hand and take some of our books along and read some of the comforting things in these books and some of the encouraging things. We must not give ourselves right up to ourselves. This institution must spread as a great blessing.

This is a good school for children if you make it so; but if you do not make it so, why, then it is worse than if they had not been here. We want to be in a position where we will honor and glorify God every day. Why are we here? What have we this institution for? To bring relief to the sick. This is according to our mission and just the work which should be carried on and the Lord wants every one of us to be in working order. And if we will come under discipline to God, we will be as happy a people as you will wish to see. Why? We see the devil working on one side, and that is his side, and he can bring the most entrancing things of heaven that he is acquainted with. He brings these things into his work, but we can have a great deal more knowledge in these things than we possess and we can be the happiest people of any in the world. And right in this institution we can be continually at work on the right side. And do not let us look on the dark side. If you have children, here is a good place for you to learn how to bring them up and how to teach them and how to guide them. You can do this right here. But that is not enough. There are other places and other towns. We have seen these places being worked and we have felt thankful for it and we expect there is a work being done more or less all around. What you want, every one of you and every one of us, is to keep the Saviour in view. Jesus told His disciples just before He left them not to mourn about it, but He said, "Let not your hearts be troubled: ye believe in God, believe also in Me. In My Father's house are many mansions: if it were not so, I would have told you. I go to prepare a place for you. And if I go and prepare a place for you, I will come again, and receive you unto Myself: that where I am, there ye may be also." —*April 5, 1910. (p. 893, 894)*

Well, now He tells them just what He is going to do. We want to say we are a people now that have to have a religious experience for ourselves, and we can never enter heaven unless we have that experience. We may have our names on the church book, but have we a daily experience in the things of God? "Let not your heart be troubled: ye believe in God, believe also in Me". And thus He comforts and encourages them with the cross right in view.

Our dear Saviour says again, "I am the true vine," and "ye are the branches," "and My Father is the husbandman." "Every branch in Me that beareth not fruit He taketh away." Now we want to know what fruit we are bearing. We want our fruits to be right before the world in the ministry of Christ on the earth, and they can be if we will. We have all these advantages and how thankful we should be. The Lord brought this place right into our hands. What advantages we have in this very place! But there are other places where they need help, and let every one who can, take his Bible in his hand and see what missionary work he can do; carry with him some of the little books that we have published, and if the people do not want to buy, leave the books with them, and tell them to read them whether they want to buy or not; and if any of you want to give some away, just do that. There is a chance to let our light shine and we want to do so. Now Satan has the advantage in many things. He can quote those glories that he had in the heavenly sanctuary just as though they belonged to him, and he will quote those things. He is working upon human minds and he will bring in all the sophistries that he can bring in and mix it in with some of his wonderful learning, an agency that he had in the heavenly courts. The world will certainly think that he is excellent. We want all that excellency and power, but we shall have the light of the truth which is to shine. But Satan will present that light that he had in the heavenly courts, and many will think that it must be the truth, and they are intelligent men and good women, and he leads them right along to perdition.

But we have a Saviour Who wants to make this institution a perfect success; he wants us to do the work intelligently, and he wants us to praise His holy name. We can do it if we will. Satan grasps the minds every time we come into a meeting where they have the love of the truth in its beauty and its charms. We want to be full of usefulness every one of us and God can make a success of this institution, but it depends upon us to make this all and in all.

"Cry aloud, spare not, lift up thy voice like a trumpet, and show My people their transgression, and the house of Jacob their sins. Yet they seek Me daily, and delight to know My ways, as a nation that did righteousness, and forsook not the ordinance of their God.

Well, now you see those who had not believed in the commandments of God. They did not believe in the Sabbath commandment. They did not obey this. We want to be in a situation where we can give these commandments so that our lives will teach the people we believe just what we profess to believe. I want to say that it will be well for you to become acquainted with these books. (Vols. of Test.)

We have seen the application. We have been placed where we had to see it. God meant we should see it.

A lady was passing by—one of our highest teachers in Battle Creek, and it was icy and she didn't know how to drive and neither did her husband, and the sleigh slipped and jerked the lines right out of their hands. "Jump, jump," said the husband and she jumped and was caught right on the side of the sleigh and struck her head on the ice and the blood poured out of her ears and nose and eyes and they thought it would be impossible to save her, but we gathered her up and took her into the house. We said we will take care of her but it is a question of how long she can live. There must be no noise around anywhere. It may be possible to save her life.

The doctor was sent for and when he came, he said, "What are you doing?" We said, "giving her a hot foot bath right under the bed clothes." "Well," he said, "you know better than I," and he turned on his heel and walked off and that was the last we saw of the doctor. Well, we kept her for four weeks and we had all the roosters removed from the neighborhood and every bit of noise excluded. And we succeeded in saving her life. Five years later in passing a woman who looked like this same teacher, and when she saw me she grasped me in her arms and said, "You saved my life and the life of this child, the only child I have, and I feel so grateful whenever I hear the name of Ellen White mentioned."

From this beginning they founded the institution in Battle Creek. It takes a great deal to break down prejudice. Tepid water will not melt cold tallow. We cannot make much impression on cold tallow with warm water.

We are intensely interested. We have a grand review before us. People are watching us everywhere and they are watching to see how much higher our piety is than the piety of those who have no connection with an institution. We want to be in a position where we can let our piety pour over outside when we can. There will be opportunities. You cannot neglect things here; you cannot do that; but you can find opportunities where you can let the light of this institution shine forth. God wants you to do it. I believe that you will try to do it. What we want is a greater work of faith that we may show forth the praises of God in what He is doing and what He will do for us. If we will show this faith, it will have as much influence as any treatment you can give to those who are looking on to see what we are doing. Let us get into that position where we will lay all on Jesus Christ, for there is a grand review to take place; only a little while and there is to be an examination of what we believe and what we are. Are we prepared to be transferred to higher grades? To a higher school where Christ will lead us to the tree of life and there will continue to teach us in regard to the ages of the eternal life. Are we prepared for that grand review? Are we fashioning our characters to that divine similitude? God help us that we may be Christians in every sense of the word. If we will obey God, let me tell you, the way is already open; the angels of God will be our respresentatives wherever we go.

The angels of God are round about us. Every one is in communication with Jesus Christ; they are one with Him and we want to do the works of God. We want to be wide awake, full of zeal, and live for God and advance step by step heavenward. Are we prepared for the grand review? It is coming on. Satan is gathering all of his beautiful knowledge that he had when he was an angel of light and he is coming in to deceive the very elect with that very knowledge, and we want to be in a position where we can work intelligently, where we can work in faith and bring souls to a knowledge of the truth of the grand review that will take place when he tells them that he is going to have the whole world as his subjects and they will gather under his banner, but we must stand higher. Young men and young women, teachers, doctors, do not put on pompous (manners) positions, as though you knew everything worth knowing, but act as little children coming to ask God to let His blessing rest upon you, that you may teach others; for if you do that the will of God will be revealed and it will follow you wherever you go. We have a whole Saviour; He is not a piece of a Saviour. He will save every soul that comes unto Him. Now, let us have that working faith, have that believing faith, have that intelligent faith that it is our privilege to have. —*April 5, 1910. (pp. 895-898)*

You may ask, "Why does Sister White read all this (Matthew 6)?" I answer, "because there are lessons here that we have not yet learned." God wants us to recognize every gift we receive as coming from Him. When we do this, and gratitude for the goodness of God fills our hearts, a heavenly atmosphere will surround the soul. My brethren and sisters, shall we not strive to order our lives by the truth of God as it is found in His Word? We need to be more diligent in the study of the Scriptures. They must be to us, not a make-believe story, but the truth of the living God, the foundation of our faith, the assurance on which we build our hope of eternal life in the kingdom of heaven.

I wish to bring before you this morning some things that have been presented to me, showing wherein some of us are making serious mistakes. The minds of many are occupied with the consideration of worldly matters, often to the exclusion of the religion of God's Word. The thoughts are more often upon the matter of eating and drinking and dressing than upon the great and important duty of serving God with humility and prayer. The Lord has shown me that in many families decided changes must be brought about. They need to know what they must do to be saved. If they will inquire diligently the way of life, God will impart to them an understanding of His Word, and teach them to value at their true worth the things of eternity. Then the heart will no longer reach out covetously for worldly benefits and the pleasures of this life.

Shall we not give diligent heed to the lessons that I have read? There is an individual work for us to do in union with Christ. We are to put on Christ, put on His qualities of character to represent Him in all our words and actions. When we are willing thus to follow on to know the Lord, walking in humility before Him and being taught of Him daily, the Holy Spirit will work through us, giving us power to represent to the world a better way.

"Therefore I say unto you, Take no (*anxious*) thought for your life, what ye shall eat, or what ye shall drink; nor yet for your body, what ye shall put on. Is not the life more than meat, and the body than raiment?" While you do your best, weary not your body and mind with the cares of this life; do not spoil your religious experience by worry; but trust the Lord to work for you, and to do for you what you cannot do for yourself. The life is more than meat, and the body is more than raiment.

There is much needless worrying, much trouble of mind, over things that cannot be helped. The Lord would have His children put their trust fully in Him. Our Lord is a just and righteous God. His children should acknowledge His goodness and His justice in the large and the small things of life. Those who cherish the spirit of worry and complaint are refusing to recognize His guiding hand. Needless anxiety is a foolish thing; and it hinders us from standing in a true position before God. When the Holy Spirit comes into the soul, there will be no desire to complain and murmur because we do not have everything we want; rather, we will thank God from a full heart for the blessings that we have. There is great need of more thankfulness among our workers today; and until they have this spirit they will be unprepared for a place in the kingdom of heaven. There is a mighty work to be done for every one of us. We comprehend but little of what God desires to work out through us. We should seek to realize the breadth of His plans, and profit by every lesson that He tries to teach us.

A great deal of mischief is wrought in the imagination of our hearts and minds when we seek to carry our own way contrary to the law of kindness. Here is where many fail. We do not cultivate a disposition to kindness; we want everything to come in an easy way to ourselves. But the question of greatest importance to each one of us should be, not how we can carry our own plans against the plans of others, but how we can have the power to live for Christ every day. Christ came to earth and gave His life that we might have eternal salvation. He wants to encircle each of us with the atmosphere of heaven, that we may give to the world an example that will honor the religion of Christ.

There is one blessing all may have who seek for it in the right way. It is the Holy Spirit of God; and this is a blessing that brings all others in its train. If we will come to God as little children, asking for His grace and power and salvation, not for our own uplifting, but that we may bring blessing to those around us, our petitions will not be denied. Then let us study the Word of God that we may know how to take hold of His promises, and claim them as our own. Then we shall be happy. The enemy will be unable to destroy our peace. As we come into right relation to God, we shall see of His salvation.

In our schools we do not see the mighty working of the Holy Spirit as we ought. Although we have worked hard that they might be conducted on right lines, and advance in the fear of God, we do not see that willingness to be guided by the Spirit of God that opens the way for its working in the fullness of its power. God desires that His rich blessing shall rest upon teachers and students. When they have the experience of being daily converted to God, the perverse disposition will be overcome; there will be no place for it. The converting power of God will come in to lead the students to act for Christ, to serve and glorify Him Who by His infinite sacrifice has made it possible for them to be saved. We need to appreciate more than we do the wonderful condescension of Christ, that we may work out in our lives His gracious character.

The Lord has a very special work to do for all who shall become citizens of His kingdom. Here are many young people associating together day after day in labor and in study, and in all things their conduct should reveal that they are controlled by the Spirit of God. They are to receive an education that will result in full consecration to God. And their own conversion is not the end of this education; they are to learn how to win others to the truth. This they will best accomplish by a life that reveals the transforming power of truth. Christ is to be formed within the hope of glory.

To those having families I will say, there is a work to be done for your children in your homes. Speak kindly to them. They are the Lord's property, His heritage. You have no right to create unhappiness in their lives. In the home it is the privilege of these children to prepare for the heavenly mansions. By no better way than by their own example can parents help the youth to gain this preparation. They are to learn by example as well as by precept that there must be no coarseness, no unkindness where angels of God dwell.

General Instruction

In this life we are to be controlled by the Spirit that rules in the heavenly courts. Righteousness and truth are to go before us. And the glory of the Lord will be the rearward of all who serve Him acceptably. They obtain Christ's righteousness.

We want our children to be saved, but we must save them in God's appointed way. They must be made to understand that they have something to do if they would win heaven. When I see so many of our children who are receiving no preparation to meet temptation, I feel that I cannot do enough in the line of helping to provide places where they can receive an education in the things of God. But unless, when we gather the youth into such places as this we give them the education that will fit them to be overcomers, we had better not gather them into our institutions. Do we want these children and youth to enter the courts of heaven and enjoy the blessings of eternal life? Then let us work to this end understandingly, and we shall see blessed results for our labors.

Great is our need of the saving grace of Christ. Everywhere we turn we see more or less clearly revealed the spirit of strife for place and position, a reaching out for honor and recognition. My brethren and sisters, if you desire honor, seek it in the right way. How shall you seek it, do you ask?—in obedience to the word of truth. Our ambition in this life should be to honor Christ at every step. The hasty temper, the cruel speech, the unkind thought, are not to be indulged. It is not for us to exalt this one, and condemn that one. In right words, words that bless and encourage, we are to reveal the fruits of righteousness.

Have you determined to be rich? Then let these words recorded in the sixth chapter of Matthew impress your heart and direct your life. They will teach you to be content, and to yield your will to the control of the Holy Spirit. You will not then be elbowing your fellow-workers that you may make room for your plans. But your greatest desire will be to work in just the place that God assigned you, and where He can look upon you with approval. Shall we not come into right relation to God? Shall we not put away all strife, which is a manifestation of unconverted self? When you feel sore because you think that somebody else is getting ahead of you, take the matter to the Father in prayer. Ask Him to put the impress of His Spirit upon your mind and character. When you feel like complaining at your lot, look about for some soul who does not have all the blessings that you enjoy. Speak to him words of hope and comfort and encouragement. Such ministry will be a blessing to him, and a greater blessing to yourself. We need to reach the place where as a people we shall reveal in word and work that the Spirit of God is dwelling within, that we are overcomers by the blood of the Lamb and the word of our testimony. It is our privilege to make the battle of life easier for those with whom we associate. Shall we not endeavor to do this? If we will partake of Christ's labors for the uplifting and redemption of souls, we shall hear His words of benediction, "Well done, thou good and faithful servant; ... enter thou into the joy of thy Lord."

Pure and undefiled religion—this is our great need. When the religion of Christ is permitted to hold sway in our lives, there will be advance moves made that will reveal to all in this place the working of divine power. Our lives will be unselfish, thoughtful lives, as we unitedly follow heavenward the path of self-denial and crossbearing.

There is a great work for our people to do in this place. You have great advantages here—advantages that have cost much labor and prayer to secure. I remember how hard we labored to secure this property. Now additional property has come to us. We are glad of this addition, for we need every foot of this land. Our duty in regard to this matter is very clear to my mind; and I mean to work in harmony with the light given to me. We are talking of enlarging our facilities, of adding more buildings; but I would not urge that this work go forward unless a different spiritual atmosphere shall pervade the institution. There is a spirit of strife for position with some. This must be overcome. When the soul is truly converted, all questions of promotion will be decided in the light of eternal interests.

It has been presented to me that unless changes are wrought in the dispositions of many who are here, they will never enter the kingdom of heaven. With some, self is uppermost. Contention and emulation are being cherished, the Spirit of God cannot control, but the enemy comes in to suggest and advise. My brethren and sisters, you cannot afford to permit this condition to continue. You cannot afford to make self service first. This will destroy our work. It must not be that we have taken all these large reponsibilities upon us for naught. We must do our work intelligently, and to the very best of our ability, if we would bring glory to God. His Spirit must come in and abide.

The Lord wants us to be Christlike, to represent to the world the beauties of Christian character. This has not always been done in this place by all the workers. When the character of Christ is reflected in God's professed people, they will desire, not the place of greatest honor, but the place that God chooses for them. "Learn of Me," the great Teacher said, "for I am meek and lowly in heart: and ye shall find rest unto your souls." Christ wants us to work out the dispositions that He will work in, as we yield our lives to his fashioning.

My brethren and sisters, let us stand where heaven can cooperate with us, where the grace of God and His Holy Spirit can rest upon us, and work through us. I was going away today, but I felt that before departing I must lay before you the great need of the converting power of God if the workers in this institution are to obtain the experience that was in His purpose in the establishing of this institution. All this seeking for the highest place, all this determination to carry our individual ideas and desires should stop right now. It does not please the Master. God wants us to be converted from our ways to His way.

As a people we are being watched by the world, and we should conduct ourselves in such a way that men and women will be con-

General Instruction

vinced that we have something that they have not. We need the help of all who are located here. If any have concluded that they cannot throw their energies into this work, there is the world before them. God bids His people order their lives by the living principles that moved Christ to sacrifice Himself for the saving of the lost. The Son of God gave His life to redeem the youth. What shall we do for them? What shall we do for those older in years? My brethren, you need first to order your own lives by the plan of salvation, then gather with Christ with all the powers of your being. Then the Lord will work through your efforts.

When I consider how hard we have worked in different places to establish health institutions, I feel it my duty to impress upon the workers connected with them that they have a great responsibility to act in a way that will rightly represent the principles that are the foundation of this message. They should be righteous in word and deed. Strife and contention, which is of the devil, should find no place in their experience.

We may inherit the things prepared for God's people from the foundation of the world, if we will live in harmony with the righteous life of Christ. Let there be no contention, no strife. There is room enough in the world; there is opportunity for all to perfect a Christian character. Let us take hold of this work intelligently. Then when any change takes place in the working of the cause here, it will be seen, in the course taken by the workers, that their dispositions are being molded by the Spirit of God, that the grace of Christ is sanctifying character.

I do not want to weary you; I have spoken long enough, but, my brethren, I want you to understand how greatly I appreciate everything that is for the advantage of this place. I pray that from this institution an army of workers may go forth to glorify the One Who gave His life for us. O, that we might all show in our daily lives that we appreciate this Gift. May God bless you every one, is my prayer. —*April 16, 1912. (pp. 995-1003)*

God would have His honor exalted before men as supreme, and His counsels confirmed in the eyes of the people. The witness of the prophet Elijah on Mount Carmel gives the example of one who stood wholly for God and His work in the earth. The prophet calls the Lord by His name, Jehovah God, which He Himself had given to denote His condescension and compassion. Elijah calls Him the God of Abraham and Isaac and Israel. He does this that he may excite in the hearts of his backslidden people humble remembrance of the Lord, and assure them of His rich free grace. Elijah prays, "Be it known this day that Thou art the God of Israel." The honor of God is to be exalted as supreme, but the prophet asks further that his mission also may be confirmed. "Let it be known this day that Thou art God in Israel," he prays, "and that I am Thy servant, and that I have done all things at Thy word. Hear me, O Lord," he pleads, "hear me."

Elijah is intense. As he prayed, the silence of death seemed to be about him. As the Amen was spoken, lo, the fire of heaven descended on the sacrifice in the sight of the multitude. —*May 7, 1911. (p. 943, par. 1)*

The people were wonderfully affected by the scene. At the manifestation of God's power they fell on their faces on the earth, and extolled the God of Abraham, and gave glory to the God of Israel. With a loud voice they shouted, "The Lord, He is the God; the Lord, He is the God."

But while the people acknowledged the God of heaven, the priests, with hardened hearts, refused to be convinced. They would remain still the prophets of Baal. Thus they showed themselves ripe for destruction. And Elijah said to the people, "Take the prophets of Baal; let not one of them escape." The time had come when delusion was unveiled. The people saw the false prophets, and when the word was spoken, they fell upon the prophets, brought them down to the brook Kishon, and took part in their slaughter. Thus was Elijah's faith crowned with victory, the priests of Baal put to shame, and the worshipers of false gods confounded. —*(p. 944, pars. 1, 2)*

It should be the determination of every soul who desires to enter the pearly gates, not so much to seek to understand all about the conditions that will prevail in the future state, as to know what the Lord requires of him in this life. It is the will of God that each professing Christian shall perfect a character after the divine similitude. By studying the character of Christ revealed in the Word, by practicing His virtues, the believer will be changed into the same likeness of goodness and mercy. Christ's works of self-denial and sacrifice brought into the daily life, will develop in the soul the faith that works by love and purifies the soul. There are many who wish to evade the cross-bearing part, but the Lord speaks to all when He says, "If any man will come after Me, let him deny himself, and take up his cross daily, and follow Me." —*May 17, 1908. (p. 676, par. 3)*

The Lord will work. Great facts will be revealed in the Word. There are rich experiences to be received from the great Medical Missionary. The knowledge of salvation through faith and a full trust in a personal God and a personal Saviour, will be manifest. Those who have held the beginning of their confidence firm unto the end will have the proof of the things which they have learned by personal experience.

The gospel will be revealed and verified. The experience of the day of Pentecost will surely be repeated. Some will receive the Holy Spirit of truth; yes, some who are now in uncertainty. The Lord has given His Word. For years He has been sending messages of warning, but by many they have been unheeded. Notwithstanding the repeated urgent warnings God has given, many have been turned away from their original faith, and are lost in the fog of error. They have refused to follow the light that God has given to point out the true path. —*No date. (p. 245, pars. 5, 6)*

General Instruction

Christ is the same Christ that He has ever been. He is our Redeemer. Those who have been striving to quench their thirst at broken cisterns, which can hold no water, need to be born again that Christ may be formed within, the hope of glory.

There are those who will never receive the gospel message in its fullness; they will never see the greater light and working of the Holy Spirit. There is a depth of depravity in unbelieving human nature that will never be healed, because the true light has been misinterpreted and misapplied. The Lord has given His Spirit in abundance of assurance to enable men and women to understand the fallacies and errors of Satan, and to guard against them.

Some will soon turn from their deceptive errors and calculations. To those who will be born again, the Bible will become a new book. There is a higher elevation to reach. True faith is to take the place of unbelief. The living springs of the Word of God, with all their rich treasure, are to flow into the soul. The truth of the Christian religion depends upon the divine authority of the Word of God. The authority of the Word is Yea and Amen.

Jesus Christ is the Way, the Truth, and the Life. Our great need is to have Him formed within, the hope of glory. He is to come into our individual experience, as a personal Saviour. He is the foundation of our faith, the Rock of Ages. "Blessed is the man unto whom the Lord imputeth not iniquity." —*No date. (p. 245 all)*

If we turn unto the Lord with full purpose of heart, teaching in the places He indicates, all things that He has commanded, we may be assured of the promise, "Lo, I am with you alway, even unto the end of the world." God is able and waiting to be gracious. —*No date. (p. 249, par. 1)*

Pray to God; commune with Him. Prove the very mind of God, as those who are striving for eternal life, and who must have a knowledge of His will. You can reveal the truth only as you know it in Christ. You are to receive and assimilate His words; they are to become part of yourselves. This is what is meant by eating the flesh and drinking the blood of the Son of God. You are to live by every word that proceedeth out of the mouth of God—that is what God has revealed. Not all has been revealed; we could not bear such a revelation. We are not to leave His Word for the suppositions of men.

Obtain an experimental knowledge of God by wearing the yoke of Christ. He gives wisdom to the meek and lowly, enabling them to judge of what is truth, bringing to light the why and wherefore, pointing out the result of certain actions. The Holy Spirit teaches the student of the Scriptures to judge all things by the standard of righteousness and truth and justice. The divine revelation supplies him with the knowledge that he needs.

And the needed knowledge will be given to all who come to Christ, receiving and practicing His teachings, making His words a part of their lives. Those who place themselves under the instruction of the great Medical Missionary, to be workers together with Him, will have a knowledge that the world, with all its traditionary lore, cannot supply.

Make the Bible the man of your counsel. Your acquaintance with it will grow rapidly if you keep your mind free from the rubbish of the world. The more the Bible is studied, the deeper will be your knowledge of God. The truths of His Word will be written in your soul, making an ineffaceable impression.

Not only will the student himself be benefited by a study of the Word of God. His study is life and salvation to all with whom he associates. He will feel a sacred responsibility to impart the knowledge that he receives. His life will reveal the help and strength that he receives from communion with the Word. The sanctification of the Spirit will be seen in thought, word, and deed. All that he says and does will proclaim that God is light and in Him is no darkness at all. Of such ones the Lord Jesus can indeed say, "Ye are laborers together with God." —*October 17, 1903. (p. 101, par. 3; p. 102, pars. 1, 2)*

God has chosen a people out of the world, and has instructed them to remain forever separate from the world. While living in the world they are not to be of the world. Dr. _____ has bound up himself with worldlings by inviting them into his councils, and he has been dishonoring the sacredness of the truth by bringing worldly lawyers into connection with the work of God's people. The Lord has signified that it is His purpose to keep His people free from the contaminating influence of the world, but the leaders of the medical work at Battle Creek have been working in a way altogether different from the way marked out by the Lord. The first and the second chapters of first Peter are full of instruction in regard to the manner in which we should labor. —*October 14, 1903. (p. 103, par. 4)*

We need as workers to keep looking unto Jesus, the Author and Finisher of our faith. As workers together with God, we are to draw souls to Christ.

We are to remember that we each have a special part to act in the Master's service. Oh, how much good the members of the church might accomplish if they realized the responsibility resting upon them to point those with whom they come in contact to the Redeemer. When church members shall disinterestedly engage in the work given them of God, a much stronger influence will be exerted in behalf of souls ready to die, and much stronger efforts will be put forth in medical missionary lines. When every member of the church does his part faithfully, the workers in the field will be helped and encouraged, and the cause of God will move forward with power. Let the ministers of the gospel and the workers in medical missionary lines labor in perfect harmony. —*October 12, 1904. (p. 79, par. 1)*

We shall have to labor under difficulties, but because of this, let not our zeal flag. The Bible does not acknowledge a believer who is idle, however high his profession may be. There will be

General Instruction

employment in heaven. The redeemed state is not one of idle repose. There remaineth therefore a rest to the people of God, but it is a rest found in loving service. Some among the redeemed will have laid hold of Christ in the last hours of life, and in heaven instruction will be given to the ones, who when they died, did not understand perfectly the plan of salvation. Christ will lead the redeemed ones beside the river of life, and will open to them that which while on this earth they could not understand. —*July 18, 1905. (p. 83, par. 3)*

God's purpose for us is that we shall ever move upward. Even in the smaller duties of common life, we are to make continual growth in grace, supplied with high and holy motives, powerful because they proceed from the One who gave His life to furnish us with the incentive to be wholly successful in the formation of Christian character....

You are to be strong in the strength of God, grounded in the hope of the gospel. You are acquainted with God's requirements, and I beg you not to remain a weakling. You possess qualifications that if rightly used would make you a blessing in the world. Arise in your God-given dignity, living the truth in its purity. Christ is ready to pardon you, to take away your sins, and make you free. He is ready to purify your heart, and give you the sanctification of His spirit. As you commit yourself to His service, He will be at your right hand to help you. Day by day you will be strengthened and ennobled. Looking to the Saviour for help, you will be a conqueror, yes, more than a conqueror over the temptations that beset you. You will become more and more like Christ. The angels of heaven will rejoice to see you standing on the Lord's side, in righteousness and true holiness.

I am very hopeful that you will become all that the Lord desires you to be—a gospel medical missionary. You are to be not only an increasingly skillful physician, but one of the Lord's appointed missionaries, in all your work placing His service first. Let nothing mar your peace. Give your heart's best and holiest affections to Him Who gave His life that you might be among the redeemed family in the heavenly courts. Striving for the crown of life will not make you dissatisfied or less useful. The great Teacher desires to acknowledge you as His helping hand. He calls for your cooperation. Will you not now give Him all that you have and are? Will you not consecrate your talents to His service? —*October 18, 1903. (p. 91 all)*

Christ stood at the head of humanity in the garb of humanity. So full of sympathy and love was His attitude that the poorest was not afraid to come to Him. He was kind to all, easily approached by the most lowly. He went from house to house, healing the sick, feeding the hungry, comforting the mourners, soothing the afflicted, speaking peace to the distressed. He took the little children in His arms and blessed them, and spoke words of hope and comfort to the weary mothers. With unfailing tenderness and gentleness He met every form of human woe and affliction. Not for Himself, but for others did He labor. He was willing to humble Himself, to deny Himself. He did not seek to distinguish Himself. He was the servant of all. It was His meat and drink to be a comfort and a consolation to others, to gladden the sad and heavy laden ones with whom He daily came in contact.

Christ stands before us as the pattern Man, the great Medical Missionary—an example for all who should come after. His love, pure and holy, blessed all who came within the sphere of its influence. His character was absolutely perfect, free from the slightest stain of sin. He came as an expression of the perfect love of God, not to crush, not to judge and condemn, but to heal every weak, defective character—to save men and women from Satan's power. He is the Creator, Redeemer, and Sustainer of the human race. He gives to all the invitation, "Come unto Me, all ye that labor and are heavy laden, and I will give you rest. Take My yoke upon you, and learn of Me; for I am meek and lowly in heart: and ye shall find rest unto your souls. For My yoke is easy, and My burden is light." —*June 24, 1903. (p. 94 all)*

"Behold," Christ declares, "I come quickly; and My reward is with Me, to give every man according as his work shall be." God calls upon us to voice the words, "Even so, come, Lord Jesus." God will do much more for His people if they will have faith in Him. Infidelity is stalking abroad through the land. Satan has laid his plans to undermine our faith in the history and the cause and work of God. I am deeply in earnest as I write this. Satan is working with men in prominent positions to sweep away the foundations of our faith. Shall we allow this to be done, brethren? —*No date. (p. 108, par. 2)*

Satan is working to fill minds with the spirit of ambition and of commercialism. Those whose minds are thus diverted, will lose their opportunity of giving the last message to the world.

If a faithful work had been done during the last few years that have gone into eternity, thousands of souls would now be found with Bibles in their hands, reading the Word of God, and praying for light and guidance. Many of these would be engaged in the work of hunting for souls, and fitting up a people to stand in the great day of God. But some who ought to be missionaries, are filled with the spirit of commercialism, and with an ambition to secure for themselves certain advantages. The truth becomes to them a dead letter, not practiced nor obeyed. Jehovah is the true God. Let Him be feared and reverenced. —*November 3, 1907. (p. 565, pars. 1, 2)*

The end of all things is at hand. The signs foretold by Christ are fast fulfilling. The nations are angry, and the time of the dead has come, that they should be judged. There are stormy times before us, but let us not utter one word of unbelief or discouragement. Let us remember that we bear a message of healing to a world filled with sin-sick souls.

General Instruction

You will remember the poverty that we met when starting the work in New England, in Boston, and in New Bedford, and other places. But the difficulties we encountered only made us unite in pushing forward the harder, and we have not forgotten what wonderful victories the Lord gave us. How many times there came upon us trials that almost overpowered us. In every place, heresies came in, and every conceivable error strove for entrance. What were our weapons? Faith and prayer. We were medical missionaries, and we realized the fulfillment of the promise, "Lo, I am with you alway, even unto the end of the world." How manifest was the power of God in healing the sick! What rejoicing, what thanksgiving, was heard! —*July 5, 1905. (p. 84, pars. 1, 2)*

There is a work to be done in all our churches. The criticizing, the condemning, and the arbitrary forbiddings of men, whatever position, is displeasing to God. During the past two years, the churches have had in some lines a wrong education. God has a people whom He is leading and instructing. And the man who exercises the power to permit or to forbid, as his judgment may indicate, has given a representation of an unsanctified disposition. —*November 11, 1907. (p. 572, pars. 2, 3)*

The churches will be left powerless, if they are educated to obey the dictates of finite men instead of obeying the leading of God. They must not be made to feel that before they can engage in any enterprise, they must first obtain permission from men. God bids me say, Cease from man, whose breath is in his nostrils, for wherein is he to be accounted for? Am not I to be consulted? Are finite, impulsive human agencies to have the control of My chosen ones?

Our minds must be stayed on God, not on men who have lost their bearings, and who do not discern that position cannot give a man unerring judgment. Every man is to fear and honor God. All are to reverence Him, and to show their interest in His people. There must be a constant seeking for divine instruction. The Lord has not appointed one man to exercise his conscience for another man. —*(p. 573, par. 1)*

We have come to a time when every member of the church should take hold of medical missionary work. The world is a lazar-house filled with victims of both physical and spiritual disease. Everywhere people are perishing for lack of a knowledge of the truths that have been committed to us. The members of the church are in need of an awakening, that they may realize their responsibility to impart these truths. Those who have been enlightened by the truth are to be light bearers to the world. To hide our light at this time is to make a terrible mistake. The message to God's people today is, "Arise, shine; for thy light is come, and the glory of the Lord is risen upon thee." —*(Vol. 7, p. 62)*

The medical missionary work should be a part of the work of every church in our land. Disconnected from the church, it would soon become a strange medley of disorganized atoms. —*(Vol. 6, p. 289)*

Much good can be done by those who do not hold diplomas as fully accredited physicians. Some are to be prepared to work as competent physicians. Many, working under the direction of such ones, can do acceptable work without spending so long a time in study as it has been thought necessary to spend in the past. —*1903. (p. 611, pars. 1-3)*

In some respects there are decided changes to be made in your character. Wherever you labor, you are to understand that while you are to stand as firm as a rock to principle, you are not to be a driver, but a fellow-laborer with your brethren. You are not to seek to rule, and dictate, and compel, but to be teachable in spirit, kind in disposition, and to be one with your brethren.

It would be a serious mistake to place you again in a position which your past experience has shown that you have not wisdom to fill. The peculiar traits of your character lead you to desire to be a leader, but I have been shown that it would not be wisdom for you to occupy the position of the president of the Southern California Conference another year.... We need for the place a man who has less confidence in his own human judgment, one who will act as Christ acted, Who, though Himself the Prince of life, made Himself of no reputation, and coming to a world that was all seared and marred with the curse, placed Himself as one among the most needy and dependent. When He revealed Himself to the world as its Saviour, He said, "Learn of Me; for I am meek and lowly in heart: and ye shall find rest unto your souls."

The presidents of our conferences must be men who are not self-sufficient and dictatorial. They must not give place to the idea that the office of president comprehends a vast amount of rulership. With such ideas they will leave impression upon minds that will do injury to the work. Precious privileges will be lost to the people when presidents minutely define and direct the work of their co-laborers.

As a people we are to be purified from our natural habits and desires. Our hearts must be changed, or we cannot correctly represent the Lord Jesus Who gave His life for us. The Son of God took humanity upon Him that He might make it possible for humanity to take hold upon divinity through the exercise of a perfect faith. Christ is our example for the development of a perfect character. Through the strength we receive from Him we may be overcomers. In seeking Him for those things that we need, we must exercise faith that will not be denied.

We must represent Him by following humbly in His footsteps. Through belief in His merits and practice of the truth, we shall receive of His grace, and this will be revealed in kindness of heart and action and singleness of purpose. Courtesy and sympathy will be revealed in our daily lives. By a daily opening of the heart to truth and righteousness as they are found in Jesus, we will be able to reveal that truth and that righteousness in our dealings with others.

The Spirit of Christ is grieved when any of His followers give evidence of possessing a harsh, unfair, or exacting spirit. As laborers together with God, each should regard the other as part of God's great firm. He desires that they shall counsel together. There is to be no drawing apart, for the spirit of independence dishonors the truth we possess. One special evidence that the love of Christ is abiding in His church is the unity and harmony which exist among its members. This is the brightest witness to the possession of true religion; for it will convert and transform the natural man, and fashion him after the divine similitude.

The converting power of Christ is to have a telling influence in all our institutions, and this power is the agency that will overcome our individual defects of character and make us laborers together with God. By the truth held in its purity, souls will be reached who could not otherwise be influenced to obey. The Holy Spirit is to be our counselor and guide in every branch of the work. The will of God made manifest in the life reveals the power of the Word to overcome every natural trait of character, and to conduct the believer "from glory to glory, even as by the Spirit of the Lord."

I have a deep interest in you, my brother. I want you to receive the grace of our precious Saviour, that you may be sanctified soul, body, and spirit, through the belief of the truth. You are not required to set a standard of character for yourself, but to accept the standard, which if copied will lead you in the lowly steps of Jesus. —*September 23, 1908. (pp. 697-699)*

Section III

Training Physicians and Nurses

Great care should be exercised in the training of young people for the medical missionary work, for the mind is molded by that which it receives and retains. Too much incomplete work has been done in the education given. The most useful education is that gained by study in connection with practical work.

Our institutions are not to be so overgrown that the most important points in education do not receive the proper consideration. Instruction should be given in medical missionary work. The teachings given in medical lines should be blended with a study of the Bible. And physical training should not be neglected.

Great care should be exercised in regard to the influences that prevail in the institution. The influences under which the nurses are placed will mold their character for eternity.

In every sanitarium established, preparation must be made to train young men and women to be medical missionaries. The Lord will open the way before them as they go forth to work for Him.

We must provide educational advantages in the different conferences. All our medical workers must not receive the stamp of one man's mind. In different places, there should be sanitariums of a high order, where our young people can receive a thorough training. We are not to countenance the carrying on of sanitariums of an inferior order, in which incompetent instructors will do slipped work and call it educational work. The instructors in our medical missionary training schools must be picked men and women of ability. —*1903. (p. 612, pars. 1-4)*

In training workers to care for the sick, let the minds of the students be impressed with the thought that their highest aim should always be to look after the spiritual welfare of their patients. To this end they should learn to repeat the promises of God's Word, and to offer fervent prayers daily, while preparing for service. Let them realize that they are always to keep the sweetening, sanctifying influence of the great Medical Missionary before their patients. If those who are suffering can be impressed with the fact that Christ is their sympathizing, compassionate Saviour, they will have rest of mind, which is so essential to the recovery of health.

In new places where schools are being set in operation, arrange to have a treatment-room or rooms connected with the school. Let this place be outside the main school building, so that the sick will be where it is quiet. Let those who are qualifying to teach, give lessons in treating the sick. Soon much permanent fruit will be gathered, in physical improvement and in spiritual advancement which, combined, will be of great advantage.

Over the medical missionary department, as well as over every other department of the school, there should be a head instructor to teach those under him. The beginning may be small. There may be only a few patients, but as the head instructor gives treatment to those, quite a number of students can look on to see how he does this work, and they can help him in many ways. Thus they will learn to do this kind of work themselves.

We must certainly arouse from our passive position along these lines. Much may be learned by visiting the hospitals. In these hospitals not a few of our young people should be learning to be successful medical missionaries in caring for the sick intelligently. Observation, and the practice of that which has been learned, will result in consecrated youth becoming active, efficient medical missionary workers. But the surgical work must be done by faithful, skillful physicians. —*1903. (p. 615, pars. 1-4)*

God will not require of man a more strict account of anything than of the way in which he has occupied his time. Have its hours been wasted and abused? God has granted to us the precious boon of life, not to be devoted to selfish gratification. Our work is too solemn, our time to serve God and our fellow men too short, to be spent in seeking for fame. Oh, if men would stop in their aspirations where God has set the bounds, what different service would the Lord receive. —*October 1, 1909. (p. 761, par. 3)*

Students who are in training for medical missionary work, should be willing to learn under those of experience, to heed their suggestions, to follow their advice. There are many who are in such haste to climb to distinction, that they skip some of the rounds of the ladder, and, in so doing, lose essential experience which they must have in order to become intelligent workers. In their zeal, the knowledge of many things look unimportant to them. They skim over the surface, and do not go deep into the mine of truth, thus by a slow and painstaking process gaining an experience that will enable them to be of special help to others. We want our medical students to be men and women who are most thorough and who feel it their duty to improve every talent lent them, that they may finally double their entrusted capital.

The light that God has given in medical missionary lines will not cause His people to be regarded as inferior in scientific medical knowledge, but will fit them to stand upon the highest eminence. God would have them stand as a wise and understanding people because of His presence with them. In the strength of Him Who is the source of all wisdom, all grace, defects and ignorance may be overcome.

Let every medical student aim to reach a high standard. Under the discipline of the greatest of all Teachers, our course must ever tend upward to perfection. All who are connected with the medical missionary work must be learners. Let no one stop to say, "I cannot do this." Let him say instead, "God requires me to be perfect; He expects me to work away from all commonness and cheapness, and to strive after that which is of the highest order."

There is only one power that can make medical students what they ought to be, and keep them steadfast—the grace of God and the power of the truth exerting a saving influence upon life and character. These students, who intend to minister to suffering humanity, will find no graduating place this side of heaven. That knowledge which is termed science should be acquired, while the seeker daily acknowledges that the fear of God is the beginning of wisdom. Everything that will strengthen the mind should be cultivated to the utmost of their power, while at the same time they should seek God for wisdom; for unless they are guided by the wisdom from above, they will become an easy prey to the deceptive power of Satan. They will become large in their own eyes, pompous, and self-sufficient. —*October 1, 1909. (p. 762, pars. 1-4)*

God-fearing physicians speak modestly of their work; but novices with limited experience in dealing with the bodies and souls of men will often speak boastingly of their knowledge and attainments. These need a better understanding of themselves; then they would become more intelligent in regard to their duties and would realize that in every department where they have to labor, they must possess a willing mind, and earnest spirit, and a hearty, unselfish zeal in trying to do others good. They will not study how best to preserve their dignity, but by thoughtfulness and caretaking will earn a reputation for thoroughness and exactitude, and by sympathetic ministry will gain the hearts of those whom they serve.

In the medical profession there are many skeptics and atheists who exalt the works of God above the God of science. Comparatively few of those who enter worldly medical colleges come out from them pure and unspotted. They have failed to become elevated, ennobled, sanctified. Material things eclipse the heavenly and eternal. With many, religious faith and principles are mingled with worldly customs and practices, and pure and undefiled religion is rare. But it is the privilege of every student to enter college with the same fixed, determined principles that Daniel had when he entered the court of Babylon, and throughout his course, to keep his integrity untarnished.

The strength and grace of God have been provided at an infinite sacrifice that men might be victorious over Satan's suggestions and temptations, and come forth unsullied. The life, the words, and the deportment are the most forcible argument, the most solemn appeal to the careless, irreverent, and skeptical. Let the life and character be the strong argument for Christianity; then men will be compelled to take knowledge of you that you have been with Jesus and have learned of Him. —*October 1, 1909. (p. 763, pars. 2, 3)*

Let not medical students be deceived by the wiles of the devil or by any of his cunning pretexts which so many adopt to beguile and ensnare. Stand firm to principle. At every step inqure, "What saith the Lord?" Say firmly, "I will follow the light. I will respect and honor the Majesty of truth."

Training Physicians and Nurses

Especially should those who are studying medicine in the schools of the world guard against contamination from the evil influences with which they are constantly surrounded. When their instructors are worldly-wise men, and their fellow students infidels who have no serious thought of God, even Christians of experience are in danger of being influenced by these irreligious associations. Nevertheless, some have gone through the medical course, and have remained true to principle. They would not continue their studies on the Sabbath, and they have proved that men may become qualified for the duties of a physician, and not disappoint the expectations of those who have encouraged them to obtain an education.

It is because of these peculiar temptations that our youth must meet in worldly medical schools, that provision should be made for preparatory and advanced medical training in our own schools, under Christian teachers. Our larger Union Conference training schools, in various parts of the field, should be placed in the most favorable position for qualifying our youth to meet the entrance requirements specified by State laws regarding medical students. The very best teaching talent should be secured, that our schools may be brought up to the proper standard. The youth and those more advanced in years who feel it their duty to fit themselves for work requiring the passing of certain legal tests, should be able to secure at our Union Conference training schools all that is essential for entrance into a medical college. —*October 1, 1909. (p. 764, pars. 1-3)*

Prayer will accomplish wonders for those who give themselves to prayer, watching thereunto. God desires us all to be in a waiting hopeful position. What He has promised, He will do; and inasmuch as there are legal requirements making it necessary that medical students shall take a certain preparatory course of study, our colleges should arrange to carry their students to the point of literary and scientific training that is necessary. —*October 1, 1909. (p. 765, par. 1)*

"Great care should be exercised in the training of young people for the medical missionary work, for the mind is molded by that which it receives and retains." —*October 1, 1909. (p. 774, par. 6)*

It is not necessary for so many of our youth to study medicine. But for those who should take medical studies our Union Conference training schools should make ample provision in facilities for preparatory education." —*October 15, 1903. (p. 776, par. 1)*

The standard set for our sanitariums and schools is a high one, and a great responsibility rests upon the physicians and teachers connected with these institutions. Efforts should be made to secure teachers who will instruct after Christ's manner of teaching, regarding this of more value than any human methods. Let them honor the educational standards established by Christ, and following His instruction give their students lessons in faith and in holiness.

Christ was sent of the Father to represent His character and will. Let us follow His example in laboring to reach the people where they are. Teachers who are not particular to harmonize with the teachings of Christ, and who follow the custom and practices of worldly physicians are out of line with the charge that the Saviour has given us. —*April 27, 1910. (p. 900, pars. 2, 3)*

All our denominational colleges and training schools should make provision to give their students the education essential for evangelists and for Christian business men. The youth and those more advanced in years will feel it their duty to fit themselves for work requiring the passing of certain legal tests and should be able to secure at our Union Conference training schools all that is essential without having to go to Battle Creek for their preparatory education.

If there are legal requirements making it necessary that medical students shall take a certain preparatory course of study, let our colleges teach the required additional studies in a manner consistent with Christian education. They should arrange to carry their students to the point of literary and scientific training that is necessary. Many of these requirements have been made because so much of the preparatory work done in ordinary schools is superficial. Let all our work be thorough, faithful and true.

In our training schools, the Bible is to be made the basis of all education. And in the required studies, it is not necessary for our teachers to bring in the objectionable books that the Lord has instructed us not to use in our schools. From light that the Lord has given me, I know that our training schools in various parts of the field should be placed in the most favorable position possible for qualifying our youth to meet the tests specified by State laws regarding medical students. To this end the very best teaching talent should be secured that our schools may be brought up to the required standard...

Let me repeat: It is not necessary for so many of our youth to study medicine. But for those who should take medical studies our Union Conference training schools should make ample provision in facilities for preparatory education. —*October 15, 1903. (p. 613 all)*

A great work is to be done in a short time, and God forbids that we should encourage so many of our youth to bind themselves up for three, or four, or six years' training, before engaging in active work. Men and women should gain an education by working along practical lines in different places, in accordance with the light that God has given, and under the direction of experienced leaders.

Let not our young men be deterred from entering the ministry. There is danger that through glowing representations some will be drawn out of the path where God bids them walk. Some have been encouraged to take a course of study in medical lines, who ought to be preparing themselves to enter the ministry. The Lord calls for more men to enter His vineyard. —*1899. (General Conference Bulletin, p. 614, pars. 1, 2)*

Those who expect to become medical missionary workers must be thoroughly educated in Bible lines. They should have the very best spiritual advantages, in order that they may be fitted to teach and to train others. —*1903. (p. 616, par. 1); (See also Testimonies for the Church, Vol. VIII, pp. 163-166)*

I have been instructed that we are not to delay to do the work that needs to be done in health reform lines. Through this work we are to reach souls in the highways and byways. I have been given special light that in our sanitariums many souls will receive and obey present truth. In these institutions men and women are to be taught how to care for their own bodies, and at the same time how to become sound in the faith. They are to be taught what is meant by eating the flesh and drinking the blood of the Son of God. Said Christ, "The words that I speak unto you, they are spirit, and they are life."

Our sanitariums are to be schools in which instruction shall be given in medical missionary lines. They are to bring to sin-sick souls the leaves of the tree of life, which will restore to them peace and hope and faith in Christ Jesus. Forbid not those who have a desire to extend this work. Let the light shine forth. All worthy health productions will create an interest in health reform. Forbid them not. The Lord would have all opportunities to extend the work taken advantage of. —*July 18, 1905. (p. 82, pars. 2, 3)*

"Break up the large centers," has been the word of the Lord. "Carry the light to many places." Those who are desirous of receiving a training for effective medical missionary work, should understand that large sanitariums will be conducted so much like institutions of the world, that students laboring in such sanitariums cannot obtain a systematic training for Christian medical missionary work. —*September 21, 1903. (p. 89, par. 3)*

No arrangements should be made to gather a large number of students at any one place. For just as surely as this is done, the stamp of the educator's mold will be imparted to the student's mind and character. If the mind of the teacher is radical, or if it is not complete, where it ought to be perfect through Christ Jesus, the students will show the defective stamp.

There should be companies organized, and educated most thoroughly to work as nurses, as evangelists, as ministers, as canvassers, as gospel students, to perfect a character after the divine similitude. To prepare to receive the higher education in the school above, is now to be our purpose. —*April 9, 1903. (p. 105, pars. 1, 2)*

By the character that he is forming, every man is deciding his future destiny. In the books of heaven is made the record. There the character is photographed. There is seen a picture of the unclothed soul. —*June 25, 1905. (p. 170, par. 4)*

The Lord must be given an opportunity to show men their duty, and to work upon their minds. No one is to bind himself to serve for a term of years under the direction of one group of men or in one specified branch of the Master's work; for the Lord Himself will call men, as of old He called the humble fishermen, and will Himself give them instruction regarding their field of labor and the methods they should follow. He will call men from the plow and from other occupations, to give the last note of warning to perishing souls. There are many ways in which to work for the Master, and the great Teacher will open the understanding of these workers, enabling them to see wondrous things in His Word.

I have repeatedly been instructed that no one should be advised to pledge himself to spend two, three, four, five, or six years under any one man's supervision. Let students stand where they can follow the will of God. Their service belongs to Him. Their capabilities and talents are to be refined, purified, ennobled. In this lower school—the school of earth—they are to be prepared for translation into the school of heaven, where their education will be continued under the personal supervision of Christ, the great Teacher, Who will lead them beside the living waters, and open to them the mysteries of the kingdom of God. —*September 21, 1903. (p. 87, pars. 3, 4)*

Kind of Workers Needed in Our Medical Institutions

The workers connected with our medical institutions should have the full confidence of the patients. Let them remember that this will be gained, not by elegant dress or by smartness of speech, but by living the life of Christ. Warm-hearted, unselfish workers are needed in our sanitariums—workers who can speak words of tenderness and compassion to the sick and suffering. The physicians and nurses are not to be stiff and unsocial, neither are they to be light and trifling. They are to be bright and cheerful, bringing sunshine to the hearts of the sick. They are to talk of the Saviour and His power to save. In Him there is healing for soul and body. —*April 15, 1904. (p. 61, par. 2)*

In the establishment and carrying forward of sanitarium work, the strictest economy is ever to be shown. Workers are to be employed who will be producers as well as consumers. In no case is money to be invested for display. Gospel medical missionary work is today to be carried forward in simplicity, even as it was carried forward by the Majesty of heaven, Who, seeing the necessities of a lost, sinful world, laid aside His royal robe and kingly crown, and clothed His divinity with humanity, that He might stand at the head of humanity. In His way of working, He has left us a perfect example.

"If any man will come after Me," He declared, "let him deny himself, and take up his cross, and follow Me." The true medical missionary will obey these words. He will not strain every nerve to make a display, thinking thus to win souls to the Saviour. The Son of God left His heavenly home to come to a world all seared and marred by the curse, that He might seek and save the lost. Ought we not, His followers, to show the same self-denial and self-sacrifice that His life revealed? For us He endured the privations of poverty. Shall we refuse to deny ourselves for His sake? —*April 15, 1904. (p. 62, par. 1)*

In order for successful work to be done in the field or in our institutions, workers with harmonious elements of character are needed. The work can be carried forward only by patience and harmony of action. It has been a lack of harmony, a lack of determination on the part of the workers to lift with one purpose in view, that has delayed the establishment of a sanitarium in Southern California. There has been so much variance that means which should have been invested in a sanitarium have been turned into other channels. —*June 30, 1904. (p. 71, par. 2)*

Those connected with them (our schools and sanitariums) are to labor with earnest alacrity. The work that is done under the ministration of the Holy Spirit, out of love for God and for humanity, will bear the signature of God, and will make its impression on human minds. —*October 12, 1904. (p. 77, par. 2)*

It is the part of a medical missionary to minister to the needs of the soul as well as to the needs of the body. The precious truth of Christ's power to save, spoken in season will give hope and courage, and may save soul and body. The Lord waters and watches over the seed thus sown. The promises of the Bible, repeated to those who are sick and discouraged, will be the means of saving many souls. The Holy Spirit cooperates with the worker who labors in the fear and love of God. God gives such workers wisdom and success. —*October 12, 1904. (p. 78, par. 4)*

The purest example of unselfishness is now to be shown by our medical missionary workers. With the knowledge and experience gained by practical work, they are to go out to give treatment to the sick. As they go from house to house, they will find access to many hearts. Many will be reached who otherwise would never have heard the gospel message.

Much good can be done by those who do not hold diplomas as fully accredited physicians. Some are to be prepared to work as competent physicians. Many workers under the direction of such ones, can do acceptable work without spending so long a time in study as it has been thought necessary to spend in the past.

Many will go out to labor for the Master who have not been able to take a regular course of study in school. God will help these workers. They will obtain knowledge from the higher school, and will be fitted to take their position in the rank and file of workers as nurses. The great Medical Missionary sees every effort that is made to find access to souls by presenting the principles of health reform.

Decided changes are taking place in our world. The Lord has declared that He will turn and overturn. Humble men, who hitherto have been in obscurity, must now be given opportunity to become workers. —*October 16, 1903. (p. 107, pars. 1-4)*

Into the medical missionary work there must be brought more of a yearning for souls. It was this yearning that filled the hearts of those who established our first medical institution. Christ is to be present in the sickroom, filling the heart of the physician with the fragrance of His love. When his life is such that Christ can go with him to the bedside of the sick, there will come to them the conviction that He, the compassionate Saviour, is present, and this conviction will do much to restore them to health.

In word and deed the physicians and nurses of our medical institutions are to say, so plainly that it cannot be misunderstood, "God is in this place," to save, not to destroy. Christ invites our physicians to become acquainted with Him. When they respond to His invitation, they will know that they receive the things they ask for. Their minds will be enlightened by wisdom from above. Constantly beholding the Saviour, they will become more and more like Him, till at last it can be said of them in the heavenly courts, "Ye are complete in Him." Christ has pledged Himself to give His disciples what they ask for in His name. As they labor in harmony with Him, they can ask Him to aid them in every time of need. —*February 3, 1904. (pp. 114, 115 to first line)*

Medical missionary workers are needed in the Southern field, who can engage in sanitarium work. Sanitariums are needed, in which successful medical and surgical work can be done. These institutions, conducted in accordance with the will of God, would remove prejudice, and call our work into favorable notice.

The highest aim of the workers in these institutions is to be the spiritual health of the patients. Successful evangelistic work can be done in connection with medical missionary work. It is as these lines of work are united that we may expect to gather the most precious fruit for the Lord.

From the instruction that the Lord has given me from time to time, I know that there should be workers who make medical evngelistic tours among the towns and villages. Those who do this work will gather a rich harvest of souls, both from the higher and the lower classes. The way for this work is best prepared by the efforts of the faithful canvasser.

Many will be called into the field to labor from house to house, giving Bible reading, and praying with those who are interested.

It is of the utmost importance that harmony exist in our institutions. Better for the work to go crippled than for workers who are not fully devoted to be employed. It is unconsecrated, unconverted men who have been spoiling the work of God. The Lord has no use whatever for men who are not wholly consecrated to His service. —*September 11, 1903. (p. 116, pars. 1-3)*

Kind of Workers Needed

The hearts and interests of God's workers should be one. The workers should be bound up with Christ, and should esteem one another highly for their works' sake. —*September 11, 1903. (p. 117 to line)*

In our Washington work, wise, competent physicians, efficient managers, and nurses with the very best qualifications will be needed. Earnest, devoted young peopole also will be needed, to enter the work as nurses. These young men and women will increase in capability as they use conscientiously the knowledge they gain, and they will become better and better qualified to be the Lord's helping hand. They may become successful missionaries, pointing souls to the Lamb of God, which taketh away the sin of the world, and whose healing efficiency can save both soul and body.

The Lord wants wise men and women, acting in the capacity of nurses, to comfort and help the sick and suffering. Through the ministrations of these nurses, those who have heretofore taken no interest in religious things will be led to ask, "What must I do to be saved?" The sick will be led to Christ by the patient attention of nurses who anticipate their wants, and who bow in prayer and ask the great Medical Missionary to look with compassion upon the sufferer, and to let the soothing influence of His grace be felt and His restoring power be exercised.

O, that all who are sick and afflicted could be ministered to by Christ-like physicians and nurses, who could help them to place their weary, pain-racked bodies in the care of the great Healer in faith looking to Him for restoration.

The nervous timidity of the sick will be overcome as they are made acquainted with the intensive interest that the Saviour has for all suffering humanity. O, the depth of the love of Christ! To redeem us from death, He died on the cross of Calvary.

Let our physicians and nurses ever bear in mind the words, "We are laborers together with God." Let every physician and every nurse learn how to work for the alleviation of mental as well as physical suffering. At this time, when sin is so prevalent and so violently revealed, how important it is that our sanitariums be conducted in such a way that they will accomplish the greatest amount of good. How important that all the workers in these institutions know how to speak words in season to those who are weary and sin-sick.

Physicians and nurses should ever be kind and cheerful, putting away all gloom and sadness. Let faith grasp the hand of Christ for His healing touch.

As our nurses minister patiently to those who are sick in body and soul, let them ask God to work for the suffering ones, that they may be led to know Christ, and let them believe that their prayers will be answered. In all that is done, let the love of Christ be revealed.

Every sincere Christian bows to Jesus as the true Physician of souls. When He stands by the bedside of the afflicted, there will be many, not only converted, but healed. He Who declared, "I am the Way, the Truth, and the Life," will be with His faithful physicians and nurses as they strive to cooperate with Him. If through judicious ministration the patient is led to give his soul to Christ, and to bring his thought into obedience to the will of God, a great victory is gained.

O, how I long to see the work going with power in New Bedford and Fairhaven, and in many other places just as greatly in need of the truth as these places. We hope that sometime a sanitarium may be established in New Bedford. Medical missionary workers are needed in such cities. But, dear sister, it requires talent of no ordinary ability to manage a sanitarium. Men of experience, tried and tested, must take hold of the work. That part of the workers who undertake to establish such an institution are experienced and qualified, is not sufficient. For their own sake, for the sake of the institution, and for the sake fo the cause at large, it is important that a complete corps of well qualified men and women be found to enter upon the work. The Lord's eye is over the whole field, and when the time is ripe for an institution to be started in a certain field, He can turn toward that place the minds of the men and women best prepared to enter the institution. —*January 1, 1905. (pp. 120-122)*

There are many lines of work to be carried forward. There is an opening for well-trained nurses to go among families, and awaken in households an interest in the truth. There is urgent need of many evangelists and Bible workers in such cities as Boston and New Bedford. Such workers would find many opportunities to sow the good seed. There is work for every energetic, thorough, earnest worker. The teaching of Christ, the simple truths taught by His parables, are just as much needed today as they were when He was in the world in person. —*January 1, 1905. (p. 123 to line)*

The nurses connected with these institutions should be prepared to exert a soul-saving influence. Those who are not rooted and grounded in the truth should not be employed. Let them first become established in the truth. Then let them learn to be ever on guard, ever seeking to make the right impression on the minds of the sick.

Nurses should always be pleasant and cheerful, and should show thoughtful consideration. They are ever to strive to do their work wisely and well, realizing that they are serving the Lord, and that in the discharge of their duties they are to live out before unbelievers their faith in the truth for this time. —*February 4, 1905. (p. 124 all below line)*

Great care should be shown in choosing young people to connect with our sanitariums. Those who have not the love of the truth in the soul should not be chosen. The sick need to have wise words spoken to them. The influence of every worker should make an impression on the minds in favor of the religion of Christ. Light has

Kind of Workers Needed

been given me that the young people chosen to connect with our sanitariums should be those who have evidence that they have been apt learners in the school of Christ.

Nurses should have regular Bible instruction, that they may be able to speak to the sick words that will enlighten and help them. Angels of God are in the rooms where the suffering ones are to take treatment, and the atmosphere surrounding the soul of the one giving treatment should be pure and fragrant. In the lives of the physicians and nurses the virtues of Christ are to be seen. His principles are to be lived. Then, by what they do and say, the sick will be drawn to the Saviour.

It is to save the souls, as well as to cure the bodies of men and women, that our sanitariums are at much expense established. God designs that by means of them, the rich and the poor, the high and low, shall find the bread from heaven and the water of life.

An experienced Christian nurse in the sickroom will use the best remedies within her knowledge for restoring the sufferer to health. And she will pleasantly and successfully draw the one for whom she is working to Christ, the Healer of the soul as well as of the body. The lessons given, line upon line, here a little and there a little, will have their influence. The older nurses, whether they be men or women, should lose no opportunity of calling the attention of the sick to Christ. Those who care for the sick should be prepared to blend spiritual healing with physical healing. Let the nurses in our sanitariums show that in the solemn work of caring for the sick, they do not rely on drug medication, but on the power of Christ, and the use of the simple remedies that He has provided—the application of hot and cold water and simple, nourishing food, without intoxicating liquor of any kind, with judicious exercise, and a putting away of all injurious practices. In treatment such as this there is health for the sick. —*February 4, 1905. (pp. 125, 126 all)*

One night we seemed to be in a council meeting, and the question being considered was, how can the sanitarium work in Southern California be best advanced? One present proposed one thing and still another proposed something entirely opposite.

One of dignity and authority arose and said, "I have words of counsel for you. Never, never repeat the mistakes of the past."

Men have placed too much confidence in themselves, and have allowed cultivated and hereditary tendencies to wrong, which ought to have been overcome, to control and to bear away the victory. Various lines of work are to be earnestly carried forward, for the enlightening of those who are in spiritual darkness. Evangelical work must receive first attention, and is to be intelligently carried forward, in all lines of your medical work.

"You have," said our Instructor, "come to an important place in the history of your work. Who shall be chosen to carry responsibilities in the sanitarium at the beginning of its work? No mistake must be made in this matter. Men are not to be placed in positions of trust who have not been tested and tried. Men and women who understand the will of the Lord are to be chosen—men who can discern the work that needs to be done, and prayerfully do it, that the mistakes and errors of the past need not be repeated."

"The one who is placed in the position of business manager," he said, "must daily be managed by the Lord. He occupies a very important place and he must possess the necessary qualifications for the work. He should have dignity and knowledge, blended with a clear sense of how to use his authority. Christ must be revealed in his life. He must be a man who can give religious instruction and exert a spiritual influence. He must know how to deal with minds, and he must allow his own mind to be controlled by the Spirit. Wisdom is to come forth from his lips in words of encouragement to all with whom he is connected. He must know how to discern and correct mistakes. He must be a man who will harmonize with his fellow-workers, a man who possesses adaptability. He should be able to speak of the different points of our faith, as occasion requires. His words and acts should reveal justice." —*December 12, 1904. (p. 129, pars. 5, 6; p. 130 all)*

There must be connected with our sanitariums in various places ample facilities for the training of workers, and great care should be taken in the selection of young people to connect with our sanitariums. We cannot afford to accept anyone who is willing to come. Great injury is done to our medical institutions when we connect with them inexperienced youth, who do not understand what it means to do faithful service for God.

Every soul connected with our institutions is to be tested and tried. If self is not hid with Christ in God, the workers will blindly do many things that will hinder the precious work of God. —*1905. (p. 244, pars. 3, 4)*

The workers in our sanitariums should understand that each has an individual work. Each should realize his duty to keep his soul and body under discipline to the great Physician, Who gave His life to rescue us from the control of a powerful foe. After He had burst the fetters of the tomb, He said to His disciples, "I am the resurrection and the life." And before He ascended to heaven, He declared, "All power is given unto Me in heaven and in earth. Go ye therefore, and teach all nations, baptizing them in the name of the Father, and of the Son, and of the Holy Ghost: teaching them to observe all things whatsoever I have commanded you: and, lo, I am with you alway, even unto the end of the world."

Here is your work. Teach the sick. Proclaim the gospel to them, persuading them to become Christ's disciples. The Father, the Son, and the Holy Spirit are pledged to be with you in every emergency. Act as Christians having divine orders. God is to be trusted, believed, obeyed. His character is to be represented in every household.

Kind of Workers Needed

A wonderful responsibility rests upon these connected with the sanitariums established in His name for the treatment of the sick. —*February 12, 1907. (p. 344, pars. 2-4)*

This is to be done without the use of poisonous drugs. Those who become workers in the sanitariums are to believe the words of Christ. "Lo, I am with you alway, even unto the end of the world." Those who have the fear of God in the heart will cultivate a sweet disposition. Forbearance and courtesy will be manifested in the life. Duties will be faithfully discharged and in a way that will not leave a disagreeable impression on the minds of the sick or the well.

In order to maintain a right influence, the workers must reveal that they are one in sentiment. Do not let it be seen that there is disunion among the helpers.

If you have any care of the sick, act tenderly, kindly, faithfully, that you may have a converting influence upon them. You have need of the grace of Christ in order to properly represent the service of Christ. And as you present the grace of truth in true, disinterested service, angels will be present to sustain you. The Comforter will be with you to fulfill the promise of the Saviour, "Lo, I am with you alway, even unto the end of the world."

I have a charge to give, a message to bear to our sanitarium workers. Keep your souls in purity. Do a work that will have a winning influence on those placed in your charge. You can speak often to the sick of the great Physician, Who can heal the diseases of the body as verily as He heals the sickness of the soul. Pray with the sick, and try to lead them to see in Christ, their Healer. Tell them that if they will look to Him in faith, He will say to them, "Thy sins be forgiven thee." It means very much to the sick to learn this lesson. —*February 12, 1907. (p. 345 all)*

I am bidden to say to the sanitarium family, Let your social meetings, and all your religious exercises be characterized by a deep earnestness and a joy that expresses the love of God in the soul. Such meetings will be profitable to all, for they will bind heart to heart. Let there be earnest seasons of prayer, for prayer will give strength to the religious experience. Confess Christ openly and bravely, and manifest at all times the meekness of Christ.

The Lord would have the family of workers at Loma Linda channels of light. If we will keep the heart and mind opened heavenward, cherishing the comfort of His grace in the heart, the presence of Christ will be revealed. Let earnestness and zeal come into your lives. Make no backward movements. The Lord is our Helper, our Guide, our Shield, our exceeding great reward. Do not allow levity to come into your experience, but cultivate cheerfulness, for this is an excellent grace. We cannot afford to be unmindful of our words and deportment.

During the past night I seemed to be standing before a large congregation, speaking to the people the words of life. I long to understand more perfectly about this meeting that was presented to me. I seemed to hear the sweet melody of praise to God, and expressions of gratitude were coming from souls that were the recipients of the grace of Christ. The voice of praise and thanksgiving was heard, and countenances were aglow with the light of the love of God. It seemed that angels' voices united with those in the meeting who were offering praise to God. —*August 29, 1907. (p. 432, pars. 2-4)*

We all have very much to be thankful for. Let us open our lips in praise and thanksgiving to God. Let us come nearer to the Lord Jesus, and acknowledge our daily obligations to Him. He has made it possible for us to secure for ourselves a very happy life even in this world of sin, and holds out the hope of being continually in His presence in the kingdom He is preparing for His people. Should not these thoughts call forth from us praise and thanksgiving? May the Lord bless you, and bless the sanitarium family, is my prayer. —*August 29, 1907. (p. 433, par. 2)*

There should be at our sanitariums intelligent men and women who can instruct in Christ's methods of ministry. Under the instruction of competent, consecrated teachers, the youth may become partakers of the divine nature, and learn how to escape the corruptions that are in the world through lust. I have been shown that we should have many more women who can deal especially with the diseases of women, many more lady nurses who will treat the sick in a simple way and without the use of drugs. —*November 3, 1907. (p. 560, par. 1)*

The work which you propose will require wise business men and efficient physicians. If you had the talent and means to carry such responsibilities, we would be glad to see your plans carry. But the sanitarium must be your first consideration. May the Lord give you wisdom and grace to bear these responsibilities as He would have you. This institution must have all the talent that is needed to make it a success. —*February 20, 1908. (p. 635, par. 3)*

In all our sanitariums the work done should be of such character as to win souls to Jesus Christ. We have a wide missionary field in our health institutions, for here people of all countries come to regain their health. The best helpers to have connected with our sanitariums are those men who desire to make the Bible their guide, those who will put forth their mental and moral powers to advance the work in correct ways.

Let the workers in the sanitariums remember that the object of the establishment of these institutions is not alone the relief of suffering and the healing of diseases, but also the salvation of souls. Let the spiritual atmosphere of these institutions be such that men and women who are brought to the sanitariums to receive treatment for their bodily ills, shall learn the lessons that their diseased souls need healing. —*February 23, 1908. (p. 638, pars. 1, 2)*

If ever there was a time when our work should be done under

Kind of Workers Needed

the special direction of the Spirit of God, it is now. Let those who are living at their ease, arouse. Let our sanitariums become what they should be—homes where healing is ministered to sin-sick souls. And this will be done when the workers have a living connection with the great Healer. —*February 23, 1908. (p. 643, par. 2)*

The teachers employed in our schools should be men who are acquainted with God through an experimental knowledge. They know Him because they obey all the commandments He has given them. Jehovah engraved His ten commandments on tables of stone, that all the inhabitants of the earth might understand His eternal and unchangeable character. These teachers who desire to advance in learning and proficiency, need to lay right hold of these wonderful revelations of God. But it is only as heart and mind are brought into harmony with God that they will understand the divine requirements. —*May 17, 1908. (p. 676, pars. 1, 2)*

None need concern themselves about these things which the Lord has not revealed to us. In these days speculations will abound, but the Lord declares, "The secret things belong unto the Lord." The voice that spoke to Israel from Sinai is speaking in these last days to men and women, saying, "Thou shalt have no other gods before Me." The law of God was written with His own finger on tables of stone, thus showing that it could never be changed or abolished. It is to be preserved through the eternal ages immutable as the principles of His government in heaven and in earth. Men have set their will against the will of God; but this will not silence His words of wisdom and command, though they may set their speculative theories in opposition to the teachings of revelation, and exalt human wisdom above a plain, "Thus saith the Lord." —*May 17, 1908. (p. 676, par. 2)*

The Lord has given us a wonderful advantage in enabling us to secure Loma Linda for the establishment of the work in progress there. A school is to be built up at Loma Linda that will train Bible workers and missionary nurses for efficient service. The Lord calls for the best talents to be united at this center for the carrying on of the work as He has directed, not the talent that will demand the largest salary, but the talent that will place itself on the side of Christ to work in His lines. —*June 20, 1908. (p. 696, par. 1)*

Our workers are to become intelligent in regard to Christ's life and manner of working. The Lord will help those who desire to cooperate with Him as physicians, if they will become learners of Him how to work for the suffering. He will exercise His power through them for the healing of the sick.

Intemperance and ungodliness are increasing everywhere. The work of temperance must begin in our own hearts. And the work of the physician must begin in an understanding of the works and teachings of the great Physician. Christ left the courts of heaven that He might minister to the sick and suffering of earth.

We must cooperate with the Chief of physicians, walking in all humility of mind before Him. Then the Lord will bless our earnest efforts to relieve the suffering of humanity. It is not by the use of poisonous drugs that this will be done, but by the use of simple remedies. We should seek to correct false habits and practices and teach the lessons of self-denial. The indulgence of appetite is the greatest evil with which we have to contend.

The truth brought to light by Christ teaches that humanity through obedience to the truth as it is in Jesus, may realize power to overcome the corruptions that are in the world through lust. Through living faith in the merits of Christ the soul may be converted and transformed into Christlikeness. Angels of God will be by the side of those who in humbleness of mind learn daily the lessons taught by Christ. —*November 5, 1909. (p. 798, pars. 2-4)*

I have decided words to speak to all who shall act a part in bearing responsibilities in our sanitariums. We are intensely desirous that all connected with our sanitariums shall give evidence that they are men and women who believe in Christ as the world's Redeemer. They are to show that they are laborers together with the Saviour, seeking to save souls of those who are not truly converted, and working to save their own souls by striving to exert a correct example. Do not gather to your working forces men who, if they are tempted, give way to their feelings, men who will not understand that if they are influenced by wrong principles, they will be sure to sow seeds of distrust in others, minds.

Christ came to our world to set His followers an example of perfection of character, that in His strength they might become Christlike, building for time and for eternity. I am bidden to give all our workers, men and women, a most solemn charge. If you are not truly converted, God cannot use you. In word, in spirit, and in all your works you are to bear testimony to the truth, making straight paths for your feet lest the lame be turned out of the way by your walking in strange paths. —*September 10, 1910. (p. 922, pars. 1, 2)*

"Beloved, I wish above all things that thou mayest prosper and be in health, even as thy soul prospereth.... I have no greater joy than to hear that my children walk in truth. Beloved, thou doest faithfully whatsoever thou doest to the brethren and to strangers; which have borne witness of thy charity before the church: whom if thou bring forward on their journey after a godly sort, thou shalt do well: because that for His name's sake they went forth, taking nothing of the Gentiles. We therefore ought to receive such, that we might be fellowhelpers to the truth." Read slowly the whole of the first chapter of second Peter, and grasp by faith the precious truths given for our encouragement. —*September 10, 1910. (p. 923, pars. 1, 2)*

I have been instructed to say to our leading sanitarium workers throughout our ranks: the work must move forward on a higher plane, and after a more sacred order than it has heretofore if it is to accomplish all that God designs should be accomplished by it in our churches and for the world. We need to pray, and to consider earnestly what is the great spiritual need of men and women in this age. Strange things are being done which are not after the Lord's counsel, but after the devising of men. As wicked practices increase among those who are determined to do wickedly, there is great need that our people bring into prominence before the world a pure, untainted work. The Lord says to us, "Be ye clean that labor in the health institutions." Work under the influence of the Holy Spirit of God. Let the men holding positions of sacred trust view the work from a high standpoint. —*May 7, 1911. (p. 941, par. 4)*

I ask you who stand as leaders in this work to read prayerfully chapters four to eleven of the book of Deuteronomy, for there is instruction that all need who would understand God's dealings with His people. And I wish to impress upon all who read these chapters that they mean much to every soul who carries responsibilities in connection with sanitarium work. "Thou art an holy people unto the Lord thy God," the Lord declares, "and the Lord hath chosen thee to be a peculiar people unto Himself, above all nations that are upon the earth." All the directions He has given are to be carefully observed, from the greatest to that which may seem the least.

The Lord says to all, Purify your souls from all commonness. Set before your children and households an example in word and deportment that will lead them to desire above all things to render to God consecrated loving service. Pray for your home; instruct your family; sanctify the Lord God of Israel in your hearts and in your lives.

I am deeply pained as I see with some a spirit of carelessness in speech and deportment. This is a hindrance to spirituality. The Lord declared to Israel: "What doth the Lord require of thee, but to fear the Lord thy God, to walk in all His ways, and to love Him, and to serve the Lord thy God with all thy heart and with all thy soul, to keep the commandments of the Lord, and His statutes, which I command thee this day for thy good? Behold the heaven and the heaven of heavens is the Lord's thy God, the earth also, with all that therein is. Only the Lord had a delight in thy fathers to love them, and He chose their seed after them, even you above all people, as it is this day." Read these words thoughtfully, and consider how great are the privileges of the people whom the Lord chose to serve Him. To all connected with sacred duties I am charged to say, Seek the Lord. Take heed to your conversation; lay off all cheapness of speech; for the Lord would have you become intelligent workers and wise counselors. Let those with whom you associate see nothing of frivolity in your words and works. You have the knowledge of sacred truth, and you are to honor these truths as men and women who must give an account for the talents entrusted to them. —*May 7, 1911. (p. 942, pars. 1-3)*

Elijah's whole life was devoted to the work of reform. He was a voice crying in the wilderness to rebuke sin and press back the tide of moral evil. And while he came to the people as a reprover of sin, his message offered the balm of Gilead for the sin-sick souls of all who would be healed. His zeal for God's glory and his deep love for the house of Israel present lessons for the instruction of all who stand today as representatives of God's work in the earth. Let the conductors of our institutional work catch the spirit of zeal felt by Elijah and learn its intensity. Let them seek for the grace of God that will give them an experience in advance of that which they have heretofore enjoyed. Let them love the work of God, and pray for its advancement in the world. —*May 7, 1911. (p. 944, par. 3)*

Definite instruction has been given concerning the part that the medical missionary workers are to act in the work of God. They are to stand as God's witnesses, to represent the work of the great Medical Missionary, Jesus Christ—God's Gift to our world to save men from the very mistakes that have brought the rebuke of God upon this people. Not a thread of selfishness is to be woven into the web. —*March 1, 1904. (p. 80, par. 1)*

... seeking to treat the sick by correct methods, and to impart to those coming to the institution the sound doctrines of the gospel.

Under the hallowed influence of such teachings souls will be converted. The truth practiced and taught by medical missionaries will be received in the heart of some, and will lead to conversion and the establishment in the heart of the true principles of righteousness. —*January 23, 1905. (p. 80, par. 2)*

The purest example of unselfishness is now to be shown by our medical missionary workers. With the knowledge and experience gained by practical work, they are to go out to give treatment to the sick. As they go from house to house, they will find access to many hearts. Many will be reached who otherwise would never have heard the gospel message.

To those who are tired of a life of sinfulness, but who know not where to turn to obtain relief, present the compassionate Saviour, full of love and tenderness, longing to receive those who come to Him with broken hearts and contrite spirits. Take them by the hand, lift them up, speak to them words of hope and courage. Help them to grasp the hand of Him Who has said, "Let him take hold of My strength, that he may make peace with Me; and he shall make peace with Me." —*1903. (p. 108, par. 1)*

We shall need the very best physicians that can be secured, men and women who are faithful and true, and who will live in constant dependence upon the great Healer, men and women who will humble their hearts before God, and believe His Word, men and women who will keep their eyes fixed on their Leader and Counselor, the Lord Jesus Christ. —*June 23, 1905. (p. 165, par. 3)*

This work must be carried on right. In the past, decided failures have been made in the institutions established for the care of the sick because so much business has been crowded in that the main object for which our sanitariums are established has been lost sight of. Great loss has thus been sustained. I am to urge upon our people that the proclamation of the principles of truth must be kept prominent as the main line of work for which our sanitariums were instituted.

The Lord calls for a solemn dedication to Him of the sanitariums that shall be established. Our object in the establishment of these institutions is that the truth for this time may through them be proclaimed. In order that this may be done, they must be conducted on right lines. In them, business interests are not to be crowded in to take the place of spiritual interests. Every day devotional exercises are to be held. The Word of God is in no case to be given a secondary place. Those who come to our sanitariums for treatment must see the Word of God, which is the bread of life, exalted above all common, earthly considerations. A strong religious influence is to be exerted. It must be plainly shown that the glory of God and the uplifting of Christ are placed before all else. —*June 23, 1905. (p. 166, pars. 1, 2)*

I wish I could see you and talk with you. Let nothing draw you to Battle Creek. It is presented to me that every effort is being made to draw to Battle Creek our young people and those who should be engaged in missionary work elsewhere. Men must be placed in charge of the educational branches of our work who are sound in the faith and as firm as a rock to principle. —*July 10, 1905. (p. 176, par. 3)*

The Lord has need of all kinds of skillful workmen. "He gave some, apostles; and some, prophets; and some, evangelists; and some, pastors and teachers; for the perfecting of the saints, for the work of the ministry, for the edifying of the body of Christ: till we all come in the unity of the faith and of the knowledge of the Son of God, unto a perfect man, unto the measure of the stature of the fullness of Christ." —*No date. (p. 602, par. 2)*

Location of Schools and Sanitariums

The Lord has ordained that memorials for Him shall be established in many places. He has presented before me buildings away from the cities, and suitable for our work, which can be purchased at a low price. We must take advantage of the favorable openings for sanitarium work in Southern California, where the climate is so favorable for this work. —*April 15, 1904. (p. 60, par. 2)*

The buildings secured for this work should be out of the cities, in rural districts, so that the sick may have the benefit of outdoor life. By the beauty of flower and field, their minds will be diverted from themselves, from their aches and pains, and they will be led to look from nature to the God of nature, Who has provided so abundantly the beauties of the natural world. The convalescent can lie in the shade of the trees, and those who are stronger can, if they wish, work among the flowers, doing just a little at first, and increasing their efforts as they grow stronger. Working in the garden, gathering flowers and fruit, listening to the birds praising God, the patients will be wonderfully blessed. Angels of God will draw near to them. They will forget their sorrows. Melancholy and depression will leave them. The fresh air and sunshine, and the exercise taken, will bring them life and vitality. The wearied brain and nerves will find relief. Good treatment and wholesome diet will build them up and strengthen them. They will feel no need for health-destroying drugs or for intoxicating drink. —*April 15, 1904. (p. 61, par. 1)*

Southern California is world-renowned as a health resort. Every year many thousands of tourists go there. These must hear the last warning message. We are called upon by God to explain the Scriptures to these people. We are not to build hotels for the accommodation of tourists, and we are not to establish sanitariums in the cities. We are to establish our work where we shall be able to do the most good to those who come to our sanitariums for treatment.

Workers who can speak to the multitudes are to be located where they can meet the people where they are, and give them the message of truth. —*May 15, 1904. (p. 67, pars. 2, 3)*

There is a special work to be done just now. A sanitarium should be established near Los Angeles. My brethren, will you not remember that it is the expressed will of God that this shall be done? Why this work should be delayed from year to year, is a great mystery. This is a matter that has long been kept before you, my brethren. Again and again sanitarium work has been pointed out as an important means of reaching people with the truth. Had the light given by God been followed, this institution might now be in running order, exerting a strong influence for good. Arrangements could have been made to utilize for sanitarium work buildings already erected. —*June 30, 1904. (p. 71, par. 1)*

I am very grateful to my heavenly Father that you have secured a building near Los Angeles for sanitarium work. Your description of the building shows the truth of the testimonies I have borne— that buildings suitable for our work will be offered to us at a low price. We must make earnest efforts to improve the opportunities that God sends us, that His work may advance as rapidly as possible. —*July 15, 1904. (p. 75, par. 2)*

The proclamation of the truth in all parts of the world calls for small sanitariums in many places, not in the heart of cities, but in places where city influence will be as little felt as possible.

I am obliged to say that the making of so large a plant in Battle Creek, and the calling together of those who should be engaged in medical missionary work in many places, is doing just what God has specified should not be done. —*September 21, 1903. (p. 89, pars. 4, 5)*

Location of Schools and Sanitariums

I am much encouraged by the letters that I have received from you regarding Loma Linda. From your description of the place, I believe it meets the representation which I have seen of what we should seek for as sanitarium locations. Such a place was presented to me a few miles from an important city. The city has recently been built up.

I have tried to place before our people the representation given me regarding sanitariums in the country, and I have urged upon them the necessity of establishing our sanitariums outside of the cities. I have had repeatedly presented to me the advantages of securing locations some miles out of the cities. Those who follow the counsel of God in providing places where the sick and suffering can receive proper treatment will be guided to the right places for the establishment of their work.

Let our sanitariums be located where there is an abundance of land. I can see the advantage of such a place as Loma Linda. The Lord worked to help us to secure this property. The work of this institution is to be carried forward on pure, elevated lines. It can be conducted in such a way that the truth will be presented as the rock upon which to build. —*June 2, 1905. (p. 161, pars. 1-3)*

Out of the cities, has been my constant advice. But it has taken years for our people to become aroused to an understanding of the situation. It has taken years for them to realize that the Lord would have them leave the cities and do their work in the quiet of the country, away from the turmoil and noise and confusion. We are thankful to God for Loma Linda. It is one of the best locations for sanitarium work that I have ever seen. At this place the sick can be given every natural advantage for regaining health and strength. —*July 1905. (p. 182, par. 2)*

Out of the cities, is my message. Those who have had the light, but have neglected to follow the instruction that the Lord has given regarding the location of our health institutions and our schools, will one day see the folly of a clinging to the cities. They will realize how kind the Lord was to point out the right way.

Let your schools, the high and the lowly, be out of the cities. If you desire to live a heavenly life in this world, place yourselves in right relation to God. Let your aspirations be Christlike. Christ lived much in contact with nature. God's missionaries are to form their lives after the diving similitude. They are to have a close connection with Christ. His life is to be their example. —*July 1905. (p. 183, pars. 3, 4)*

For the past twenty years the Lord has been giving the message that plants are to be made in many places. He will greatly bless us as we endeavor to carry out His will. Out of the city into the country, is the word that has been given, and this word is to be obeyed. Our sanitariums are to be established in the most healthful surroundings. We have tried to follow closely the Lord's directions in this matter, and He has let light shine on our pathway, as we have endeavored to establish sanitariums where sin-sick souls may be led to the great Healer. God declared that we should find buildings suitable for our work, and that these buildings would be offered to us at a very low price. Has not our recent experience in Southern California proved this true? —*July 1905. (p. 184, par. 1)*

Our young men and young women should be encouraged to attend schools away from the cities, that under intelligent teachers, they may receive a training that will fit them to stand on vantage ground. How can our young people advance spiritually, while working as servants simply to prepare food for and serve worldings? They often do unnecessary work in the preparation of foods that are not even wholesome. Shall our youth be encouraged to rest satisfied with such an education? —*September 27, 1905. (p. 225, par. 2)*

The advantage of outdoor life must never be lost sight of. How thankful we should be that God has given us beautiful sanitarium properties at Paradise Valley, Glendale, and Loma Linda. "Out of the cities! Out of the cities!" This has been my message for years. And yet how slow some are to realize that the crowded cities are not favorable places for sanitarium work.

Even in Southern California not many years ago, there were some who favored the erection of a large sanitarium building in the heart of Los Angeles. In the light of the instruction God has given we could not consent to the carrying out of any such plan. In the visions of the night, the Lord had shown me unoccupied properties in the country, suitable for sanitarium purposes, and for sale at a price far below the original cost.

It was some time before we found these places. First, we secured the Paradise Valley Sanitarium, near San Diego. A few months later in the good providence of God, the Glendale property came to the notice of our people, and was purchased and fitted up for service. But light came that our work of establishing sanitariums in Southern California was not complete, and on several different occasions Testimonies were given that medical missionary work must be done somewhere in the vicinity of Redlands.

"On our way to Redlands, as our train passed through miles of orange groves, I recognized this section of Southern California as one of the places that had been presented to me with the word that it should have a fully equipped sanitarium.

"As I looked from the car window, and saw the trees laden with fruit, there arose before me a vision of what the spiritual harvest might have been had earnest, Christlike efforts been put forth for the salvation of souls." —*April 6, 1905. (p. 280, pars. 1-5)*

Sanitariums must be established in various places away from the cities. Schools must be established in connection with the sanitariums. As far as possible, these organizations must be blended, each helping

Location of Schools and Sanitariums

the other, and yet each doing its special work. —*May 1, 1906. (p. 284, par. 2)*

The light of truth must be held up in Battle Creek. Faithful watchmen must be stationed there. The truth must go forth by the exposition of the Word, to saints and to sinners. Laborers are now needed there, who will distinguish the difference between eating of the fruit of the forbidden tree, and the eating of the fruit of the tree bearing the gospel message.

I am instructed to say, Prepare places where will be given true education free from deceptive theories. Let the plain words of Christ, uncontaminated by false science, be taught. It will require no elaborate preparations to engage sincerely, humbly, prayerfully in this work.

Will we now make thorough work for eternity? We have no time to criticize another soul. Do not consider it your duty to chastise another. See that your own soul is right with God. —*May 1, 1906. (p. 285, pars. 1-3)*

Clear light has been given that our educational institutions should be connected with our sanitariums wherever this is possible. The work of the two institutions is to blend. I am thankful that we have a school at Loma Linda. The educational talent of competent physicians is a necessity to the schools where medical missionary evangelists are to be trained for service. The students in the school are to be taught to be strict health reformers. The instructions given in regard to disease and its causes, and how to prevent disease, and the training given in the treatment of the sick, will prove an invaluable education, and one that the students in all our schools should have. —*February 20, 1908. (p. 635, par. 4)*

The blending of our schools and sanitariums will prove an advantage in many ways. Through the instruction given by the sanitarium, students will learn how to avoid forming careless, intemperate habits in eating. Let the instruction be given in simple words. We have no need to use the many expressions used by worldly physicians which are so difficult to understand that they must be interpreted by the physician. These long names are often used to conceal the character of the drugs being used to combat disease. We do not need these. —*February 20, 1908. (p. 636, par. 1)*

I am thankful when I think of the advantages enjoyed by the schools that are established near our sanitariums, so that the work of the two educational institutions can blend. The students in these schools, while gaining an education in the knowledge of present truth can also learn how to be ministers of healing to those whom they go forth to serve. The prayer of Christ includes such work as this: "Neither pray I for these alone," He said, "but for them also which shall believe on Me through their word; that they all may be one; as thou, Father, art in Me, and I in Thee, that they also may be one in Us: that the world may believe that Thou hast sent Me. And the glory which Thou gavest Me, I have given them; that they may be one, even as We are one: I in them, and Thou in Me, that they may be made perfect in one; and that the world may know that Thou hast sent Me, and hast loved them as Thou hast loved Me." —*February 23, 1908. (p. 642, par. 1)*

I have clear instruction that wherever it is possible, schools should be established near to our sanitariums, that each institution may be a help to the other. —*October 17, 1903. (p. 733, par. 4)*

"At the 1901 General Conference, in an article entitled, "Instruction Regarding the School Work," read before the delegates April 22, 1901, it was pointed out that all our medical students were not to receive their training at the one medical college in Battle Creek. Of our schools that were introducing educational reforms, Sister White read:

"We are thankful that an interest is being shown in the work of establishing our schools on a right foundation, as they should have been established years ago. If the proper education is given to students, it is a positive necessity to establish our schools at a distance from cities, where the students can do manual work."

Although there may be few students at first, do not be discouraged. The school will win its way. Introduce the medical missionary work. Some of the students are to be educated as nurses and some as physicians. It is not necessary for our students to go to Ann Arbor for a medical education. They may obtain at our schools all the education that is essential to perform the work for this time.

It will take some time to get a right understanding of the matter, but just as soon as we begin to work in the lines of true reform the Holy Spirit will lead us and guide us if we are willing to be guided.

All must place themselves under the influence of the Holy Spirit. When they place themselves under the influence of the Spirit, they will accommodate themselves to Bible lines. When the Word of God takes possession of the minds of teachers, then they are fitted to deal with the education of others. The Word of God is to stand as the foundation of all education. It is to be made the basis of all the schools that we establish. —*April 22, 1901. (p. 731, pars. 2-4)*

It will be a great advantage to have our buildings in retired locations so far as possible. The healthfulness of the surroundings should be fully considered. Locations should be selected a little out from the noisy cities. Those who labor in the large cities need special advantages, that they may not be called to sacrifice life or health unnecessarily. —*December 1, 1909. (p. 808, par. 3)*

I write these things because it has been presented to me as a matter of importance that our workers should so far as possible avoid everything that would imperil their health. We need to exercise the best of judgment in these matters. Feeble or aged men and women should not be sent to labor in unhealthful crowded cities. Let them labor where their lives will not be needlessly sacrificed. Our brethren who bring the truth to the cities must not be obliged to imperil their health in the noise and bustle and confusion, if retired places can be secured. —*December 1, 1909. (p. 809, par. 1)*

"Those who have true wisdom, will plan to establish our sanitarium in the country, where the patients can have the benefit of out-of-door life, where they can sit in the sunshine, or, when the sunshine is too warm, under the shade of the trees. The patients are to be given the advantage of the Lord's health-giving remedies to be found out-of-doors. And the treatments given them in other lines are to be conducted on the same natural, health-restoring principles." —*March 12, 1902. (p. 834, par. 5)*

During the past three nights light has been given me that in the medical missionary work we have lost great advantages by failing to realize the need of a change in our plans in regard to the location of sanitariums. It is the Lord's will that our sanitariums shall be established outside the city. The surroundings of a santarium should be as attractive as possible. Out-of-door life is a means of obtaining health and happiness. In flower gardens and orchards, the sick will find health, cheerfulness and happy thoughts."

"All those representations, and many more, passed as living reality before me. I felt grateful to God, as I realized what an influence an out-of-door life among the flowers and fruit-laden trees has upon those who are sick, both in body and in mind. "Let our medical institutions be established on extensive tracts of land, where the patients can have opportunity for out-of-door exercise. This will prove to be one means for their restoration to health. Encourage the patients to live out-of-doors. Devise plans to keep them out-of-doors, where they will become acquainted with God through nature. As they take exercise in the open air, restoration will begin in body, mind, and soul. Jesus expects those who believe in Him to give to the patients in our medical institutions the messages of God's Word as healing leaves from the tree of life."
—*March 17, 1902. (p. 835, pars. 1, 2)*

In another communication, dated March 14, 1902, I read: "In visions of the night I have been writing letters, and I dare not put off longer the work to be done. Night after night, I have been wakened at eleven, twelve, and one o'clock with a message from the Lord, and I arise at once, and begin to write, fearing that if I do not, I shall forget the instruction given me. Thus it was when I was at Los Angeles. In the night season I was in a council meeting and the question under consideration was the establishment of a sanitarium in Southern California. One brother urged that it would be best to have a sanitarium in the city of Los Angeles, and he pointed out the objections to establishing the sanitarium out of the city. —*(p. 835, par. 3)*

"There was among us One Who presented this matter very clearly, and with the utmost simplicity. He told us it would be a mistake to establish a sanitarium within the city limits. A sanitarium should have the advantage of plenty of land, so that the invalids can work in the open air. For nervous, gloomy, feeble patients, out-of-door work is invaluable. Let them have flowerbeds to care for. In the use of rake and hoe and spade they will find relief for many of the maladies. Idleness is the cause of many diseases.

"Life in the open air is good for body and mind. It is God's medicine for the restoration of health. Pure air, good water, sunshine, beautiful surroundings—these are God's means for restoring the sick to health in natural ways. It is worth more than silver or gold to sick people to lie in the sunshine or in the shade of the trees." —*March 14, 1902. (p. 836, pars. 1, 2)*

Southern California is world-renowned as a health resort. Every year thousands of tourists go there. These must hear the last warning message. We are called upon by God to explain the Scriptures to these people. We are not to build hotels for the accommodation of tourists, and we are not to establish sanitariums in the cities. We are to establish our work where we shall be able to do the most good to those who come to our sanitariums for treatment. —*1902. (p. 842, par. 6)*

The Lord has ordained that memorials for Him shall be established in many places. He has presented before me buildings away from cities, suitable for our work, which can be purchased at a low price. We must take advantage of the favorable openings for sanitarium work in Southern California, where the climate is so favorable for this work. —*October 19, 1902. (p. 840, par. 3)*

Light has been given that it is best to establish our sanitariums outside the cities. Some of our physicians have spoken in favor of locating our sanitariums in the cities. It is difficult to understand why any one should plan to establish a large sanitarium in the city. The very atmosphere of the cities is objectionable. We must conduct our sanitarium work in places suitable for the recovery of the sick. The more attractive the surroundings, the better. In the gardens of nature, the sick rapidly find something to please. Their thoughts are uplifted to the Creator. Let us thank God that so many of our sanitariums are established in pleasing country locations, and yet within easy reach of important centers of population where there are many people to whom we are to communicate a knowledge of saving truth. —*January 27, 1910. (p. 854, par. 2)*

(To the questions, "Should such an educational center be established in every one of our Union Conferences?" Sister White gave the following reply): In one sense, yes. A beginning should be made in every Conference, and these schools can gradually attain to perfection. In every Conference educational advantages should be provided for young people. —*Ms. 169, 1902. (p. 612, par. 5)*

Kind of Students Needed in Our Institutions

We are to seek for students who will plow deep into the Word of God, and who will conform the life practice to the truths of the Word. Let the education given be such as will qualify consecrated young men and women to go forth in harmony with the great commission, "Go ye therefore, and teach all nations, baptizing them in the name of the Father and of the Son and of the Holy Ghost: teaching them to observe all things whatsoever I have commanded you." —*October 30, 1907. (p. 535, par. 3)*

All who desire to enter the medical missionary work, and who are worthy should be given an opportunity to learn. Giving the common treatments to the sick will accomplish much, and will give opportunity to those who administer these hygienic treatments to labor with earnestness for the spiritual recovery of their patients. Let the hearts of all who are working along these lines be softened and subdued. Let the workers learn to consult the great Physician in prayer much more than they have done. Pray, watch, wait, believe. —*1903. (p. 614, par. 4)*

While seeking a preparation for his life-work, the medical student should be encouraged to attain the highest possible development of all his powers. His studies, taxing though they are, need not necessarily undermine his physical health, or lesson his enjoyment of spiritual things. Throughout his course of study, he may continually grow in grace and in a knowledge of the truth, while at the same time he may be constantly adding to the store of knowledge that will make him a wise practitioner.

To medical students I would say, Enter upon your course of study with a determination to do right and to maintain Christian principles. Flee temptations, and avoid every influence for evil. Preserve your integrity of soul. Maintain a conscientious regard for truth and righteousness. Be faithful in the smaller responsibilities, and show yourselves to be close, critical thinkers, having soundness of heart and uprightness, being loyal to God, and true to mankind.

Opportunities are before you; if studious and upright, you may obtain an education of the highest value. Make the most of your privileges. Be not satisfied with ordinary attainment; seek to qualify yourselves to fill positions of trust in connection with the Lord's work in the earth. United with the God of wisdom and power, you may become intellectually strong, and increasingly capable as soul-winners. You may become men and women of responsibility and influence if by the power of your will, coupled with divine strength, you earnestly engage in the work of securing a proper training. —*October 1, 1909. (p. 760, pars. 1-3)*

Students should go as far as possible in thought, training, and intelligent enterprise, but they should never infringe upon a rule, never disregard one principle, that has been interwoven into the upbuilding of the institution. The dropping down is easy enough; the disregard of regulations is natural to the heart inclined to selfish ease and gratification. It is much easier to tear down than to build up. One student with careless ideas may do more to let down the standard, than ten men with all their efforts can do to counteract the demoralizing influence. —*October 1, 1909. (p. 766, par. 3)*

In order for you to become men and women that can be depended upon, there must be a growth of the powers, the exercise of every faculty, even in little things; then greater power is acquired to bear larger responsibilities. Individual responsibility and accountability are essential. In putting into practice that which you are learning during your student days, do not shrink from bearing your share of responsibility because there are risks to take, because something must be ventured. Do not leave others to be brains for you. You must train your powers to be strong and vigorous; then the entrusted talents will grow as a steady, uniform, unyielding energy is exercised in bearing individual responsibility. God would have you add, day by day, little by little, to your stock of ideas, acting as if the moments were jewels to be carefully gathered and discreetly cherished. You will thus acquire breadth of thought and strength of intellect.

God will not require of man a more strict account of anything than of the way in which he has occupied his time. Have its hours been wasted and abused? God has granted to us the precious boon of life, not to be devoted to selfish gratification. Our work is too solemn, our time to serve God and our fellow men too short, to be spent in seeking for fame. Oh, if men would stop in their aspirations where God has set the bounds, what different service would the Lord receive!

Students who are in training for medical missionary work, should be willing to learn under those of experience, to heed their suggestions, to follow their advice. There are many who are in such haste to climb to distinction, that they skip some of the rounds of the ladder, and in so doing, lose essential experience which they must have in order to become intelligent workers. In their zeal, the knowledge of many things looks unimportant to them. They skim over the surface, and do not go deep into the mine of truth, thus by a slow and painstaking process gaining an experience that will enable them to be of special help to others. We want our medical students to be men and women who are most thorough, and who feel it their duty to improve every talent lent them, that they may finally double their entrusted capital.

The light that God has given in medical missionary lines will not cause His people to be regarded as inferior in scientific medical knowledge, but will fit them to stand upon the highest eminence. God would have them stand as a wise and understanding people because of His presence with them. In the strength of Him Who is the Source of all wisdom, all grace, defects and ignorance may be overcome.

Kind of Students Needed in Our Institutions

Let every medical student aim to reach a high standard. Under the discipline of the greatest of all teachers, our course must ever tend upward to perfection. All who are connected with the medical missionary work must be learners. Let no one stop to say, "I cannot do this." Let him say instead, "God requires me to be perfect. He expects me to work away from all commonness and cheapness, and to strive after that which is of the highest order."

There is only one power that can make medical students what they ought to be, and keep them steadfast—the grace of God and the power of the truth exerting a saving influence upon life and character. These students, who intend to minister to suffering humanity, will find no graduating place this side of heaven. That knowledge which is termed science should be acquired, while the seeker daily acknowledges that the fear of God is the beginning of wisdom. Everything that will strengthen the mind, should be cultivated to the utmost of their power, while at the same time they should seek God for wisdom; for unless they are guided by wisdom from above, they will become an easy prey to the deceptive power of Satan. They will become large in their own eyes, pompous, and self-sufficient.

God-fearing physicians speak modestly of their work; but novices with limited experience in dealing with the bodies and souls of men will often speak boastingly of their knowledge and attainments. These need a better understanding of themselves; then they would become more intelligent in regard to their duties and would realize that in every department where they have to labor, they must possess a willing mind, and earnest spirit, and a hearty, unselfish zeal in trying to do others good. They will not study how best to preserve their dignity, but by thoughtfulness and caretaking will earn a reputation for thoroughness and exactitude, and by sympathetic ministry will gain the hearts of those whom they serve.

In the medical profession there are many skeptics and atheists who exalt the works of God above the God of science. Comparatively few of those who enter worldly medical colleges come out from them pure and unspotted. They have failed to become elevated, ennobled, sanctified. Material things eclipse the heavenly and eternal. With many, religious faith and principles are mingled with worldly customs and practices, and pure and undefiled religion is rare. But it is the privilege of every student to enter college with the same fixed, determined principles that Daniel had when he entered the court of Babylon, and throughout his course, to keep his integrity untarnished. The strength and grace of God has been provided at an infinite sacrifice that men might be victorious over Satan's suggestions and temptations, and come forth unsullied. The life, the words, and the deportment are the most forcible argument, the most solemn appeal to the careless, irreverent, and skeptical. Let the life and character be the strong argument for Christianity; then men will be compelled to take knowledge of you that you have been with Jesus and have learned of Him.

Let not medical students be deceived by the wiles of the devil or by any of his cunning pretexts which so many adopt to beguile and ensnare. Stand firm to principle. At every step inquire, "What saith the Lord?" Say firmly, "I will follow the light. I will respect and honor the Majesty of truth."

Especially should those who are studying medicine in the schools of the world, guard against contamination from the evil influences with which they are constantly surrounded. When their instructors are worldly-wise men and their fellow students infidels who have no serious thought of God, even Christians of experience are in danger of being influenced by these irreligious associations. Nevertheless, some have gone through the medical course, and have remained true to principle. They would not continue their studies on the Sabbath, and they have proved that men may become qualified for the duties of a physician, and not disappoint the expectations of those who have encouraged them to obtain an education.

It is because of these peculiar temptations that our youth must meet in worldly medical schools, that provision should be made for preparatory and advanced medical training in our own schools, under Christian teachers. Our larger Union Conference training schools, in various parts of the field, should be placed in the most favorable position for qualifying our youth to meet the entrance requirements specified by state laws regarding medical students. The very best teaching talent should be secured, that our schools may be brought up to the proper standard. The youth and those more advanced in years who feel it their duty to fit themselves for work requiring the passing of certain legal tests, should be able to secure at our Union Conference training schools all that is essential for entrance into a medical college.

The medical school at Loma Linda is to be of the highest order because those who are in that school have the privilege of maintaining a living connection with the wisest of all physicians from whom there is communicated knowledge of a superior order. And for the special preparation of those of our youth who have clear convictions of their duty to obtain a medical education that will enable them to pass the examinations required by law of all who practice as regularly qualified physicians, we are to supply whatever may be required, so that these youth need not be compelled to go to medical schools conducted by men not of our faith. Thus we shall close a door that the enemy would be pleased to have left open, and our young men and young women, whose spiritual interests the Lord desires us to safeguard, will not feel compelled to connect with unbelievers in order to obtain a thorough training along medical lines.

The teachers in our medical college should encourage the students to gain all the knowledge they can in every department. If they find the students deficient in caretaking, in a comprehension of their responsibilities, they should lay the matter frankly before such ones,

Kind of Students Needed in Our Institutions 169

giving them an opportunity to correct their habits and to reach a higher standard.

Students should go as far as possible in thought, training, and intelligent enterprise, but they should never infringe upon a rule, never disregard one principle that has been interwoven into the upbuilding of the institution. The dropping down is easy enough; the disregard of regulations is natural to the heart inclined to selfish ease and gratification. It is much easier to tear down than to build up. One student with careless ideas may do more to let down the standard, than ten men with all their efforts can do to counteract the demoralizing influence.

Failure or success will be read in the course the students pursue. If they stand ready to question rules and regulations and order, if they indulge self, and by their example encourage a spirit of rebellion, give them no place. The institution might better close its doors than to suffer this spirit to leaven the helpers and break down the barriers that it has cost thought, effort, and prayer to establish.

In training workers to care for the sick, let the student be impressed with the thought that his highest aim should always be to look after the spiritual welfare of his patients. He could learn to repeat the promises of God's Word, and to offer fervent prayers, daily, while preparing for service. Help him to realize that he is always to keep the sweetening, sanctifying influence of the great Medical Missionary before his patients. If those who are suffering can be impressed with the fact that Christ is their sympathizing, compassionate Saviour, they will have rest of mind, which is so essential to recovery of health.

If medical students will study the Word of God diligently they will be far better prepared to understand their other studies, for enlightenment always comes from an earnest study of the Word of God. Nothing will so help to give a retentive memory as study of the Scriptures. Let our medical missionary workers understand that the more they become acquainted with God and with Christ, and the more they become acquainted with Bible history, the better prepared will they be to do their work.

Christ, the great Medical Missionary, came to this world at infinite sacrifice to teach men and women the lessons that would enable them to know God aright. He lived a perfect life, setting an example that all may safely follow. Let our medical students study the lessons that Christ has given. It is essential that they have a clear understanding of these lessons. It would be a fearful mistake for them to neglect the study of God's Word for a study of theories which are misleading, which divert minds from the words of Christ to the fallacies of human production. God would have all who profess to be gospel medical missionaries learn diligently the lessons of the Great Teacher. This they must do if they would find rest and peace. Learning of Christ, their hearts will be filled with the peace that He alone can give.

These things God has been opening to me for many years. In our medical missionary training schools we need men who have a deep knowledge of the Scriptures, men who have learned the lessons taught in the Word of God, and who can teach these lessons to others clearly and simply, just as Christ taught His disciples that which He deemed most essential.

And the needed knowledge will be given to all who come to Christ, receiving and practicing His teachings, making His Word a part of their lives. The Holy Spirit teaches the student of the Scriptures to judge all things by the standard of righteousness and truth and justice. The divine revelation supplies him with the knowledge that he needs. Those who place themselves under the instruction of the great Medical Missionary to be workers together with Him, will have a knowledge that the world, with all its traditionary lore, cannot supply. —*October 1, 1909. (pp. 761-769)*

Failure or success will be read in the course the students pursue. If they stand ready to question rules and regulations and order, if they indulge self, and be their example encourage a spirit of rebellion, give them no place. The institution might better close its doors than to suffer this spirit to leaven the helpers and break down the barriers that it has cost thought, effort, and prayer to establish. —*October 1, 1909. (p. 767, par. 1)*

Work for Students

I do not see the wisdom of the school depending on the second tithe to meet so much of its expenses. I fear that, if the brethren rely so much upon this, difficulties will rise. You should labor patiently to develop those industries by which students can partly work their way through school. —*June 30, 1904. (p. 70, par. 2)*

Amusements

There are some who feel that if there is prosperity here it will be necessary to get up some amusement. Let us not cherish such thoughts as this. Rather let the people see that you have a mind for usefulness and duty, and that to the saving of the soul. The amusements that consume time just to gratify self do not pay.

Some will think that by having amusements here we will gain more influence. But what we want is to go steadily forward, with our hands firmly holding the divine promises, believing that Christ will lead and guide and bless, and place a heavenly stamp upon our work. Do not feel that there is not enough in all that we have to do in this place for Christ and heaven, and that you must reach out for some amusement outside of your God-given work. Do not do it, for this will not harmonize with Christ's example. Stand solidly for God. Tell the students, here we have Riverside and other places. If you want to do a good work, take our publications, and carry them to these places. Hold meetings, and let the people see that you have a living connection with heaven. If you are a child of God, your prayers, and your work to strengthen and build up will have an influence, and God will bestow His blessing upon you.

I have felt so thankful regarding the improvements that I see here. God has prospered you, and He will continue to prosper. And we must give ourselves to the education of those who do not appreciate these things. We must keep it before them in the living light. Regarding the securing of means for the development of the work, you must exercise that living faith that takes hold from above. Some here know what a battle we have had in order to secure harmonious action, and we thank the Lord that when the enemy comes in like a flood, then the Spirit of the Lord lifts up for us a standard against the enemy.

We need not feel that we must provide amusements to gratify the desires of some who come in here hoping to attract attention to themselves. It would be better that such ones should go elsewhere. We are here to give the last message of warning to a perishing world, and every jot of our influence is to be consecrated to God. It is not His will that frivolous, unsanctified amusements shall be instituted here. We have a heaven to win, a hell to shun; let us work solidly in behalf of ourselves and others for eternal life in the kingdom of God. —*No date. (p. 934, pars. 2-4)*

It is our privilege to be co-workers with God. Let no one feel that he must secure the highest place in order that he may do the greatest amount of acceptable service. Do not fear that you will lose patronage unless you enter into some of the world's fashions and amusements. Your eyes must be fixed on the Pattern, Christ Jesus. Imitate Him, in works, in conversation, in your deportment before the people. If you will follow in the footsteps of Jesus, you will have an everlasting reward. The way is open for you to work in unison with Christ, and He Who gave His precious life for you will help and strengthen you, and guide you step by step, if you desire to be led. —*No date. (p. 936, par. 1)*

Competing with Worldly Medical Schools

The education that meets the world's standard is to be less and less valued by those who are seeking for efficiency in carrying the medical missionary work in connection with the work of the third angel's message. They are to be educated from the standpoint of conscience, and as they conscientiously and faithfully follow right methods in their treatment of the sick, these methods will come to be recognized as preferable to the methods of nursing to which many have become accustomed, which demand the use of poisonous drugs.

We should not at this time seek to compete with worldly medical schools. Should we do this, our chances of success would be small. We are not now prepared to carry out successfully the work of establishing large medical institutions of learning. Moreover, should we follow the world's methods of medical practice, exacting the large fees that worldly physicians demand for their services, we would work away from Christ's plan for our ministry to the sick. —*November 3, 1907. (p. 559, pars. 3, 4)*

Conforming to Legal Requirements

"If there are legal requirements making it necessary that medical students shall take a certain preparatory course of study, let our colleges teach the required additional studies in a manner consistent with Christian education.... They should arrange to carry their students to the point of literary and scientific training that is necessary. Many of these requirements have been made because so much of the preparatory work done in ordinary schools is superficial." —*October 1909. (p. 775, par. 2)*

Some questions have been asked me regarding our relation to the laws governing medical practitioners. We need to move understandingly, for the enemy would be pleased to hedge up our work so that our physicians would have only a limited influence. Some men do not act in the fear of God, and they may seek to bring us into trouble by placing on our necks yokes that we could not consent to bear. We cannot submit to regulations if the sacrifice of principle is involved, for this would imperil the soul's salvation.

But whenever we can comply with the law of the land without putting ourselves in a false position, we should do so. Wise laws have been framed in order to safeguard the people against the imposition of unqualified physicians. These laws we should respect, for we are ourselves by them protected from presumptuous pretenders. Should we manifest opposition to these requirements, it would tend to restrict the influence of our medical missionaries.

We must carefully consider what is involved in these matters. If there are conditions to which we could not subscribe, we should endeavor to have these matters adjusted so that there would not be strong opposition against our physicians. The Saviour bids us be wise as serpents, and harmless as doves. —*November 5, 1909. (p. 797, pars. 1-3)*

Unequally Yoked Together

"Be not unequally yoked together with unbelievers: for what fellowship hath righteousness with unrighteousness? and what communion hath light with darkness? and what concord hath Christ with Belial? or what part hath he that believeth with an infidel? and what agreement hath the temple of God with idols? for ye are the temple of the living God; as God hath said, I will dwell in them, and walk in them; and I will be their God, and they shall be My people. Wherefore come out from among them, and be ye separate, saith the Lord, and touch not the unclean thing; and I will receive you, and will be a Father unto you, and ye shall be My sons and daughters, saith the Lord Almighty." —*May 7, 1909. (p. 722, par. 3)*

There is constant danger among our people that those who engage in labor in our schools and sanitariums will entertain the idea that they must get in line with the world, study the things which the world studies, and become familiar with the things that the world becomes familiar with. This is one of the greatest mistakes that could be made. We shall make grave mistakes unless we give special attention to the searching of the Word. —*May 7, 1909. (p. 723, par. 1)*

E. G. White: We want none of that kind of "higher education" that will put us in a position where the credit must be given, not to the Lord God of Israel, but to the god of Ekron. The Lord designs that we shall stand as a distinct people, so connected with Him that He can work with us. Let our physicians realize that they are to depend wholly upon the true God.

E. G. White: I felt a heavy burden this morning when I read over a letter that I found in my room, in which a plan was outlined for having medical students take some work at Loma Linda, but to get the finishing touches of their education from some worldly institution. I must state that the light that I have received is that we are to stand as a commandment-keeping people, and this will separate us from the world. The Sabbath is a great distinguishing line. As God's peculiar people we should not feel that we must acknowledge our dependence upon the transgressors of God's law to give us influence in the world. It is God that gives us influence. He will give us advantages that are far above all the advantages we can receive from worldlings.

Elder _____: I know that these thoughts are what you have presented to us before. We do not want to cause you to carry a heavy burden. We simply wanted to be sure that we were moving in right lines. If the Lord gives you light, well and good; we will wait.

E. G. White: If we follow on to know the Lord, we shall know that His going forth is prepared as the morning. There are some who may not be able to see that here is a test as to whether we shall put our dependence on man, or depend upon God. Shall we by our course seem to acknowledge that there is a stronger power with the unbelievers than there is with God's own people? When we take hold upon God, and trust in Him, He will work in our behalf. But we are to stand distinct and separate from the world.

E. G. White: I feel a decided interest in the work at Loma Linda, and I desire that it shall exert a powerful influence for the truth. Your success depends upon the blessing of God, not upon the views of men who are opposed to the law of God. When they see that God blesses us, then people will be led to give consideration to the truths we teach.

E. G. White: We need not to tie to men in order to secure influence. We need not think that we must have their experience and their knowledge. Our God is a God of knowledge and understanding, and if we will take our position decidedly on His side, He will give us wisdom. I would that all our people might see the inconsistency of our being God's commandment-keeping people, a peculiar people zealous of good works, and yet feeling that we must copy after the world in order to make our work successful. Our God is stronger than any human influence. If we will accept Him as our Educator, if we will make Him our strength and righteousness, He will work in our behalf.

E. G. White: These principles may result in a condition of things that is not just as we should like them to be. We may like to have certain conditions, that in the end would result in bondage which we do not anticipate.

E. G. White: Jesus Christ is our Saviour today, and He is willing to work in our behalf if we will not put our dependence upon some other power. If we are sustained by the living God, the superiority of His power will be manifested in His people. This is the testimony that I have borne all the way along.

Elder _____: We love to hear the truth over and over again, that we may be sure it is the truth.

E. G. White: You have the Word which tells you that God's commandment-keeping people are to have His special favor, and that they are to be sanctified through obedience to the truth. Shall we unite ourselves with those that are full of error, who have no respect for God's commandments, and shall our students go forth to obtain the finishing touches of their education from them?

Elder _____: What is to be the final outcome? Will all our medical missionaries be simply nurses? Shall we have no more physicians, or shall we have a school in which we can ourselves give the finishing touches?

E. G. White: Whatever plan we follow, take your position that you will not unite with those that do not respect God's commandments.

Unequally Yoked Together

Elder _____: Does that mean that we are not to have any more physicians, but that our people will work simply as nurses, or does it mean that we shall have a school of our own to educate physicians?

E. G. White: We shall have a school of our own. But we are not to be dependent upon the world; we must place our dependence upon a power that is higher than all human power. If we honor God, He will honor us.

Elder _____: The governments of earth provide that if we conduct a medical school we must take a charter from the government. That in itself has nothing to do with how the school is conducted. It is required, however, that certain studies shall be taught. There are ten required subjects. Physiology is one. It is required that those who labor as physicians shall be proficient in these studies. In starting our sanitariums for the care of the sick, we must secure a charter from the government; our printing office must do the same. Would the securing of a charter for a medical school, where our students might obtain an education, militate against our dependence upon God?

E. G. White: No, I do not see that it would. Only see that you do not exalt men above God. If you can gain force and influence that will make your work more effective without tying yourselves to worldly men, that would be right.

Elder _____: That is the vital point, where we have been hanging for three years. The only thing that we have asked for in this matter is to take advantage of the government provision that would give standing room for our students when they are qualified.

E. G. White: I do not see anything wrong in that as long as you do not in any way lift men above the Lord God of Israel, or throw discredit upon His power.

Elder _____: In planning our course of study, we have tried to follow the light in the Testimonies, and in doing so it has led us away from the requirements of the world. The world will not recognize us as standing with them. We will have to stand distinct, by ourselves.

E. G. White: We shall always have to stand distinct. God desires us to be separate.

Elder _____: Now the proposition in this letter was to deviate from that so that standing as we do would enable us to stand with them and to have their advantages. From the instruction that has come it has seemed to me from the very first, that we were to stand by ourselves in a distinct light, following the light that God has given with reference to physical healing and that when we do that, God will open the way before us, and give us prestige with the people. But if we deviate and connect with those other schools, we would find ourselves being thrown more and more into the very things that they are doing, and our students would be molded after their similitude instead of after the similitude of the truth.

E. G. White: That is what I am trying to guard against all the time. As we read the Bible we see that God is dishonored when His people go to any worldly power, or put their trust in a worldly power. That is where God's people spoiled their history. You must arrange the matter the best you can, but that which is presented to me is that you are not to acknowledge any power as above that of our God. Our influence is to be acknowledged of God, because we keep His commandments, and His commandments are not grievous.

Elder _____: Jesus said at one time, "The scribes and the Pharisees sit in Moses' seat: all therefore whatsoever they bid you observe, that observe and do; but do not ye after their works." Now the law says that a man shall not practice medicine unless he has a diploma from a college, and unless he has passed the examination of the state board, and has a certificate. The law would not recognize the diplomas of our physicians unless they have studied some things that we do not think are really essential. For instance, in their preparation they have to study a number of things that we think they might get along without, but we can teach them. We do not have to teach these subjects in their way; we can teach them in our way. When it comes to the study of drugs, they teach how to give them. We teach the dangers of using them, and how to get along without them. In some other schools they teach geology on the evolution basis. We can teach geology and show that evolution is false.

E. G. White: Well, you must plan these details yourselves. I have told you what I have received, but these details you will have to work out for yourselves.

Elder _____: It seems clear to me that any standing we can lawfully have without compromising, is not out of harmony with God's plan.

E. G. White: No it is not. All I can say is that I have had very distinct light, however, that there is danger of our limiting the power of the Holy One of Israel. He is the God of the universe. Our influence is dependent upon our carrying out the Word of the living God. We weaken our powers by not placing our dependence upon God, and taking hold of His strength. This is our privilege. —*September 20, 1909. (pp. 754-759)*

Opportunities are before you; if studious and upright, you may obtain an education of the highest value. Make the most of your privileges. Be not satisfied with ordinary attainment; seek to qualify yourselves to fill positions of trust in connection with the Lord's work in the earth. United with the God of wisdom and power, you may become intellectually strong, and increasingly capable as soul winners. You may become men and women of responsibility and influence, if, by the power of your will, coupled with divine strength, you earnestly engage in the work of securing a proper training. —*October 1, 1909. (p. 760, par. 3)*

Unequally Yoked Together

I am instructed to say that in our educational work, there is to be no compromise in order to meet the world's standards. God's commandment-keeping people are not to unite with the world, to carry various lines of work according to worldly plans and worldly wisdom.

Our people are now being tested as to whether they will obtain their wisdom from the greatest Teacher the world ever knew or seek to the god of Ekron. Let us determine that we shall not be tied by so much as a thread to the educational policies of those who do not discern the voice of God, and who will not hearken to His commandments.

We are to take heed to the warnings: "Enter ye in at the strait gate: for wide is the gate, and broad is the way, that leadeth to destruction, and many there be which go in thereat: because strait is the gate, and narrow is the way, which leadeth unto life, and few there be that find it." Those who walk in the narrow way are following in the footprints of Jesus. The light from heaven illuminates their path.

Shall we represent before the world that our physicians must follow the pattern of the world, before they can be qualified to act as successful physicians? This is the question that is now testing the faith of some of our brethren. Let not any of our brethren displease the Lord by advocating in their assemblies the idea that we need to obtain from unbelievers a higher education than that specified by the Lord. —*October 11, 1909. (p. 788, pars. 1-4)*

The representation of the great Teacher is to be considered an all-sufficient revelation. Those in our ranks who qualify as physicians are to receive only such education as is in harmony with these divine truths. Some have advised that students should, after taking some work at Loma Linda, complete their medical education in worldly colleges. But this is not in harmony with the Lord's plan. God is our wisdom, our sanctification, and our righteousness. Facilities should be provided at Loma Linda, that the necessary instruction in medical lines may be given by instructors who fear the Lord, and who are in harmony with His plans for the treatment of the sick.

I have not a word to say in favor of the world's ideas of higher education in any school that we shall organize for the training of physicians. There is danger in their attaching themselves to worldly institutions, and working under the ministrations of worldly physicians. Satan is giving his orders to those whom he has led to depart from the faith. I would now advise that none of our young people attach themselves to worldly institutions, in the hope of gaining better success, or stronger influence as physicians.

"When Israel was a child, then I loved him, and called My son out of Egypt. As they called them, so they went from them: they sacrificed unto Baalim, and burnt incense to graven images. I taught Ephraim also to go, taking them by their arms; but they knew not that I healed them. I drew them with cords of a man, with bands of love: and I was to them as they that take off the yoke on their jaws, and I laid meat unto them." —*October 11, 1909. (p. 789, pars. 1-3)*

"Verily My Sabbaths ye shall keep: for it is a sign between Me and you throughout your generations." Connect with those who honor God by keeping His commandments. If the recommendation goes forth from our people that our workers are to seek for success by acknowledging as essential the education which the world gives, we are virtually saying that the influence the world gives is superior to that which God gives. God will be dishonored by such a course. God has full knowledge of the faith and trust and confidence that His professed people have in His providence. —*November 5, 1909. (p. 798, par. 1)*

The work of Elder _____ and others who have labored in Oakland and the nearby places might have been a much greater blessing, had they not been obliged to meet wrong influences in opposition to the counsels that God has given to build up and prepare a people for the final conflict that is before us. —*December 6, 1909. (p. 818, par. 5)*

It is not in harmony with the plan of God that men who are working counter to the spirit of the messages that the Lord gives to bless and strengthen His people, should be given places of large influence in our churches. Such men are not a help, but a hindrance. Their work is to unsettle minds, and they sow the seed which will spring up and bear its fruit to make of none effect the counsels that the Lord has so graciously given to His people. —*December 6, 1909. (p. 819, par. 1)*

Higher Education

The question is asked, "What is the higher education?" There is no education higher than that contained in the principles laid down in the words that I have read to you from the sixth chapter of second Corinthians. Let our students study diligently to comprehend this. Through His own chosen messengers God has given us light and instruction as to what constitutes the higher education. There is no higher education to be gained than that which was given to the early disciples, and which is given to us through the Lord. May the Holy Spirit of God impress your minds with the truth that there is nothing in all the world in the line of education that is so exalted as the instruction contained in the chapters to which I have referred. Let us advance just as far as the work will take us. Let us work intelligently for this higher education. Let our righteousness be the sign of our understanding of the will of God committed to us through His messengers.

It is the privilege of every believer to take the life of Christ and the teachings of Christ as His daily study. Christian education means the acceptance, in sentiment and principle, of the teachings of the Saviour. It includes a daily conscientious walking in the footsteps of Christ, Who consented to lay off His royal robe and crown

Higher Education 179

and to come to our world in the form of humanity, that He might give to the human race a power that they could gain by no other means. What was that power? It was the power resulting from the human nature uniting with the divine, the power to take the teachings of Christ and follow them to the letter. In His resistance of evil, and His labor for others, Christ was giving to men an example of the highest education that it is possible for anyone to reach. —*May 7, 1909. (p. 723, pars. 2, 3)*

Strong temptations will come to many who place their children in our schools because they desire the youth to secure what the world regards as the most essential education. Who knows what the most essential education is unless it is the education to be obtained from the Book which is the foundation of all true knowledge. Those who regard as essential the knowledge to be gained along the line of worldly education are making a great mistake, one which will cause them to be swayed by individual opinions that are human and erring. To these who feel that their children must have what the world calls the essential education, I would say, Bring your children to the simplicity of the Word of God, and they will be safe. We are going to be greatly scattered before long, and what we do must be done quickly.

The light has been given me that tremendous pressure will be brought upon every Seventh-day Adventist with whom the world can get into close connection. We need to understand these things. Those who seek the education that the world esteems so highly are gradually led farther and farther from the principles of truth until they become educated worldlings. At what a price have they gained their education! They have parted with the Holy Spirit of God. They have chosen to accept what the world calls knowledge in the place of the truths which God has committed to men through His ministers and prophets and apostles. And there are some who, having secured this worldly education, think that they can introduce it into our schools, but let me tell you that you must not take what the world calls the higher education and bring it into our schools and sanitariums and churches. I speak to you definitely; this must not be done. —*May 7, 1909. (p. 724, pars. 2, 3)*

Upon the mind of every student should be impressed the thought that education is a failure unless the understanding has learned to grasp the truths of divine revelation, and unless the heart accepts the teachings of the gospel of Christ. The student who, in the place of the broad principles of the Word of God, will accept common ideas, and will allow the time and attention to be absorbed in commonplace, trivial matters, will find his mind becoming dwarfed and enfeebled; he will lose the power of growth. The mind must be trained to comprehend the important truths that concern eternal life. —*(p. 725, par. 1)*

I am instructed that we are to carry the minds of our students higher than it is now thought by many to be possible. Hearts and minds are to be trained to preserve their purity by receiving daily supplies from the fountain of eternal truth. The divine mind and hand has preserved through the ages the record of creation in its purity. It is the Word of God alone that gives to us an authentic account of the creation of our world. This Word is to be the chief study in our schools. Here we may hold converse with patriarchs and prophets; here we may learn what our redemption has cost One Who was equal with the Father from the beginning, and Who sacrificed His life that a people might stand before Him redeemed from every common, earthly thing, and renewed in the image of God. —*May 7, 1909. (p. 725, par. 2)*

If we are to learn of Christ, we must pray as the apostles prayed when the Holy Spirit was poured upon them. We need a baptism of the Spirit of God. We are not safe for one hour while we are failing to render obedience to the Word of God. —*(p. 726, par. 1)*

The Lord wants us to come into harmony with His Spirit. If we will do this, His Spirit can rule our minds. If we have a true understanding of what constitutes the essential education, and endeavor to teach its principles, Christ will stand by to help us. He promised His followers that when they should stand before councils and judges, they were to take no thought what they should speak. I will instruct you, He said; I will guide you. Knowing what it is to be taught of God, when words of heavenly wisdom are brought to our mind, we will distinguish them from our own thoughts. We will understand them as the words of God, and we will see in them life and power that is for us.

"I will give you tongue and utterance." Of all the precious assurances God has given me regarding my work, none has been more precious to me than this, that He would give me tongue and utterance. wherever I should go. In places where there was the greatest opposition, every tongue was silenced. I have spoken the plain message to our own people and to the multitude, and my words have been accepted as coming from the Lord. —*May 7, 1909. (p. 727, pars. 2, 3)*

Do not regard as most essential the theoretical part of our education. Medical students will have to follow the prescribed studies. They will listen to many theories that are contrary to truth. The Lord would have our medical students connect closely with those who believe and teach the truth. And as helpers with them they can learn how to treat the sick, and how to become faithful ministers to the sick. There are many ways by which the Lord would have us connect with these who honor and teach His Word, and He will give us through this connection a most valuable education. —*May 7, 1909. (p. 728, par. 3)*

"God would have all who profess to be gospel medical missionaries, learn the lessons of the great Teacher. The one book that is essential for all to study is the Bible. Study it with reverence and godly fear, and it is the greatest of all educators. Study the Bible more and the theories of the medical fraternities less, and you will have greater spritual health. Your mind will be clearer and more vigorous. Much that is embraced in the medical course is positively unnecessary. Those who take a medical training spend a great deal of time in learning that which is merely rubbish. Many of the theories that they learn may be compared in value to the traditions and maxims taught by the scribes and Pharisees. Many of the intricacies with which they have to become familiar are an injury to their minds.

"These things God has been opening before me for many years. In our medical schools and institutions, we need men who have a deeper knowledge of the Scriptures. Because the Word of God has been neglected, strange things have been done in our medical missionary work of late. The Lord cannot accept the present showing." —*October 17, 1903. (p. 732, par. 2 beginning at quotation marks)*

Endeavor to place yourself where you will not be confused by the representations and forbiddings of human agencies who would misinterpret the true meaning of the higher education. Lift up the Man of Calvary. By the work of teaching and by earnest prayer endeavor to place the students where they will receive the inspiration of heaven. Jesus Christ is to be presented before them as the Source of all light and knowledge. Let none dishonor Him by choosing to accept the world's interpretation of what the higher education means. Let us leave that to those who do not acknowledge the truths of the Word of God as the source of all true knowledge.

Give to the teachers all the advantages possible, to secure a clear understanding of what constitutes the essential education. —*June 9, 1909. (p. 737, pars. 3, 4)*

Teach the students to look for wisdom to the One Who gave His life for the salvation of the world. Now is your time to work. That same Jesus Who walked with His disciples on earth, and Who taught them from day to day, will teach His servants in this age. —*June 9, 1909. (p. 738, par. 1)*

The whole of the book of Acts should receive careful study. It is full of precious instruction; it records experiments in evangelistic work, the teachings of which we need in our work today. This wonderful history deals with the highest education which the students in our schools are to receive. —*June 9, 1909. (p. 739, par. 3)*

I am intensely in earnest that our people shall realize that the only true education lies in walking humbly with God. The teachings of the Word of God are opposed to the ideas of those who think that our students must receive the mold of an education that is according to human ideas. Some are departing from the faith, as the result of receiving from the world what they regard as a "higher education." The Word of God just as it reads contains the very essence of truth. The highest education is the keeping of the law of God. —*October 11, 1909. (p. 791, par. 2)*

Institutions in which medical missionary work can be done are to be regarded as especially essential to the advancement of the Lord's work. The sick and suffering are to be relieved, and then, as opportunity offers, they are to be given instruction in regard to the truth for this time. Thus we can bring present truth before a class of people who could be reached in no other way. —*April 16, 1904. (p. 60, par. 5)*

Word of God Basis of All Education

The one book that is essential for all to study is the Bible. Studied with reverence and godly fear, it is the greatest of all educators. In it there is no sophistry. Its pages are filled with truth. Would you gain a knowledge of God and Christ, Whom He sent into the world to live and die for sinners? An earnest diligent study of the Bible is necessary in order to gain this knowledge.

Many of the books piled up in the great libraries of earth confuse the mind more than they aid the understanding. Yet men spend large sums of money in the purchase of such books, and years in their study, when they have within their reach a book containing the words of Him Who is the Alpha and Omega of wisdom. The time spent in a study of these books might better be spent in gaining a knowledge of Him Whom to know aright is life eternal. Those only who gain this knowledge will at last hear the words, "Ye are complete in Him." —*October 17, 1903. (p. 99, pars. 2, 3)*

Make the Bible the man of your counsel. Your acquaintance with it will grow rapidly if you keep your mind free from the rubbish of the world. The more the Bible is studied, the deeper will be your knowledge of God. The truths of His Word will be written in your soul, making an ineffaceable impression.

Not only will the student himself be benefited by a study of the Word of God; his study is life and salvation to all with whom he associates. He will feel a sacred responsibility to impart the knowledge that he receives. His life will reveal the help and strength that he receives from communion with the Word. The sanctification of the Spirit will be seen in thought, word and deed. All that he says and does will proclaim that God is light and in Him is no darkness at all. Of such ones the Lord Jesus can indeed say, "Ye are laborers together with God." —*October 17, 1903. (p. 102, pars. 1, 2)*

"It will take some time to get a right understanding of the matter, but just as soon as we begin to work in the lines of true reform the Holy Spirit will lead us and guide us if we are willing to be guided.... All must place themselves under the influence of the Holy Spirit. When they place themselves under the influence of the Spirit, they will accommodate themselves to Bible lines. When the Word of God takes possession of the minds of teachers, then they are fitted to deal with the education of others. The Word of God is to stand as the foundation of all education. It is to be made the basis of all the schools that we establish. —*1901. (p. 731, par. 4)*

Christ, the great Medical Missionary, came to this world at infinite sacrifice to teach men and women the lessons that would enable them to know God aright. He lived a perfect life, setting an example that all may safely follow. Let our medical students study the lessons that Christ has given. It is essential that they have a clear understanding of these lessons. It would be a fearful mistake for them to neglect the study of God's Word for a study of theories which are misleading, which divert minds from the words of Christ to the fallacies of human production. God would have all who profess to be gospel medical missionaries learn diligently the lessons of the Great Teacher. This they must do if they would find rest and peace. Learning of Christ their hearts will be filled with the peace that He alone can give.

"Their work should be more decidedly combined with the study of God's Word. Ideas are inculcated that are not at all necessary, and the necessary things do not receive sufficient attention. While students are being educated in this way, they are being made less able to do acceptable work for the Master. The taxation that they undergo to obtain an extended knowledge in medical lines, unfits them for work, as they should, in ministerial lines.... Thus some are disqualified for the work that they might have done had they begun missionary work where it is needed, and let the medical line come in as an essential part connected with the work of the gospel ministry as a whole, as the hand is connected with the body." —*October 1909. (p. 775, par. 1)*

"God would have all who profess to be gospel medical missionaries learn the lessons of the Great Teacher. The one book that is essential for all to study is the Bible. Study it with reverence, and godly fear. It is the greatest of all educators. In our medical schools and institutions we need men who have a deeper knowledge of the Scriptures. Because the Word of God has been neglected, strange things have been done in our medical missionary work of late. The Lord cannot accept the present showing." —*October 17, 1903. (p. 777, par. 4)*

Kind of Teachers

These things God has been opening before me for years. In our medical schools and institutions we need men who have a deeper knowledge of the Scriptures, men who have learned the lessons taught in the Word of God, and who can teach these lessons to others, clearly and simply, just as Christ taught His disciples the knowledge that He deemed most essential.

If, during the remainder of this year, our medical missionary workers would follow the great Physician's prescription for obtaining rest, a healing current of peace would flow through their souls. Here is the prescription:

"Come unto Me, all ye that labor and are heavy laden, and I will give you rest. Take My yoke upon you, and learn of Me; for I am meek and lowly in heart: and ye shall find rest unto your souls. For My yoke is easy, and My burden is light."

When our medical missionary workers follow this prescription, gaining from the Saviour power to reveal His characteristics, their scientific work will have a greater soundness. Because the Word of God has been neglected, strange things have been done in the medical missionary work of late. The Lord cannot accept the present showing. —*October 17, 1903. (p. 100, pars. 2-5)*

The teachers in our medical college should encourage the students to gain all the knowledge they can in every department. If they find the students deficient in caretaking, in a comprehension of their responsibilities, they should lay the matter frankly before such ones, giving them an opportunity to correct their habits and to reach a higher standard.

The teachers should not become discouraged because some are slow to learn. Neither should they discourage the students when mistakes are made. As errors and defects are kindly pointed out, the students in turn should feel grateful for any instruction given. A haughty spirit on the part of the students should be discouraged. All should be willing to learn, and the teachers should be willing to instruct, training the students to be self-reliant, competent, careful, painstaking. As the students study under wise instructors, and unite with them in sharing responsibilities, they may, by the aid of the teachers, climb to the topmost round of the ladder. —*October 1, 1909. (p. 766, pars. 1, 2)*

In training workers to care for the sick, let the student be impressed with the thought that his highest aim should always be to look after the spiritual welfare of his patients. He could learn to repeat the promises of God's Word, and to offer fervent prayers, daily, while preparing for service. Help him to realize that he is always to keep the sweetening, sanctifying influence of the great Medical Missionary before his patients. If those who are suffering can be impressed with the fact that Christ is their sympathizing, compassionate Saviour, they will have rest of mind, which is so essential to recovery of health. —*October 1, 1909. (p. 767, par. 2)*

Faithful teachers should be placed in charge of the Bible classes, teachers who will strive to make the students understand their lessons, not by explaining everything to them, but by requiring them to explain clearly every passage they read. Let these teachers remember that little good is accomplished by skimming over the surface of the Word. Thoughtful investigation and earnest, taxing study are necessary to an understanding of this Word. —*October 1, 1909. (p. 768, par. 1)*

A time will come when medical missionaries of other denominations will become jealous and envious of the influence exerted by Seventh-day Adventists who are working in these lines. They will feel that influence is being secured by our workers which they ought to have. We should have in various places, men of extraordinary ability, who have obtained their diplomas in medical schools of the best reputation, who can stand before the world as fully qualified and legally recognized physicians. Let God-fearing men be wisely chosen to go through the training essential in order to obtain such qualifications. They should be prudent men who will remain true to the principles of the message.

These should obtain the qualifications, and the authority to conduct an educational work for our young men and our young women who desire to be trained for medical missionary work.

Now while the world is favorable toward the teaching of the health reform principles, moves should be made to secure for our own physicians the privilege of imparting medical instruction to our young people who would otherwise be led to attend the worldly medical colleges. The time will come when it will be more difficult than it is now, to arrange for the training of our young people in medical missionary lines. —*April 27, 1910. (p. 903 all)*

I have words of instruction for you and your co-workers who are ministers and physicians and counselors at Loma Linda. During my visit to Southern California, light was given me that many of the leaders in our sanitariums were failing of meeting the requirements of God; and more than this, they did not realize their lack. I was instructed that those who stand in positions of responsibility in these important institutions are engaged in a most sacred work, that they have little time in which to do the work committed to their trust, and that it was of the utmost importance that faithfulness and consecration mark their efforts in every line.

In a remarkable way God has brought into our possession some of the institutions through whose agency we are to accomplish the work of reformation to which we as a people are called. At this time every talent of every worker should be regarded as a sacred trust to be used in extending the work of reform. —*May 7, 1911. (p. 939, pars. 1, 2)*

The Son of God is made unto us wisdom, and righteousness, and sanctification and redemption. Teachers should bear in mind that He is the great standard for all teachers. Beholding Christ, and studying His teachings, you will learn to appreciate their originality, their authority, their spirituality, their tenderness, their benevolence, and their practicability. All who dig for the treasure of truth will be imbued with the Spirit of Christ. By beholding Him, they will be changed into the same image.

Those who make the Word of God their counselor, will realize the weakness of the human heart, but they will find courage in the assurance that the power of the grace of God is sufficient to subdue every unsanctified, unholy impulse. When the enemy comes in like a flood, the Spirit of the Lord will lift up a standard against him. And when the Spirit of the Lord lifts up for His blood-bought heritage a standard against the enemy, the principles of the Word of truth will bear sway in the life. Having surrendered themselves to the will of God, they reveal a faith that works by love, and purifies the soul. —*August 8, 1907. (p. 398, pars. 1, 2)*

Those who would be safe teachers of the truth, must first be learners in the school of Christ. You must recognize in Christ a personal Saviour if you would lead those whom you instruct to Him. Christ invites, "Come unto Me, all ye that labor and are heavy laden, and I will give you rest. Take My yoke upon you, and learn of Me; for I am meek and lowly in heart: and ye shall find rest unto your souls. For My yoke is easy, and My burden is light." Learning the lessons of Christ you will find rest.

Christ is the great fountainhead of all wisdom, the One Who never makes a mistake. All the treasures of heaven were committed to Him that He might impart them to the persevering seeker after truth. —*August 6, 1907. (p. 397, pars. 3, 4)*

One night this week, I think it was Sunday, I did not sleep any through the entire night; and again on Wednesday I had a wakeful night. I slept for a short time before three o'clock. While I lay awake, I spent the time in prayer that God would give to His people sanctified and converted minds, that individually they might comprehend their duty, and learn to reveal the power of the truth in sound speech that cannot be condemned.

The talent of speech is a precious talent. The riches of the grace of Christ, which He is ever ready to bestow upon us, we are to impart in true, hopeful words. "Rejoice in the Lord alway: and again I say, Rejoice." If we would guard our words, so that nothing but kindness shall escape our lips, we will give evidence that we are preparing to become members of the heavenly family. In words and works we shall show forth the praises of Him Who has called us out of darkness into His marvelous light. O, what a reformative influence would go forth if we as a people would value at its true worth the talent of speech and its influence upon the human souls. —*August 29, 1907. (p. 431, pars. 2, 3)*

Care Workers Should Have for Own Health

We do not look upon you, my brother, as a man who has put only half of his heart into this grand work. We take the opposite view of this, knowing that you put heart, mind, soul, and strength into your work. The only fear that I have had in regard to you is that you will try to carry too heavy a burden.

Those who put their whole soul into the medical missionary work, who labor untiringly, in peril, in privation, in watchings oft, in weariness and painfulness, are in danger of forgetting that they must be faithful guardians of their own mental and physical powers. They are not to allow themselves to be overtaxed. But they are filled with zeal and earnestness, and they sometimes move unadvisedly, putting themselves under too heavy a strain. Unless such workers make a change, the result will be that sickness will come upon them, and they will break down. —*October 12, 1904. (p. 77, pars. 3, 4)*

While God's workers are to be filled with a noble enthusiasm, and with a determination to follow the example of the divine worker, the great Medical Missionary, they are not to crowd too many things into the day's work. If they do, they will soon have to leave the work entirely, broken down because they have tried to carry too heavy a load. My brother, it is right for you to make the best use of the advantages given you of God in earnest efforts for the relief of suffering and for the saving of souls, but do not sacrifice your health.

We have a calling as much higher than common, selfish interests as the heavens are higher than the earth, but this thought should not lead the willing, hardworking servants of God to carry all the burdens they can possibly bear, without periods of rest.

How grand it would be if among all who were engaged in carrying out God's wonderful plan for the salvation of souls, there were no idlers. How much more would be accomplished if everyone would say, "God holds me accountable to be wide awake, and to let my efforts speak in favor of the truth I profess to believe. I am to be a practical worker, not a daydreamer." It is because there are so many daydreamers that true workers have to carry double burdens. —*October 12, 1904. (p. 78, pars. 1-3)*

Out-of-door Work for Patients

The buildings secured for this work should be out of the cities in rural districts, so that the sick may have the benefit of outdoor life. By the beauty of flower and field, their minds will be diverted from themselves, from their aches and pains and they will be led to look from nature to the God of nature, Who has provided so abundantly the beauties of the natural world. The convalescent can lie in the shade of the trees, and those who are stronger can, if they wish, work among the flowers, doing just a little at first, and increasing their efforts as they grow stronger. Working in the garden, gathering flowers and fruit, listening to the birds praising God, the patients will be wonderfully blessed. Angels of God will draw near to them. They will forget their sorrows. Melancholy and depression will leave them. The fresh air and sunshine, and the exercise taken, will bring them life and vitality. The wearied brain and nerves will find relief. Good treatment and wholesome diet will build them up and strengthen them. They will feel no need for health-destroying drugs or for intoxicating drink. —*April 15, 1904. (p. 61, par. 1)*

Everything at Loma Linda is fresh and wholesome and attractive. The patients could live out-of-doors a large part of the time. The land will serve as a school for the education of patients. By outdoor exercise and working in the soil, men and women will regain their health. Rational methods for the cure of disease will be used in a variety of ways. Drugs will be discarded. —*July 1905. (p. 182, par. 1)*

"In the night season I was given a view of a sanitarium in the country. The institution was not large, but it was complete. It was surrounded by beautiful trees and shrubbery, beyond which were orchards and groves. Connected with the place were gardens, in which the lady patients, when they chose, could cultivate flowers of every description, each patient selecting a special plot for which to care. Outdoor exercise in these gardens was prescribed as a part of the regular treatment.

"Scene after scene passed before me. In one scene a number of suffering patients had just come to one of our country sanitariums. In another scene I saw the same company, but, O, how transformed their appearance! Disease had gone, the skin was clear, the countenance joyful; body and mind seemed to be animated with new life. God will work wonders for us if we will in faith cooperate with Him. Let us, then, pursue a sensible course, that our efforts may be blessed of heaven, and crowned with success." —*1909. (p. 834, pars. 1, 2)*

There was among us One Who presented this matter very clearly, and with the utmost simplicity. He told us it would be a mistake to establish a sanitarium within the city limits. A sanitarium should have the advantage of plenty of land, so that the invalids can work in the open air. For nervous, gloomy, feeble patients, out-of-door work is invaluable. Let them have flowerbeds to care for. In the use of rake and hoe and spade they will find relief for many of their maladies. Idleness is the cause of many diseases.

Life in the open air is good for body and mind. It is God's medicine for the restoration of health. Pure air, good water, sunshine, beautiful surroundings—these are God's means for restoring the sick to health in natural ways. It is worth more than silver or gold to sick people to lie in the sunshine or in the shade of the trees. —*1909. (p. 836, pars. 1, 2)*

Institutions in which medical missionary work can be done are to be regarded as a special essential to the advancement of the Lord's work. The buildings secured for this work should be out of the cities, in rural districts, so that the sick may have the benefit of out-of-door life. By the beauty of flower and field, their minds will be diverted from themselves, from their aches and pains, and they will be led to look from nature to the God of nature, Who has provided so abundantly the beauties of the natural world. The convalescent can lie in the shade of the trees, and those who are stronger can, if they wish, work among the flowers, doing just a little at first, and increasing their efforts as they grow stronger. Working in the garden, gathering flowers and fruit, listening to the birds praising God, the patients will be wonderfully blessed. The angels of God will draw near to them. The fresh air and sunshine, and the exercise taken, will bring them life and vitality. —*October 19, 1902. (p. 841, par. 1)*

Dealing with Sanitarium Workers

There is a great necessity for decided reforms to be made in regard to our dealings with the workers in our sanitariums. Faithful, conscientious workers should be employed, and when they have performed a reasonable amount of work in a day, they should be relieved that they may secure needed rest.

Only a reasonable amount of labor should be required; for this the worker should receive a reasonable wage. If helpers are not given proper periods for rest from their taxing labor, they will lose their strength and vitality. They cannot possibly do justice to the work, nor can they represent what a sanitarium employee should be. More helpers should be employed if neccssary and the work should be so arranged that when one has performed a day's labor he may be freed to take the rest necessary to the maintenance of his strength. —*September 27, 1905. (p. 225, pars. 4, 5)*

Let no man consider it his place to judge of the amount of labor a woman should perform. A competent woman should be employed as matron, and if any one does not perform her work faithfully, the matron should deal with the matter. Just wages should be paid, and every woman should be treated kindly and courteously, without reproach.

And let those who have charge of the men's work be careful lest they be too exacting. The men should have regular hours for service, and when they have worked full time, they are not to be begrudged their periods of rest. A sanitarium is to be all that the name indicates.

Every worker should seek to educate himself to perform his work expeditiously. The matron should teach those under her charge how to make quick, careful movements. Train the young to perform the work with tact and thoroughness. Then when the hours of work are over, all will feel that the time has been faithfully spent, and the workers are rightfully entitled to a period of rest.

Educational advantages should be provided for the workers in every sanitarium. The workers should be given every possible advantage consistent with the work assigned them. —*September 27, 1905. (p. 226, pars. 1-4)*

The Lord instructed me that our sisters who have received training that has fitted them for positions of responsibility, are to serve with faithfulness and discernment in their calling, using their influence wisely, and, with their brethren in the faith, obtaining an experience that will fit them for still greater usefulness. The instruction of the apostle Peter, "Add to your faith virtue; and to virtue knowledge," they are to bring into their individual experience, and this work of daily sanctification through cooperation with the Spirit of God, will develop their knowledge and capabilities. —*May 7, 1911. (p. 939, par. 3)*

In ancient times the Lord worked in a wonderful way through consecrated women who united in His work with men whom he had chosen to stand as His representatives. He used women to gain great and decisive victories. More than once, in times of emergency, He brought them to the front and worked through them for the salvation of many lives. Through Esther, the queen, the Lord accomplished a mighty deliverance for His people. At a time when it seemed that no power could save them, Esther, and the women associated with her, by fasting and prayer and prompt action, met the issue, and brought salvation to their people.

A study of women's work in connection with the cause of God in the Old Testament times will teach us lessons that will enable us to meet emergencies in the work today. We may not be brought into such a critical and prominent place as were the people of God in the time of Esther, but often converted women can act as an important part in more humble positions. This, many have been doing, and are still ready to do. It is a woman's duty to unite with her husband in the disciplining and training of her sons and daughters, that they may be converted, and their powers consecrated to the service of God. There are many who have ability to stand with their husbands in sanitarium work, to give treatments to the sick and to speak words of counsel and encouragement to others. There are those who should seek an education that will fit them to act the part of physicians.

In this line of service a positive work needs to be done, women as well as men are to receive a thorough medical training. They should make a special study of the diseases common to women, that they may understand how to treat them. It is considered most essential that men desiring to practice medicine shall receive the broad training necessary for the following of such a profession. It is just as essential that women receive such a training, and obtain their diplomas certifying their right to act as physicians. —*May 7, 1911. (p. 940, pars. 1-3)*

Our institutions should be especially thorough in giving the women a training that will fit them to act as midwives. There should be in our sanitariums lady physicians who understand well their profession, and who can attend women at the time of childbirth. Light has been given me that women instead of men should take the responsibility in such cases. I was directed to the Bible plan, in which at such times women acted the part of the physician. This plan should be carried out by us, for it is the Lord's plan.

Again and again light has been given me that women should be chosen and educated for this line of work. Now the time has come when we should face the matter clearly. More women should be educated for this work, and thus a door of temptation may be closed. We should allow no unnecessary temptation to be placed in the way of physicians and nurses, or the people for whom they minister.

The Lord has greatly favored us in providing suitable buildings at Loma Linda for the carrying forward of the work as it should be carried. Let us be in earnest in following the counsel we have received.

I have been instructed to say to our leading sanitarium workers throughout our ranks: The work must move forward on a higher plane, and after a more sacred order than it has heretofore if it is to accomplish all that God designs should be accomplished by it in our churches and for the world. We need to pray, and to consider earnestly what is the great spiritual need of men and women in this age. Strange things are being done, which are not after the Lord's counsel, but after the devising of men. As wicked practices increase among those who are determined to do wickedly, there is great need that our people bring into prominence before the world a pure, untainted work. The Lord says to us, "Be ye clean that labor in the health institutions." Work under the influence of the Holy Spirit of God. Let the men holding positions of sacred trust view the work from a high standpoint. —*May 7, 1911. (p. 942, pars. 1-4)*

I have written to you the instruction that has been given me regarding the special work to be done by the lady physicians in our sanitariums. It is the Lord's plan that men shall be trained to treat men, and women trained to treat women. In the confinement of women, midwives should take the responsibility of the case. In Bible times it was not considered a proper thing for men to act in this capacity, and it is not the will of God that men should do this work today. Very much evil has resulted from the practice of men treating women and women treating men. It is a practice according to human devising, and not according to God's plan. Long has the evil been left to grow, but now we lift our voice in protest against that which is displeasing to God. —*June 7, 1911. (p. 948, par. 3)*

Use of Drugs in Our Institutions

Workers—gospel medical missionaries—are needed now. We cannot afford to spend years in preparation. Soon doors now open to the truth will be forever closed. Carry the message now. Do not wait, allowing the enemy to take possession of fields now open before you. Let little companies go forth to do the work to which Christ appointed His disciples. Let them labor as evangelists, scattering our publications, and talking of the truth to those they meet. Let them pray for the sick, ministering to their necessities, not with drugs, but with nature's remedies, and teaching them how to regain health and avoid disease. —*September 21, 1903. (p. 90, par. 5)*

An experienced Christian nurse in the sickroom will use the best remedies within her knowledge for restoring the sufferer to health. And she will pleasantly and successfully draw the one for whom she is working to Christ, the Healer of the soul as well as of the body. The lessons given, line upon line, here a little and there a little, will have their influence. The older nurses, whether they be men or women, should lose no opportunity of calling the attention of the sick to Christ. Those who care for the sick should be prepared to blend spiritual healing with physical healing. Let the nurses in our sanitariums show that in the solemn work of caring for the sick, they do not rely on drug medication, but on the power of Christ, and the use of the simple remedies that He has provided—the application of hot and cold water and simple, nourishing food, without intoxicating liquor of any kind, with judicious exercise, and a putting away of all injurious practices. In treatment such as this there is health for the sick. —*February 4, 1905. (p. 125, par. 4)*

The character of the buildings, the terraced hill, covered by graceful pepper trees, the profusion of flowers and shrubs, the tall shade trees, the orchards and field—all combine to make this place meet fully the descriptions that I have given in the past of the place presented to me as the most perfect for sanitarium work. Everything at Loma Linda is fresh and wholesome and attractive. The patients could live out-of-doors a large part of the time. The land will serve as a school for the education of patients. By outdoor exercises and working in the soil, men and women will regain their health. Rational methods for the cure of disease will be used in a variety of ways. Drugs will be discarded. —*July 1905. (p. 182, par. 1)*

Christ is no longer in this world in person, to go through our cities and towns and villages, healing the sick. He has commissioned us to carry forward the medical missionary work that He began, and in this work we are to do our very best. Institutions for the care of the sick are to be established, where men and women suffering from disease may be placed under the care of God-fearing physicians and nurses, and be treated without drugs. —*October 27, 1905. (p. 233, par. 2)*

Be careful not to do anything that would restrict the work at Loma Linda. It is in the order of God that this property has been secured, and He has given instruction that a school should be connected with the sanitarium. A special work is to be done there in qualifying young men and young women to be efficient medical missionary workers. They are to be taught how to treat the sick without the use of drugs. Such an education requires an experience in practical work. —*August 19, 1906. (p. 315, par. 3)*

Let the students be given a practical education. And the less dependent you are upon worldly methods of education, the better it will be for the students. Special instruction should be given in the art of treating the sick without the use of poisonous drugs, and in harmony with the light that God has given. Students should come forth from the school without having sacrificed the principles of health reform.

The education that meets the world's standard is to be less and less valued by those who are seeking for efficiency in carrying the medical missionary work in connection with the work of the third angel's message. They are to be educated from the standpoint of conscience, and as they conscientiously and faithfully follow right methods in their treatment of the sick, these methods will come to be recognized as preferable to the methods of nursing to which many have become accustomed, which demands the use of poisonous drugs. —*November 3, 1907. (p. 559, pars. 2, 3)*

There should be at our sanitariums intelligent men and women, who can instruct in Christ's methods of ministry. Under the instruction of competent, consecrated teachers, the youth may become partakers of the divine nature, and learn how to escape the corruptions that are in the world through lust. I have been shown that we should have many more women who can deal especially with the diseases of women, many more lady nurses who will treat the sick in a simple way and without the use of drugs. There are many simple herbs, which, if our nurses would learn the value of, they could use in the place of drugs, and find very effective.

I write these things that you may know that the Lord has not left us without the use of simple remedies which when used will not leave the system in the weakened condition in which the use of drugs so often leaves it. We need well-trained nurses who can understand how to use the simple remedies that nature has provided for restoration to health, and who can teach those who are ignorant of the laws of health how to use these simple but effective cures.

He Who created men and women has an interest in those who suffer. He has directed in the establishment of our sanitariums and in the building up of schools close to our sanitariums, that they may become efficient mediums in training men and women for the work of ministering to suffering humanity. In the treatment of the sick, poisonous drugs need not be used. Alcohol or tobacco in any form must not be recommended, lest some soul be led to imbibe a taste for these evil things. There will be no excuse for the liquor dealers in that day when every man shall receive according to his works. Those who have destroyed life will by their own life have to pay the penalty. God's law is holy and just and good. —*November 3, 1907. (p. 560, pars. 1-4)*

The blending of our schools and sanitariums will prove an advantage in many ways. Through the instruction given by the sanitarium, students will learn how to avoid forming careless, intemperate habits in eating. Let the instruction be given in simple words. We have no need to use the many expressions used by worldly physicians which are so difficult to understand that they must be interpreted by the physician. These long names are often used to conceal the character of the drugs being used to combat disease. We do not need these.

Nature's simple remedies will aid in recovery without leaving the deadly aftereffects so often felt by those who use poisonous drugs. They destroy the power of the patient to help himself. This power the patients are to be taught to exercise by learning to eat simple, healthful foods, by refusing to overload the stomach with a variety of foods at one meal. All these things should come into the education of the sick. Talks should be given showing how to preserve health, how to shun sickness, how to rest when rest is needed. —*February 20, 1908. (p. 636, pars. 1, 2)*

We must have medical instructors who will teach the science of healing without the use of drugs. If physicians refuse to give their services unless they can be paid the highest wage, we shall not bribe them. We are to prepare a company of workers who will follow Christ's methods. —*June 20, 1908. (p. 696, par. 2)*

The education that meets the world's standard is to be less and less valued by those who are seeking for efficiency in carrying the medical missionary work in connection with the work of the third angel's message. They are to be educated from the standpoint of conscience, and as they conscientiously and faithfully follow right methods in their treatment of the sick, these methods will come to be recognized as preferable to the methods to which many have become accustomed, which demand the use of poisonous drugs." —*April 23, 1908. (p. 735, par. 4)*

Intemperance and ungodliness are increasing everywhere. The work of temperance must begin in our own hearts. And the work of the physician must begin in an understanding of the works and teachings of the great Physician. Christ left the courts of heaven that He might minister to the sick and suffering of earth. We must cooperate with the Chief of physicians, walking in all humility of mind before Him. Then the Lord will bless our earnest efforts to relieve the suffering of humanity. It is not by the use of poisonous drugs that this will be done, but by the use of simple remedies. We should seek to correct false habits and practices, and teach the lessons of self-denial. The indulgence of appetite is the greatest evil with which we have to contend. —*November 5, 1909. (p. 798, par. 3)*

It is not necessary that our medical missionaries follow the precise track marked out by medical men of the world. They do not need to administer drugs to the sick. They do not need to follow the drug medication in order to have influence in their work. The message was given me that if they would consecrate themselves to the Lord, if they would seek to obtain under men ordained of God, a thorough knowledge of their work, the Lord would make them skillful. Connected with the divine Teacher, they will understand that their dependence is upon God and not upon the professedly wise men of the world. —*April 27, 1910. (p. 900, par. 4)*

Use of Drugs in Our Institutions

Our people should become intelligent in the treatment of sickness without the aid of poisonous drugs. Many should seek to obtain the education that will enable them to combat disease in its varied forms by the most simple methods. Thousands have gone down to the grave because of the use of poisonous drugs, who might have been restored to health by simple methods of treatment. Water treatments, wisely and skillfully given, may be the means of saving many lives. Let diligent study be united with faithful ministry. Let prayers of faith be offered by the bedside of the sick. Let the sick be encouraged to claim the promises of God for themselves. "Faith is the substance of things hoped for, the evidence of things not seen." Christ Jesus, the Saviour of men, is to be brought into our labors and councils more and more. —*August 29, 1911. (p. 960, par. 1)*

Section IV

Money for Work

My brother, we need means to advance the work of the Lord in many places. We must firmly establish the work at the capital of our nation. Do you not wish to have a part in the work that God has given us to do there? Will you not do your best to help us to secure the facilities that we must have in order to advance the work in Washington, D.C. and in Southern California? —*April 15, 1904. (p. 64, par. 3)*

For two years I have been interested in the Potts' Sanitarium property, and have advised and urged our people to secure it. Two years ago we thought it could be secured for twelve thousand dollars. One year ago it was offered for eight thousand, and this spring it was offered for still less. I advised those having in charge the medical work in Southern California, to purchase the building, and when they hesitated, because of a lack of funds, I persuaded _____ and _____ to join me, and we have purchased the Potts' Sanitarium and eight acres adjoining for five thousand dollars. —*April 15, 1904. (p. 65, par. 3)*

Something similar can be done in the neighborhood of Los Angeles, if wise plans are adopted for the carrying forward of the work, and if the men whom the Lord has entrusted His talent of means will put their money into use for the honor of God and the blessing of humanity. —*April 15, 1904. (p. 66, par. 1)*

I am glad that means is in sight to make the first payment on the place (Loma Linda); for we ought to have it. I do not know just where to look for the rest of the money needed. I have asked _____ to let me know of anyone who would be willing to lend me some money without interest. He thinks that I could get means on these terms.

We will appropriate the proceeds of the sale of a certain number of copies of "Ministry of Healing" toward the purchase of this property. The book will soon be on the market. —*May 28, 1905. (p. 155, pars. 2, 3)*

Money is needed with which to establish the work in places outside of the cities, from which the cities can be worked.

We must have means with which to meet the payments on Loma Linda. I ask our brethren who have means to awake to the responsibilities resting upon them, and to do what they can to help us. Those who have the Lord's money in trust should regard it as a privilege to give of their means to help to pay for a place so well adapted for sanitarium work. Gifts and loans at a low rate of interest will be gladly received. My brethren, it is the Lord's money that you are handling, and you cannot invest it better than by putting it into the Lord's work; thus you will lay up treasure in heaven. "I beseech you therefore, brethren, by the mercies of God, that ye present your bodies a living sacrifice, holy, acceptable unto God, which is your reasonable service. And be not conformed to this world: but be ye transformed by the renewing of your mind, that ye may prove what is that good, and acceptable, and perfect, will of God." —*July 1905. (p. 184, par. 3)*

In order properly to fit the sanitarium and the school at Loma Linda to carry on the work that the Lord has plainly directed should be carried on, means must be raised. And let no man act a part in influencing our brethren and sisters in Southern California not to do that which needs to be done. —*August 19, 1906. (p. 316, par. 2)*

There are times when certain sanitariums will have to pass through a close, severe struggle for means in order to do a special work which the Lord has particularly designated should be done. In such emergencies, they are to be free to receive gifts and donations from our churches. Some who receive the truth have means, and they will aid in sustaining the good work which should be done in our sanitariums. —*August 19, 1906. (p. 317, par. 2)*

The Lord has given you your work, _____. He has not appointed _____ to tell you what your duty is; as superintendent of the sanitarium, your work is an important one. Elder _____ is not to intrude himself upon that which God has given you to do. That there shall be no more money in the sanitarium until the institution shall have earned that amount required, is not for Elder _____ to decide. Hire money, if this is necessary in order to perfect the work. —*November 2, 1906. (p. 334, par. 2)*

The Lord has greatly blessed our people in Southern California, in enabling them to secure at a very low cost valuable sanitarium properties. Through the institutions that are established here, the Lord desires to reach a class that can be reached in no other way. Therefore, I would urge upon our people to whom the Lord has entrusted the talent of means, that they make loans and gifts to place these institutions in a position where they can do without embarrassment the work that will be to the honor and glory of God. —*May 19, 1907. (p. 355, par. 1)*

The establishment of these three institutions has brought a heavy financial burden to our people in Southern California. Yet they have cheerfully responded to the calls for means that have been made. Brother _____, and Dr. _____, and others connected with these sanitariums have invested all they could spare that the work might not be hindered. —*May 19, 1907. (p. 356, par. 3)*

At our request, Brother _____ is going East to attend some of our camp-meetings, where he may come in contact with many of our brethren and sisters, and lay before them the opportunities for assisting these important branches of the Lord's work. We unite in asking those who have means to spare, to consider the matter of investing some of their money in these institutions, thus helping to provide necessary facilities, that a thorough work may be done in caring for the sick who are coming to Southern California in search of health. May the Lord give ability to help, and a willing mind. —*May 19, 1907. (p. 357, par. 1)*

Seats were arranged under the pepper trees at the back of the sanitarium. It was an interesting occasion. The Lord blessed me in speaking from the fifty-eighth chapter of Isaiah. Before I closed, I made a strong appeal to those who had means to help in the Lord's work, and I presented the needs of the Loma Linda Sanitarium. I urged them not to spend all their efforts merely in commercial lines, but to lay up treasure beside the throne of God. —*May 20, 1907. (p. 358, par. 3)*

At our request Brother _____ has consented to visit important gatherings of our people in the Middle West, and to endeavor to secure gifts or loans for some of our Southern California sanitariums. We desire that wherever he goes, he may be given opportunity to present the work and needs of the Paradise Valley and Loma Linda Sanitariums. We need help in both places. Both at Loma Linda and Paradise Valley it has been necessary to build additions to the main building for bathrooms. This has left us with debts that must be met shortly, and we greatly need financial assistance.

At Loma Linda, a school is being conducted for the training of medical missionary evangelists, and we want this school to be of the highest order. Both the sanitarium and the school can be a help one to the other.

Elder _____ has felt an earnest interest in the advancement of the Sanitarium work along right lines. He and Sister _____ have put their whole soul into an effort to make the work at Loma Linda a success. They have put into the institution all the means they could spare to keep the enterprise moving. We have the utmost confidence in the integrity of Brother _____, and have no reason to doubt that the Lord selected him as the manager of the Loma Linda Sanitarium. —*May 22, 1907. (p. 360, pars. 1-3)*

It would have been an excellent thing if the teachers of the San Fernando School during the vacation had availed themselves of this opportunity to push the work with "Christ's Object Lessons." They would have found a blessing in going out with the students and teaching them how to meet the people, and how to introduce the book. The story of the gift of the book and its object, would lead some to have a special interest in the book, and in the school for which it is sold. Why have not the teachers of our schools done more of this work? If our people would only realize it, there is no more acceptable work to be done in the home field than to engage in the sale of "Object Lessons"; for while they are thus helping to carry out the Lord's plan for the relief of our schools, they are also bringing the precious truths of the Word of God to the attention of the people.

The indifference that has been manifested by some toward this enterprise is displeasing to God. He desires that it shall be recognized by all our people as His method of relieving our schools from debt. It is because this plan has been neglected, that we now feel so keenly our lack of means for the advancing work. Had the schools availed themselves of the provision thereby made for them, there would be more money in the school treasury, and more money in the

Money for Work 199

hands of His people to relieve the necessities of other needy departments of the cause; and best of all, teachers and students would have received the very lessons that they needed to learn in the Master's service. —*September 12, 1907. (p. 474, pars. 1, 2)*

I send you these lines because I see that there is need of a deeper intuition, a wider perception, on the part of our sanitarium and education workers, if they would get all the benefit that God intends shall come to them through the use of "Object Lessons" and "Ministry of Healing." I ask you, my brethren, to read these words to our people, that they may learn to show the spirit of wisdom, and of power, and of a sound mind. —*September 12, 1907. (p. 475, par. 1)*

The Loma Linda Sanitarium needs help. It was the Lord Who placed this institution in our possession, that we might carry forward His work through its instrumentality. It should have every convenience necessary to make it a blessing to the sick. In the efforts made to build up this work, Satan has tried in every way to discourage—but we must not be discouraged, but arouse to the task of carrying this work successfully. Los Angeles can help to meet the emergency by loaning means or making gifts to provide for the present necessities.

There is need of an elevator at the sanitarium; it is also necessary that some other improvements be made, and that, as far as possible, the indebtedness be decreased. Let all who possibly can, help in the circulation of "Ministry of Healing" that means may come in for the doing of the work. If at the beginning of this new year, we will take hold of this work, the blessing of the Lord will be upon us. The pushing of this enterprise is included in the missionary work to be done for this time. Let all plan to see what can be done. —*January 13, 1908. (p. 593, pars. 1, 2)*

The Lord says to His people in America: "When I send my servants to establish My work in a new field, and build up the interests essential to give it character, I call upon My people to sustain that work with their prayers and with their means....

"When My servant whom I have called to make known My will was sent to Australia, you in America should have understood that you had a work to do in co-operation with her. Who was it that carried out My directions in laying the foundation of the institutions in America, which have grown to such large proportions? And when My servant was sent to establish the work in a new field, could you not see that He Who owns all the gold and silver was calling for your co-operation? You had obtained a standing fully abundant and ample. And when the work was to begin in another field, I would be with My servant to indicate the work, and you should have been ready to aid.

"Place your money where the work of God demands help, that the medical missionary work in that new field may be made a success. The work in Australia should have been placed on such a basis that after a time it might become self-sustaining.

"When My servants were sent to Australia, you should have understood that God would work through them, and you should have exercised liberality in apportioning means to advance the work....

"Again the word of the Lord came to me, saying: 'I have spared your life to do My work, and wherever I send you, go, and I will send My angel with you. In no case should you be feeble in your request for the advantage of means. Wherever I send you, go and speak My words. I will be thy mind; I will be thy judgment. All the advantages are Mine. The means and facilities are Mine, and there should be no withholding. But selfishness, a desire to control, has kept the advantages in one place, so that everything is overbalanced. Call for the means God designed you to have long ago. Hold up My banner. Give honor to no human instrumentality, but to God, that My name may be a praise in the earth. The Lord, He is God, and before Him there is no other. My work in Australia has been greatly hindered. But go not forth in hesitancy. I will be with you. Ask of My people the means that should have gone to advance the work in the Australasian field, and the new world to which I have sent you.'

"The work should be established in this country, and it will be; for thus the Lord has said. We might be years in advance if our brethren in America had stood unflinchingly to their duty, to hear and obey the Word of the Lord. Let no more time be lost. You have so many advantages; do your work unselfishly. It is God's work we are doing, and you will not find the work in your hands restricted, if you follow the will and Word of God. Share your advantages, with us in the field, that the work may stand on a true basis, and have the influence and character it should possess. Your minds may not now be prepared to see the importance of surrendering yourselves to do what ought to have been done when we were appointed to come to this field. You may not be able to see all the particulars involved in this request of God to impart. But the special work has been laid out, and you are called upon to do your God-given duty in our onward march in this country by furnishing us with facilities for our work.

"Our brethren have not discerned that in helping us to do this work they would be helping themselves. That which is given to start the work here will result in strengthening the work in other places. As your gifts free us from continual embarrassment, our labors can be extended; there will be an ingathering of souls, churches will be established, and there will be increasing financial strength. We shall have sufficiency, not only to carry on the work here, but to impart to other fields. Nothing is gained by withholding the very means that would enable us to work to advantage, extending the knowledge of God and the triumphs of truth, in regions beyond." —*1899. (p. 707, par. 4; p. 708)*

When Brother _____ was leaving for Southern California at the close of this conference, he inquired of me, "What shall we plan to do for Loma Linda?" "Go straight ahead," I replied. "Let the truth shine forth in every possible way. Continue to work with all your zeal in the territory surrounding your sanitarium. Help your students to learn how to labor, and keep sending them out into Redlands, and Riverside, and San Bernardino and the smaller towns and villages round about. Introduce our publications, and do thorough work. Let your light shine as a lamp that burneth. Encourage the students to greater activity in missionary labor while taking their course of study."

Our brethren at Loma Linda are in need of funds with which to carry on their work. But notwithstanding their present necessity I have encouraged them not to falter, but to go forward in the name of the Lord. And now I appeal to my brethren in Washington not to allow them to suffer. While we are planning to support the educational work in such places as Washington, we must not forget the important work that must be done at Loma Linda, and in other centers of training. —*June 11, 1909. (p. 740 all)*

I have felt so thankful regarding the improvements that I see here. God has prospered you, and He will continue to prosper. And we must give ourselves to the education of those who do not appreciate these things. We must keep it before them in the living light; you must exercise that living faith that takes hold from above. Some here know what a battle we have had in order to secure harmonious action, and we thank the Lord that when the enemy comes in like a flood, then the Spirit of the Lord lifts up for us a standard against the enemy. —*April 20, 1911.*

I would like to inquire what progress has been made in the raising of the means for the purchase of the land. My investment was not made in order to lessen the responsibility of others who could help. Do what you can to encourage those who have money that they may use in the cause, to use it wisely and not let it slip away into speculation. Secure pledges from those who have not the money in sight. We need special wisdom to move out at the right time. I thank the Lord that He encouraged me to walk by faith, and I pray that He will help you to show others their privilege in this matter. —*June 7, 1911. (p. 947, par. 3)*

I want you to keep me posted about the money coming in with which to make the payments on the Loma Linda property. I am writing to different ones, asking them to help us at this time, and I think that we shall obtain means to make every payment. Please write to me often and tell me what you are doing, and what the prospects are for obtaining means. —*July 10, 1905. (p. 176, par. 4)*

Debt and Borrowing Money

The idea that a sanitarium should not be established unless it could be started free from debt, has put the brake upon the wheels of progress. In building meeting houses we have had to borrow money, in order that something might be done at once. We have been obliged to do this, in order to fulfill the directions of God. Persons deeply interested in the progress of the work borrowed money and paid interest on it, to help establish schools and sanitariums and to build meeting houses. The institutions thus established and the churches built have been the means of winning many to the truth. —*June 30, 1904. (p. 71, par. 3)*

Thus the tithe has been increased, and workers have been added to the Lord's forces. Will my brethren consider this, and work in accordance with the light which God has given us, regarding the work in Southern California? Let that which should be done be done without delay. Do your best to remedy the neglect of the past. The word has once more come that a sanitarium is to be set in working order near Los Angeles. If this sanitarium is conducted in harmony with the will of God, it will be a means of great blessing, a means in the Lord's hands of leading souls to the truth. —*June 30, 1904. (p. 72, pars. 1, 2)*

To the managers of all our sanitariums, I would say: Let no large debts be created. Make no unnecessary move. Set aside your desire for full equipments at once. Let the best possible use be made of fewer facilities, rather than to increase debts. All that is needed may in time be obtained, but all the furnishings, and facilities need not be provided at once. Let reason, calm thought, and wise calculation be the rule of action. If success attends our institutions established for the care of the sick, it will be because the managers have preferred to get along with the most essential things rather than to pile up debts.

The Lord calls upon us to do a work in many places. We shall have sanitariums that can be carried on without involving our cause heavily in debt. A word to the wise is sufficient. Let none think they must invest in the most costly conveniences. There is a more humble way of working successfully. Provide first the simpler appliances necessary for giving treatments. We need not now go to the expense of providing swimming pools and other costly facilities.

Our sanitarium work at Loma Linda may be carried on with simplicity without incurring a heavy debt. Let our people be wise and true, and do their work in a humble way, in order that means may be saved in every line possible. This will facilitate the establishment of sanitariums in other places. My brethren, study to show yourselves approved unto God. We are laborers together with God to save the souls and the bodies of many to the glory of Christ Jesus. —*May 6, 1906. (p. 295, pars. 1-3)*

Upon the Union Conference President should rest the greater responsibilities, and I am instructed that he needs other helpers to advise him in his work. He should not cling to the idea that unless money is in hand no move should be made that calls for the investment of means. If in our past experience we had always followed this method, we would often have lost special advantages such as we gained in the purchase of the Fernando School property, and in the purchase of the sanitarium properties at Paradise Valley, Glendale, and Loma Linda.

Debt and Borrowing Money

To make no move that calls for the investment of means unless we have the money in hand to complete the contemplated work, should not always be considered the wisest plan. In the upbuilding of His work, the Lord does not always make everything plain before His servants. He sometimes tries the confidence of His people by having them move in faith. Often He brings them into straight and trying places, bidding them go forward when their feet seem to be touching the waters of the Red Sea. It is at such times, when the prayers of His servants ascend to Him in earnest faith, that He opens the way before them, and brings them out into a large place. —*September 19, 1907. (p. 478, pars. 1, 2)*

It is well that our training schools for Christian workers should be established near to our health institutions, that the students may be educated in the principles of healthful living. Institutions that send forth workers who are able to give a reason for their faith, who have that faith that works by love and purifies the soul, are of great value.

I have clear instruction that wherever it is possible, schools should be established near to our sanitariums, that each institution may be a help to the other. But I dare not advise that steps be taken at this time to branch out so largely in the educational work at Loma Linda that a large outlay of means will be required to erect new buildings. Our faithful workers at Loma Linda must not be overwhelmed with such great responsibilities that they will be in danger of becoming worn and discouraged.

I am charged to caution you against building extensively for the accommodation of students. It would not be wise to invest at this time so large a capital as would be required to equip a medical college that would properly qualify physicians to stand the test of the medical examinations of the different states.

A movement should not now be inaugurated that would add greatly to the investment upon the Loma Linda property. Already there is a large debt resting upon the institution, and discouragement and perplexity would follow if this indebtedness were to be greatly increased. As the work progresses, new improvements may be added from time to time as they are found necessary. An elevator should soon be installed in the main building. But there is need of strict economy. Let our brethren move cautiously and wisely, and plan no larger than they can handle without being overburdened. —*November 3, 1907. (p. 558, pars. 1-4)*

I dare not advise you in such large plans as you propose; you need to make the Lord your wisdom in these matters. I do not feel that you should plan for such large outlay of means without your having some certainty that you can meet your obligations. I would caution you against gathering a large load of indebtedness. There is the food factory to be completed and set in operation. I call your attention to this enterprise that you may not lay more plans than you can well carry out. —*February 20, 1908. (p. 634, par. 4)*

You are men of varied talents, and you are right on the ground. The Lord will be your Instructor in all matters if you will seek His counsel in faith. Study every step, and pray that the Lord may lead you. If He gives you light in this matter, then you can move with assurance. Now is the time for you to ask of the Lord wisdom, and to submit your plans to Him. It is an excellent opportunity for you to receive an individual experience. Plan wisely; move guardedly; and the Lord will certainly be your Helper.

I feel the deepest interest in the work at Loma Linda. The plans you suggest seem to be essential, but you need to assure yourselves that they can be safely carried. You should not make hasty moves that will involve heavy indebtedness. —*February 20, 1908. (p. 635, pars. 1, 2)*

In the providence of God there comes to this people in time of need, favorable opportunities to secure valuable facilities that can be utilized wisely for the rapid advancement of the cause. At times, the Lord has specified that we should come into possession of properties in certain localities where we needed to gain an entrance for the proclamation of the third angel's message. The idea that we are not to purchase any such properties unless first the money is in hand, is not in accordance with the mind of God. Again and again in years past the Lord has tested our faith by opening the way for us to secure places possessing advantages at a cost far below their real value, and at a time when we had no money. We have at such times met the situation by borrowing money on interest, and advancing in harmony with the command of our divine Leader Who bade us advance in faith. These experiences have been attended with many perplexing problems, but the Lord has helped us through them all, and His name has been glorified. Had we hesitated, the precious cause would have been retarded rather than advanced, and, in many cases, opportunity would have been given our enemies to triumph over our failures to secure these advantages placed within our reach. In such matters as these we are to learn to walk by faith when necessary, as some have walked in the past. —*January 27, 1910. (p. 853, par. 1)*

"Christ's Object Lessons" and "Ministry of Healing"

I wish to say a few words more about the circulation of "Christ's Object Lessons." My brethren, show our people what they can do in handling this book. As tourists from all parts of the world flock into Los Angeles and other parts of Southern California, let there be those who can call their attention to this book. It is full of precious truth, and as it is presented to unbelievers, angels of God will impress many to buy it. Let those who do this work keep in mind the words, "As unto the Lord." The purpose for which it is done will invest this work with a dignity that will improve the habits, the manners, and the address of the workers. By this effort the poorest, humblest worker is linked with the great Master Worker.

In order to be ready to receive the impressions of the Holy Spirit, in order to advance in harmony with the will of the Lord, we need consecrated minds and hearts. Let not human beings seek to put their own plans and preferences in the place of God's plans. Those who do this will hinder the Lord's work. Let no one say or do anything that will discourage Christlike effort. To each one God has given his work. If every one would be zealous to do that which will increase his ability to labor, how much would be accomplished. —*June 30, 1904. (p. 72, pars. 3, 4)*

The Lord wants you, my brethren, to arouse to action the minds of those who do not realize that God is calling them to active service. Tell them that their obedient love, in willing effort, is to flow forth as streams in the desert. Day by day what they accomplish is to give evidence that they are laborers together with God. The work that the Lord places before them may be dreaded, but they will gain courage as they advance.

Let all do something. All can do much more than they have done. Let parents and children help. The consciousness that they are co-workers with Christ will give the workers a joy and assurance that they could gain in no other way. And not only will relief be brought to the schools, but the light of truth will be widely diffused.

The experience gained by the youth who engage in this work will be of great value to them, teaching them to improve every God-given opportunity to labor with diligence and fidelity, and with perseverance under disappointment. The Lord makes a way for all who employ the means He has provided for the accomplishment of certain objects.

My brethren and sisters in Southern California, educate yourselves to work for the Master. Remember that in helping to circulate "Christ's Object Lessons," you are placing before others truths which cannot fail of being a blessing to them. Each one of God's people has a part to act in the work of the Redeemer. Those who receive Christ are to prove the sincerity of their love for Him by earnest, self-sacrificing efforts in His service. No oportunity for helping to advance the Lord's cause is to be allowed to pass by. In meekness and lowliness, yet with an earnest determination to accomplish something for the blessing of others, God's children are to take hold of His work. —*June 30, 1904. (p. 73, pars. 1-4)*

Only a small part of that which may be accomplished has yet been done in circulating "Christ's Object Lessons." Let not our people think that their duty is done, their work finished. This book is still to be taken out by God's people, and is to find its place in many more homes. Let the same territory be gone over and over again. In this there will be a blessing for the one who sells the book and for those who buy it.

Let us take hold of the work with renewed courage. Let God's people consecrate to His service the time and tact that He has given them. O, what a blessing many will obtain from the consciousness that they are working for God. This thought will help them to do their work intelligently.

My brethren and sisters, by earnest prayer brace yourselves for duty, and then expect the help of the Lord. Prove yourselves to be laborers together with God. As you go forth to sell "Christ's Object Lessons," repeat again and again the words: "Not slothful in business; fervent in spirit; serving the Lord." With this as your motto, press on with the work.

With humble hearts begin afresh, and by words and example encourage those who have never tried to sell the book to make an effort. Let all that you do be done gracefully and cheerfully and well. Learn to ask the Lord to help you and believe that He surely will. The work that is undertaken in the name of the Lord and for the purpose of placing the light before the people will be blessed by Him. What is needed is workers who are humble and contrite. He who lives near the Saviour will reveal in his life that he has held communion with Him. —*June 30, 1904. (p. 74, pars. 1-4)*

Diligent efforts should be made to lessen the debt resting on the school, but these efforts should be made by all. I have supposed that "Christ's Object Lessons," handled discreetly, would do much toward relieving our schools from debt, and I believe that this book will yet be the means of doing much to help the Fernando School.

Let each family try to pay the expenses of the students that it sends to school. Some families, in which there are several children attending school, will be hard pressed. Would it not be wisdom to create a fund by the sale of "Christ's Object Lessons" for the assistance of such ones? There are many young people who desire to be in school, and who ought to be, but who have no means. These young people can be helped through school if our people will do their duty in handling "Christ's Object Lessons." —*June 30, 1904. (p. 70, pars. 1, 3)*

A mistake was made in the methods that were adopted to clear the schools in California from debt. The book "Christ's Object Lessons" was given to relieve the indebtedness of our schools. But this plan has not been presented in our schools as it should have been; the students and teachers have not been educated to take hold of this book and push its sale for the benefit of the educational work. —*1907. (p. 457, par. 4)*

The plan that has been followed of calling on our people to support these schools must not be continued, for this is giving to the teachers and students, and to our people in general a wrong education. They must not be so instructed that they will forget the needs of other fields outside their own. —*(p. 458, par. 1)*

In the cities of Riverside, Redlands, and San Bernardino a mission field is open to us that we have as yet only touched with the tips of our fingers. A good work has been done there as far as our workers have had encouragement to do it, but there is need of means to carry the work successfully. It was God's purpose that by the sale of "Ministry of Healing" and "Christ's Object Lessons" the necessary means would be raised for the work of our sanitariums and schools, and thus our people be left free to donate of their means for the opening of the work in new fields. If our people had engaged in the sale of these books as God purposed they should, we would now have the means to carry the work in the way the Lord designed.

Wherever the work of selling "Christ's Object Lessons" has been taken hold of in earnest, the book has had a good circulation. And the lessons that have been learned by those who have engaged in this work have well repaid their efforts. Our people should all be encouraged to take a part in this missionary effort. Light has been given me that in every possible way instruction should be given to our people in the best methods of presenting this book to the people. We have been instructed that at our large gatherings, workers should be present who will teach our people how to sow the seeds of truth. This means more than instruction how to sell the "Signs of the Times" and other periodicals. —*1907. (p. 458, pars. 2, 3)*

It includes such books as "Christ's Object Lessons" and "Ministry of Healing." These are books which contain precious truths, and from which the reader can draw lessons of highest value. —*(p. 459, par. 1)*

At your recent camp-meeting, was any one appointed to present the interests of this line of work to our people? If this was not done, you lost a precious opportunity of placing large blessings within the reach of the people and an opportunity of raising means for the relief of our institutions. My brother, let us encourage our people to take up this work without further delay that those who have had experience in the sale of health foods may interest themselves in the sale of "Christ's Object Lessons" and "Ministry of Healing," for here is food unto eternal life. Los Angeles has been presented to me as a very fruitful field for the sale of these books. I know that every household in the land would be benefited by their presence in the home.

Those who bear responsibilities in our sanitariums and schools should act wisely in this matter, encouraging all by this means to gather the money required to meet the expenses of the different institutions. We have need of workers in Southern California who have clear spiritual eyesight, men who will weigh matters wisely, and can see afar off. If our workers were more fully consecrated to the cause of God, a much more effective work would be done.

God's Spirit is grieved because His people are so slow to understand that which the Lord requires of them. Our workers should present these books to our people at our large and small gatherings, and call four volunteers who will engage in the sale of them. When this work is entered into with the earnestness which the times in which we live demand, the indebtedness that now rests upon our schools and sanitariums will be wiped out, and the people who are now being called on to give of their means to support these institutions, will be free to donate their offerings to missionary work in other needy places. —*1907. (p. 459, pars. 1-3)*

Great good will result by bringing these books before the women of the W.C.T.U. Invite these workers to your meetings, and give them an opportunity to become acquainted with our people. Place these books in their hands, and tell them the story of their gift to the cause and its object. Explain how by the sale of "Ministry of Healing" patients will be brought to the sanitarium for healing who could never get there unaided, and how through this means also sanitariums are managed wisely by men and women who have the fear of God before them. The workers in the temperance cause will not be slow to see the advantage of this branch of the work. If you will in earnestness and faith work out the plan that God has laid down, angels of God will attend your steps, and the blessing of heaven will be upon your efforts.

I send you these lines because I see that there is need of a deeper intuition, a wider perception, on the part of our sanitariums that God intends shall come to them through these books. I ask you, Brother _____, to read these words to our people, that they may learn to show the wisdom of a sound mind. The Lord gave me His Holy Spirit to enable me to write the manuscript for this book, the "Review and Herald" and the Press donated the labor required to prepare it for the public, and God now calls upon our people, men and women and youth, to make the most of this gift to His cause. Let the students, under wise directors, be set to work to sell the books, and let all understand why they are engaged in this missionary enterprise. The blessing and approval of God will rest upon those who make the effort. —*1907. (p. 460, pars. 1-3)*

Our brethren should not forget that the wisdom of God has made provision for our schools in a way that will bring blessing to all who participate in the enterprise. The book "Christ's Object Lessons" was donated to the educational work that the students and other friends of the schools might handle these books, and by their sale raise much of the means needed to lift the school indebtedness. But this plan has not been presented to our schools as it should have been; the teachers and students have not been educated to take hold of this book and courageously push its sale for the benefit of the educational work.

Long ago, the teachers in our schools should have learned to take advantage of "Christ's Object Lessons." In selling these books the students will serve the cause of God, and while doing this by the dissemination of precious light, they will learn invaluable lessons in Christian experience. All our schools should now come into line, and earnestly endeavor to carry out the plan presented to us for the education of the workers, for the relief of the schools, and for the winning of souls to the cause of Christ. —*September 12, 1907. (p. 470, pars. 2, 3)*

It would have been an excellent thing if the teachers of the San Fernando School during the vacation had availed themselves of this opportunity to push the work with "Christ's Object Lessons." They would have found a blessing in going out with the students and teaching them how to meet the people, and how to introduce the book. The story of the gift of the book and its object, would lead some to have a special interest in the book and in the school for which it is sold. Why have not the teachers in our schools done more of this work? If our people would only realize it, there is no more acceptable work to be done in the home field than to engage in the sale of "Christ's Object Lessons"; for while they are thus helping to carry out the Lord's plan for the relief of our schools, they are also bringing the precious truths of the Word of God to the attention of the people.

The indifference that has been manifested by some toward this enterprise is displeasing to God. He desires that it shall be recognized by all our people as His method of relieving our schools from debt. It is because this plan has been neglected that we now feel so keenly our lack of means for the advancing work. Had the schools availed themselves of the provision thereby made for them, there would be more money in the school treasury and more money in the hands of His people to relieve the necessities of other needy departments of the cause, and best of all teachers and students would have received the very lessons that they needed to learn in the Master's service. —*September 12, 1907. (p. 474, pars. 1, 2)*

I send you these lines because I see that there is need of a deeper intuition, a wider perception, on the part of our sanitarium and educational workers, if they would get all the benefit that God intends shall come to them through the use of "Christ's Object Lessons" and "Ministry of Healing." I ask you, my brethren, to read these words to our people, that they may learn to show the spirit of wisdom, and of power, and of a sound mind. —*September 12, 1907. (p. 475, par. 1)*

The work that was done in collecting money to lift the school debt in Southern California was not a work of God's ordering. He gave our schools the precious book "Christ's Object Lessons," and He wants that book to be appreciated. The students have lost precious lessons because they have not taken up the work of pushing the sale of these books.

There is a most valuable experience to be gained by those who will aid in doing this work for the benefit of our educational institutions. If teachers and students will act their part in this missionary enterprise, angels of God will open the way before them.

In this new year let new methods be recommended. Let parents encourage their children to act a part in the circulation of "Christ's Object Lessons." This will instruct the children in acts of self-denial. The work of selling "Christ's Object Lessons" is a work that Christ would have the children engage in and they themselves will be blessed in the work. Light, precious light, is contained in the book which every family should follow. —*January 13, 1908. (p. 592, pars. 1, 2)*

"Ministry of Healing" is another book containing valuable instruction. It is also a gift to the work; its teachings will do good to those who receive them, as its title suggests. The sale of "Ministry of Healing" is one way in which the sanitarium is to receive help. Let us take a personal interest in this matter. These two books can be handled separately or together, as may be deemed advisable. And those who read them will see in them precious light. Angels will be beside those who study them, to impress minds and hearts. —*(p. 592, par. 3)*

There has been a dearth of means for our educational work because we have neglected to follow fully the Lord's directions. The Lord now asks that energy and zeal be given to the carrying out of His methods. The books "Christ's Object Lessons" and "Ministry of Healing" are the Lord's specified agencies for the financial aid of our institutions. By following the plan that He has laid down, a continual work of education may be carried on. I pray that God may teach us to understand His ways, and help us to learn daily of Christ. —*June 20, 1908. (p. 696, par. 3)*

We will appropriate the proceeds of the sale of a certain number of copies of "Ministry of Healing" toward the purchase of this property (Loma Linda). The book will soon be on the market. —*May 28, 1905. (p. 155, par. 3)*

We hope to see you soon now, but in regard to the purchase of "Loma Linda" I will say, "Go ahead." I hope to be able to help by giving the proceeds from a certain number of copies of "Ministry of Healing." I can do no more, except to borrow. I wish the place purchased. Do not neglect to tell me all I ought to know. I have been looking over your descriptive letter, and I am well satisfied that the place is one we ought to have. It is cheap at forty thousand dollars. We will not leave you but will stand back of you, and help you to raise the means. In regard to the right man to manage the institution, I am confident that we shall find some one when the right time comes. —*May 31, 1905. (p. 160 all)*

Physicians' Salaries

Have you learned how much Dr. _____ proposes to charge for his services? If a physician does his work skillfully, his talent should be recognized, but there is danger of our being brought into perplexity. If we introduce a new system of paying our surgeons high wages, there may be a hard problem to settle after a time. Other physicians will demand high wages, and our ministers will require consideration also. —*September 27, 1905. (p. 223, par. 3)*

In regard to the proposition made by Brother _____, I look at the matter as you do. We cannot afford to start out on the high-wage plan. This was the misfortune of the people in Battle Creek, and I have something to say on this point. We have before us a large field of missionary work. We are to be sure to heed the requirements of Christ, Who made Himself a donation to our world. —*November 1, 1905. (p. 235, par. 3)*

Physicians' Salaries

Nothing that we can possibly do should be left undone. There is to be neatness and order, and everything possible is to be done to show thoroughness in every line. But when it comes to paying twenty-five dollars a week and giving a large percentage on the surgical work done, light was given me in Australia that this could never be because our record is at stake. The matter was presented to me that many sanitariums would have to be established in Southern California, for there would be a great inflowing of people there. Many would seek that climate.

We must stand in the counsel of God, every one of us prepared to follow the example of Jesus Christ. We cannot consent to pay extravagant wages. God requires of His under-physicians a compliance with the invitation, "Take My yoke upon you, and learn of Me; for I am meek and lowly in heart: and ye shall rest unto your souls. For My yoke is easy, and My burden is light." —*November 1, 1905. (p. 236 all)*

If he is granted considerably more than other physicians, they will come to believe they are not treated right unless they have more also. We must move cautiously and understandingly, and not allow wages to creep up so high that many will be tempted. There may have to be a coming down rather than a going up in physicians' wages because there is a great work to be done. Unless you have some clear light from the Lord, it is not advisable to pay one man considerably more than another doing similar work. For, if you do, the other will think it perfectly proper to expect similar high wages. We must look at things on all sides, and it is of no use for us to think that we can offer a successful worker a high wage simply because he may demand it. We must, rather, consider what we can afford to do at the present time, when the fields are opening upon which we shall henceforth have to expend much more means than we have spent hitherto. These are matters that will test the faith of our people. —*December 4, 1913. (p. 1017, par. 3)*

W. C. White: They do test our faith, Mother— especially when a group of workers have labored with a man until they have learned to love him and adore him and they believe that he can do better work than any other man. Then it is natural for them to think that it is wrong for the brethren to withold from him that which he might use to advantage. They think, "What is a thousand dollars, or fifteen hundred dollars, extra, when life is involved?" They say, "Here is such and such a case that he has just brought through, and there is another whose life he has saved," and they feel as if it would be awfully mean of us not to meet his requirements. They say, "There is no one who has to work and suffer as does a surgeon. Think of the hours of arduous labor, of anxiety, of mental anguish they have to endure, when a precious life is hanging by a slender thread."

But on the other hand, in considering this matter, we must remember that other institutions are influenced by our action. We see a poor struggling sanitarium situated in a beautiful place, in a position to do a large business, and with every prospect of making money if only they can have a brilliant physician, and they can get a good physician if they are encouraged to pay only three or five hundred dollars more than the wage scale recommended. They say, "If you will only let us pay a few hundred dollars more than you have advised, we can gain five thousand dollars to cover this small additional expense for wages." And thus it seems—when we look at it from a business point of view.

You see there is a selfishness that underlies that, that the Lord is not pleased with. We must work harmoniously. It is through harmonious action that our work is to be carried forward, and some will have a very hard time. Some will have an easier time. But all these things will have to be taken just as they come, and the workers must remember what Jesus gave in coming to our world. I think of it over and over and over again, and it seems to me that we can do an excellent work, if we set a right example. But if we desire that which most of our brethren cannot receive, this injures our influence. One brother says, "Such and such a brother has a certain wage, and I must have a wage to correspond." And so the wages will climb, and keep climbing, higher and still higher. The fact is, that the wage of some may have to be lower and still lower in order that we may meet the extensive requirements of the work that is before us in warning the world.

O, I am so thankful that the Lord has given me a little strength that I may use in completing my books! I have not gotten through yet. I have not completed all that I desire to see done. I mean to take just as good care of myself as possible, that I may complete intelligently the work the Lord has entrusted to me. And in all this I desire to share with my brethren in self-denial. What we want, brethren, is to be an example in all matters, whether man sees it or not. Let us remember, brethren, that the Lord sees every sacrifice we make individually for the spread of the truth. But if you encourage some to receive a wage considerably higher than that which their brethren are receiving, others will desire to climb just as high, and if they are not allowed to do so, they will become dissatisfied. —*December 4, 1913. (p. 1019, pars. 1, 2)*

Brethren, we cannot afford to lay a stumbling block in the path of any soul simply because they think they must have matters arranged so and so. The Lord desires us to be consistent in everything. He desires us to follow the self-sacrificing example of Christ, and when we do that, His blessing rests upon us. When we go to various places and our brethren know that we have been tempted to ask for higher pay but that we have overcome this temptation, He will give us influence with the people. It is not the higher pay that brings success. Success comes through following in the footsteps of the Saviour, in self-denial and self-sacrifice. When we do this, the Lord pronounces His blessing upon us. He discerns the hidden motives, and when the work that is to be done is especially difficult and taxing, His grace will be sufficient for our every need.

Even if we as laborers of God go beyond that which seems to be for the good of our health and strength, we may look to Him in confidence, casting our helpless soul upon Him, and realizing that He Who Himself led a self-sacrificing life of toil on this earth will acknowledge our faithfulness, and will help us marvelously. When we come to hard places, the angels of God will be right there to sustain and bless. Heavenly angels will be by our side to make right impressions upon those with whom we are associated, and to whom we are ministering. —*December 4, 1913. (p. 1020, pars. 1, 2)*

Those who have the cause of God at heart, must realize that they are not working for themselves or for the small wage they may be receiving, and that God can make the little they do receive, go farther than they may think it can. He will give them satisfaction and blessings as they go forward in self-sacrificing labor. And He will bless every one of us as we labor in the meekness of Christ. And when I see some seeking for higher wages, I say to myself, they are losing a precious blessing. I know this to be a fact. I have seen it worked out again and again.

Now brethren, let us take hold and do the very best that we possibly can, without asking for higher wages except as we find that it is an impossibility to do the work given us without more, but even then let others see this necessity as well as ourselves, for God puts it into their hearts to see it, and they will speak the word that will have more influence than for us to speak a thousand words. They will speak words that will give us a proper standing before the people. The Lord is our Helper and God, our frontguard, and our rearward. —*December 4, 1913. (p. 1021, pars. 2, 3)*

As we bring ourselves into right relationship with God, we shall have success wherever we go, and it is success that we want, not money—living success, and God will give it to us because He knows all about our self-denial. He knows every sacrifice that we make. You may think that your self-denial does not make any difference, that you ought to have more consideration, and so on. But it makes a great difference with the Lord. Over and over again I have been shown that when individuals begin to reach out after higher and still higher wages something comes into their experience that places them where they stand no longer on vantage ground. But when they take the wage that carries on the face of it the fact that they are self-sacrificing, the Lord sees their self-denial and He gives them success and victory. This has been presented to me over and over again. The Lord that seeth in secret will reward openly for every sacrifice that His tried servants have been willing to make.

The brethren often leave their families and make many other sacrifices in behalf of the cause that they love more than anything else in life. They may be tempted to think that in return for this self-denial they ought to receive more remuneration, but the more they might receive would not always bring them a blessing. If they go forward in a spirit of cheerfulness, others will follow their example, and as they go forward, following on to know the Lord more perfectly, they will know that His going forth is prepared as the morning. The Lord guards the men that are willing to brave hardship and danger in order to reach precious souls in out-of-the-way places. He regards their determination to make His cause first. He honors those who are willing to endure hardness as good soldiers of Christ. He sees every sacrifice that is made; He sees the end from the beginning, and He will care for every one of His servants who remain faithful. There have been times when I have thought that my brethren might have done better than they did do in my behalf. But I have been careful about criticizing. I have thought of the great sacrifice Christ made in giving His life for a lost world. God gave His only begotten Son to save fallen man, and the offering that was made was prompted by the spirit of self-sacrifice. —*December 4, 1913. (p. 1022, pars. 1, 2)*

In years past, when this subject of wages has been under consideration, I have told my brethren that the Lord knows all about the spirit that prompts us to action, and that He can turn matters in our favor at times we do not expect it. As we set a right example, the blessing of the Lord will rest upon us. I have seen the Lord work in many ways and in many places to help the very ones that view those matters in the right light and set a self-sacrificing example. And, brethren, as you labor earnestly, prayerfully, humbly, in the spirit of Christ, God will open doors before you. The people will see your self-denial.

At times when my brethren have come to me, seeking advice as to whether they should demand a higher wage, I have told them they might gain a little means by asking for higher wages, but that the blessing of God will accompany those who follow a different course. God sees the self-denial; the Lord God of Israel sees every motive, and when you come into a hard place, the angels of God are there to help you, and to give you victory after victory.

I have been very clear in counseling my brethren not to demand large wages, for this is not the impelling motive that leads us to spend our energies in the work of soul-saving. We are not to let the wage question stand in the way of our responding to the call of duty, wherever our services may be required. The Lord can bring matters around so that a blessing will attach to our labors far exceeding any compensation we may or may not receive, and He will give to His servants words to speak that are of the highest consequence to perishing souls. —*December 4, 1913. (p. 1023, pars. 1-3)*

The people are hungering and thirsting for help from heaven. I have tried to put in practice these principles of self-sacrifice, and I know whereof I speak when I say that the blessing of God will rest upon you when you make the call of duty first. I am glad for this privilege of testifying before you this morning that the Lord has turned matters, over and over again, in such a way as to give us more than we could possibly ask for. The Lord will prove His servants, and if they prove true to Him, and leave their cases with Him, He will help them in every time of need.

We are not laborers together for God for the wages we may receive in His service. True brethren, you must have wages with which to support your families; but if you should begin to stipulate as to just how much you shall receive, you may prove a stumbling-block to someone else who does not have the disposition, perhaps, that you have to be liberal; and the result will be confusion. Others will think that all are not dealt with on an equality. You will soon find that the cause of God will become cramped; and this result you do not desire to see. You wish to see the cause of God placed on vantage ground. By your example, as well as by your words, the people are to have a living assurance that the truth received into the heart begets a spirit of self-denial. And as you go forward in this spirit, there are many that will follow.

The Lord desires His children to act in that self-denying, self-sacrificing way that will bring to us the satisfaction of having performed our duty well because it was duty. The only begotten Son of God gave Himself to an ignominious death on the cross, and should we complain at the sacrifice we are called upon to make? —*December 4, 1913. (p. 1024 all)*

During my wakeful hours through the night season, I have been pleading with the Lord to guard our brethren against a tendency to promise to go here or there on the stipulation that they are to have a little higher wage. If they go in a spirit of self-sacrifice, trusting in Him, the Lord will grant sustaining power to mind and character, and success will be the result.

In the future, our work is to be carried forward in self-denial and self-sacrifice even beyond that which we have seen in past years. God desires us to commit our souls to Him, that He may work through us in manifold ways. I feel intensely over these matters. Brethren, let us walk in meekness and lowliness of mind, and put before our associates an example of self-sacrifice. If we do our part in faith, God will open ways before us now undreamed of. —*December 4, 1913. (p. 1025, pars. 1, 2)*

_____: How shall we meet this condition? Some of our physicians, like Dr. _____ and Dr. _____ and others, who are bighearted and generous, are brought into contact with sickness and poverty and distress, and they feel intensely the importance of advance moves in the church and in the institutions with which they are connected, and they feel that they must give. They love to give. They make big donations, and they keep making big donations, and they say, "We need money so that we can keep on giving." How ought we to meet such proposals? Shall we put the money into their hands in the form of wages, or ought our institutions that have a surplus be willing to respond liberally to the requests of these men to do things for the poor and needy who greatly desire help?

Sister White: Yes, that is the way the matter should be handled. The institution should do what it can to help.

_____: Sometimes the brethren call the attention of the management to certain needy cases, and they are met with the response, "We cannot afford it; there are lots of poor people in the world, and we cannot help them all." Then the physicians say, "We must have money to use in urgent cases, and the surest way to get it is to demand a liberal wage."

That is not the best way. If matters are arranged so that the cause of God will be served to the best account, angels of God will work, and a right influence will be exerted. As those connected with the institutions share in sacrifice, the minds of the people will be impressed, and all will be inspired to do to the utmost of their ability. But if men feel that they cannot labor in our institutions unless they have large wages, they will meet with disappointment. This has been presented to me over and over again.

Let us not forget the infinite sacrifice Christ has made in our behalf. That He might obtain for us heaven, He hung on the cross and suffered death—a most shameful death. If He were willing to give Himself freely in order that we might have life everlasting, how glad we should be for the privilege of service, and how eager we should be to follow His example of self-sacrifice. —*December 4, 1913. (p. 1025; p. 1026, par. 2)*

Store, Bakery and Health Foods

Last week we had an important gathering at the sanitarium here of our health food workers. I spoke to them on Sabbath, and on Sunday I addressed them for about an hour on the subject of our restaurant work. I told them that there must be a thorough reformation in the health food business. It is not to be regarded so much as a commercial enterprise. At present but little is seen as the result of this work to lead us to recommend the establishment of more places to be conducted as our restaurants have been in the past. But few have been converted by this work in Los Angeles and in San Francisco. Many of the workers have lost the science of soul-saving.

Please read carefully what is published in Testimonies, Volume 7, regarding the health food work and the evangelical work. I feel more and more impressed that we must make diligent efforts to present the truth. I need not now write much regarding these lines of work, for the light has been in print for some time. But since these Testimonies were published, circumstances have arisen that reveal the necessity for the cautions that have been given. Health reform needs a reformation, before it shall stand as God designs it should. We need to practice true godliness in every undertaking. In all the restaurants in our cities there is danger that the combination of many foods in the dishes served, shall be carried too far. The stomach suffers when so many kinds of foods are placed in it at one meal. Simplicity is a part of health reform. There is danger that our work shall cease to merit the name which it has borne. —*September 27, 1905. (p. 224, pars. 2, 3)*

Store, Bakery and Health Foods

If we would work for the restoration of health, it is necessary to restrain the appetite, to eat slowly, and only a limited variety at one time. This instruction needs to be repeated frequently. It is not in harmony with the principles of health reform to have so many different dishes at one meal. We must never forget that it is the religious part of the work, the work of providing food for the soul, that is more essential than anything else. —*September 27, 1905. (p. 225, par. 1)*

The Lord does not design that His denominated people shall exhaust their strength to carry on restaurants in the manner in which they are now conducted. The many complicated combinations of food that are not wholesome tend to make of the health reform a health deform. —*September 27, 1905. (p. 225, par. 3)*

We were conversing in regard to erecting a store, and one of authority who was in our midst, speaking to several present, suggested the propriety of erecting such a building at a distance from the main building and all other buildings that are now standing there, so that there will be no danger to them from fire. He suggested that changes would need to be made after thorough study, and that the building should be placed where the wind would not carry the smoke or sparks to the main building. Great care is to be exercised in regard to this matter, and intelligence is to be shown in the movements made. —*December 11, 1905. (p. 252, par. 2)*

Brother _____, before closing my letter, I will finish what I intended to say about the building of the food factory. This work requires much wisdom and genuine good sense. If you can bring it about, do so. Make the best possible use of "Ministry of Healing" to aid you in your work. I believe that you can accomplish that which seems to be a necessity. I think that if we all walk humbly with God, we shall always have grateful hearts. —*December 11, 1905. (p. 255, par. 4)*

The Lord has instructed me that it would be a mistake for us to plan for the production of a large quantity of health foods at Loma Linda to be distributed through commercial channels. Loma Linda is a place that has been especially ordained of God to make a good impression upon the minds of many who have not had the light of present truth. Every phase of the work in this place, every movement made, should be so fully in harmony with the sacred character of present truth as to create a deep spiritual impression.

Everything connected with the institution at Loma Linda should, so far as possible, be unmingled with commercialism. Nothing should be allowed to come in that would in any wise lessen the favorable impression you are striving to make. If we manifest a genuine faith in eternal realities, this will have a far-reaching effect on the minds of others. We must allow nothing to hinder our efforts for the saving of souls. God requires us to leave impressions that will help awaken unbelievers to a realization of their duty. Let us use voice and pen in helping those who need clear discernment. —*May 6, 1906. (p. 286, pars. 2, 3)*

Many are now inquiring, "What shall I do to inherit eternal life?" We cannot answer this question satisfactorily by connecting with our sanitariums the production of health foods for commercial gain. By our example we are to leave upon the minds of our patients the impression that we are sustained and guided by the grace of God, and that we are keeping constantly in view the glory of the Lord.

It is not rank, or wealth, or learning, or power, that lends influence to a Christian, but a willing mind, and a heart consecrated to the cause of Christ. In the service of God there is a place for every one, and He is glorified when every one is satisfied in filling the place appointed him. To His servants He imparts grace sufficient for every duty. However humble may be their sphere of service, they may by His grace reveal that they are Christian gentlemen and Christian ladies.

In the visions of the night, these principles were presented to me in connection with the proposal for the establishment of a bakery at Loma Linda. I was shown a large building where many foods were made. There were also some smaller buildings near the bakery. As I stood by, I heard loud voices in dispute over the work that was being done. There was a lack of harmony among the workers, and confusion had come in.

Then I saw Brother _____ approach. His countenance bore a look of anxiety and distress as he endeavored to reason with the workmen, and bring them into harmony. The scene was repeated, and Brother _____ was often drawn away from his legitimate work as manager of the sanitarium to settle variances. He was carrying too heavy a load, and he looked careworn and perplexed. —*May 6, 1906. (p. 287, pars. 1-4)*

I then saw patients standing on the beautiful sanitarium grounds. They had heard the disputes between the workmen. The patients did not see me, but I could see them and hear them, and their remarks were brought to my ears. They were expressing words of regret that a food factory should be established on these beautiful grounds, in such close proximity to an institution for the care of the sick. Some were disgusted, and a most unfavorable impression was being made. How sorry I felt! All these buildings had cost money that should have been used in fitting up bathrooms, which would involve considerable expense.

Then One appeared on the scene, and said, "All this has been caused to pass before you as an object lesson, that you might see the result of carrying out certain plans. Sanitariums must help those who come to them by calling attention to the gospel truth. Commercialism must not take the place of the vital work to be done. This beautiful place came to us in the providence of God, and it should be kept as a restful, desirable, healthful retreat to which we may call the sick, where they shall be greatly blessed physically, and where they can hear the evidence of present truth and the reasons for our faith."

Store, Bakery and Health Foods

And then, lo, the whole scene changed. The bakery building was not where we had planned it, but at a distance from the sanitarium buildings, on the road toward the railway. It was a humble building, and a small work was carried on there. The commercialism idea was lost sight of, and, in its stead, a strong spiritual influence pervaded the place. A suitable helper was given Brother _____ at such times as he required help. The management of this small bakery did not bring a heavy responsibility upon Brother _____. The patients were favorably impressed by what they saw. —*May 6, 1906. (p. 288 all)*

Brother and Sister _____, you are to unite in being a blessing in spiritual lines. The Lord will bless you, and make you a blessing. You must not be encouraged to take upon yourselves the responsibility of conducting a large business in the health food line. We must all fill our appointed places, and become like-minded with God. Then we shall not fail nor be discouraged. The strength and power and influence of the Word will be revealed in Christlike tenderness, through the softening, subduing influence of the Holy Spirit of God.

Nothing of a commercial nature, as a means of lessening the debt of the sanitarium, should be brought in to burden the mind. These are many considerations in connection with this matter that I fear I shall not be able to define plainly to you. Improvements on the Loma Linda property will need to be made, but your work is not to gather in perplexities that will tax brain and nerve.

My brother, you and your wife are to be a special help to the sick and the afflicted. You can take them out to ride, and in many other ways show a genuine interest in their behalf while acting as manager of the sanitarium and as a religious instructor.

The manager and the pastor have their appointed work to do. The Lord calls upon His servants to attain unto perfection of Christian character in every line of effort. We are to see that our hearts are under the control of the Holy Spirit—under the control of a power out of and above ourselves. Let every soul take hold of the work earnestly, because he is thoroughly converted, because he discerns the methods and ways of the Lord.

The manager of the sanitarium bears important responsibilities. Let his associates who are engaged in continuous hard labor in the various handicrafts, keep their souls searched as with a lighted candle. Unity of action in diversity of labor must be maintained. —*(p. 289 all)*

The workers are to live out the prayer of Christ, Who declares, "I sanctify Myself, that they also might be sanctified through the truth." Let them read the Word of the Lord, in order that they may have the wisdom that is unto salvation. The richest treasures are to be found by searching for them in the Word. Some minds will be so impressed to seek these hidden treasures as to sell all that they have in order to buy the field and come into possession of the hidden treasure which they may impart to others.

The truths of the Word of God, applied to the heart and carried out with humility in the daily life practice, will make Christians strong in the strength of Jehovah, and happy in His peace. Christian kindness and earnest consecration are constantly to be manifested in the life. We are not always engaged in special duties connected with sacred service, but the common, daily round of duties may be done in His Spirit, and such labor will commend itself to every man, even to the unconverted who know not the doctrine. We may let our light so shine in good works that the truth which we cherish shall be, to unbelievers, spirit and life.

We shall have a work to do at Loma Linda in supplying health foods, in a limited way, to the surrounding cities, but it has been presented to me that in the establishment of a large food factory, you would be disappointed in your expectations. The influence connected with its management would not make a favorable impression upon the people. The Lord is able to make the proper impression upon human minds, when we co-operate with Him and follow the plans that He outlines. —(p. 290 all)

The light given me is that in a food business large enough to supply Southern California, it would be difficult to avoid commercialism, and if the perplexing details were not attended to most carefully, there would be more expense than income. You can ill afford to spend the time that would be required to make the business a success. The Lord calls upon us to ascend a higher platform. Our example must exert a decided influence in favor of the doctrines we profess. Let us cling close to the teaching of the Word. Let us make the Word our counselor. The truths of the Word, carried out in our daily lives, will keep the soul pure and refined, noble and elevated. Walking in the light of the truth, self will be hid in constant love and fear of God. Before the world, the truth is to become majestic, for it reveals God in word, in spirit, in character.

The words were spoken by my Instructor: "The influence to be constantly going out, is that which is created by the light shining forth with clear, convincing power from every soul who claims to believe the truth. The Lord would have you exalt the truth in language, in faith, in practice. Those who are connected with you are in no wise to be permitted to become deficient in tenderness, in mercy, in refinement of speech. The heart is ever to be obedient unto God. Cling to your heavenly Helper."

Talk these things, Brother _____, and you will be a laborer together with God. By beholding you become changed into the likeness of His image; through His grace you become a partaker of His divine nature. You can glorify God by writing helpful, encouraging letters; by engaging in conversation with the patients; by placing select reading matter in the hands of those with whom you become acquainted. The life of Christ was a life of incessant labor to prepare human beings to be members of the royal family in the mansions above. —*May 6, 1906. (p. 291 all)*

Brother _____, I have written a great deal of late in regard to the subject of food manufacture. We are not to allow Dr. _____'s plans in regard to the corn flakes cause a large investment of money that should be invested in less expensive preparations of food. We will deal in foods that will not require such an outlay of means in order to secure the privilege of using them. I will send to you copies of some things I have written on this subject.

Time is very short, and cities and towns are to be visited with judgment. Fire and water will work with their destructive forces. We should not make the food business a straining for high profits. We should work in connection with the great food manufacturer, Jesus Christ, Who fed five thousand people with five loaves and two small fishes. —*September 14, 1906. (p. 322, pars. 3, 4)*

In many places, in different sections of the country, an effort should be made to utilize natural products for healthful foods. A good work along this line may be done at Loma Linda. Our brethren there should make a beginning soon, even if all the arrangements regarding this work cannot be definitely decided upon at this time.

As our brethren at Loma Linda study how to make the health food work a means of bringing the truth for this time before the minds of unbelievers, the Lord will add His blessing and will make plain the course they should pursue in the conduct of the business.

A similar work is to be carried forward in the Southern States. Men and women who embrace the truth in the South will often need to be helped to find employment. Many will find opportunity to engage in evangelistic work, and these should learn, in connection with this work, to teach worldlings how to prepare simple, palatable food.

Outside the city of Nashville there are advantages that should be utilized in providing wholesome food for the people. —*September 26, 1906. (p. 326 all)*

In regard to the health food business, I would urge you to move slowly. Dr. _____'s proposition to sell the corn flake rights to our people for twenty years has just been considered by our brethren here, and I fear, if I had not been on the ground, this matter would have been carried through to the loss of our food business. When a thing is exalted, as the corn flakes has been, it would be unwise for our people to have anything to do with it. It is not necessary that we make the corn flakes an article of food.

I would advise you, my brother, to keep away from the influence of Dr. _____'s ingenious plans. Let us use our own ingenuity to invent the best kinds of food possible. We are living in the closing days of the earth's history; souls are starving for a knowledge of the Word of God and of healthful living. Let us seek to carry our work solidly, giving all possible instruction regarding the principles of health reform, praying with the sick and teaching the people how to care for themselves in sickness and health. —*November 2, 1906. (p. 331, pars. 1, 2)*

It has been found necessary to provide additional bathroom facilities at Loma Linda, and to make some changes greatly needed, and a small bakery should be added. We are in need of means to accomplish that which must be done, and we pray the Lord to put it into the heart of our brethren and sisters to help in this time of necessity. —*May 19, 1907. (p. 355, par. 5)*

Use of Loma Linda Land

As the Lord prospers us, we should manifest our gratitude by a willingness to advance. We should see the advantage of adding to that which we already have. I feel a burden regarding the danger of letting anybody come into the neighborhood to spoil the place:

There is a piece of land across the railroad, lying next to a piece already purchased, which should be secured. One day we drove over it, and all around it. We wanted to see all about it. And I am sure from the representations that have been made to me, that this piece of land ought to come into our possession. If you are wise, the next time I come here, you will have that land. I will try to help you all I can. Let us work intelligently.

There are several reasons why you should have this land. You need the produce from it for your cattle to subsist upon; this place is close at hand, and joins that which you already have.

Here we have our school, and here many important interests are centered. We must not permit elements to come in that will tend to hinder and retard the work. It will be pleasing to the Lord if we keep our eyes wide open, and are fully awake, ready to take advantage of every circumstance that will place us in right relation to the work we have to do. It would be a grievous error for us to allow to pass an opportunity to secure this property, for we might never again have such an opportunity. I advise you to secure it before it becomes so expensive that you could not afford to buy it.

There is danger of our becoming too narrow. These many little houses close together across the railroad do not look well. If we can get land and have room, so as not to build any more in that way, it will be better. —*April 20, 1911. (p. 930, pars. 1-5)*

You need the land, and it will be a matter of regret by and by if it is not secured. Do not make any delay to take steps that will prevent its being taken up by those who would plan for unbelievers to crowd into it. We should keep them out. If we do this, we shall have reason to rejoice.

The Lord is well pleased with what you have already done here at Loma Linda. When one sees the prosperity that has attended the

Use of Loma Linda Land

work, and the spirit of consecration that prevails, the conviction deepens that you are working in harmony with God.

I desire that all the work of this place shall be a correct representation of what our health institutions should be. Let everything that we lay our hands to, show the result of the moving of the Spirit of God upon the human heart. This will be evidence that we have the higher education. Workers whose hearts are in obedience to the movings of the Spirit of God will make this place what God desires it to be. I am surprised, happily surprised to see everything looking so well. It is beyond my expectations. And now let every one strive to keep it so, and labor for improvements.

I am highly gratified as I look upon the land we already have. This will be one of the greatest blessings to us in the future—one that we do not fully appreciate now but which we shall appreciate by and by. I hope that you will get the other land that I have spoken of, and join it to that which you already have. It will pay you to do this. As I have carried the burden of this place from the very beginning, I wanted to say this much to you. Now I leave the matter with you, and let us work in harmony. —*April 20, 1911. (p. 931, pars. 1-4)*

My mind is settled in regard to the purchase of the land in front of the Loma Linda Sanitarium. We must have that piece of land. I will pledge myself to be depended upon for one thousand dollars. I hope to be favored with an opportunity to hire some money soon, but I shall not worry in regard to this, or I shall not be able to do anything. The effort of speaking on Sabbath and of reading my letters today is all I have been able to do to the present time. But as soon as I can, I will make some movement concerning the raising of the one thousand dollars. The piece of land we must have, for it will never do to have buildings crowded in there. Do not fail to carry through the purchase of it. Do your best, and I will do my best. The money from me you may depend upon. We shall be able to send it soon. —*April 30, 1911. (p. 938, par. 2)*

I wish to say to Elder _____ that the money which I pledged to help purchase the eighty-five acres will be sent without fail. Please let me know if a couple of weeks' delay will trouble you seriously. I am truly glad that I gave my promise to help to purchase this land, under the influence of the Spirit of God. I felt that the land must be secured; otherwise we should have reason to regret that we did not obtain it. —*May 18, 1911. (p. 945 all)*

I want to say to you both that I am thankful I was moved to speak as I did concerning the piece of land in front of the Loma Linda Sanitarium. I was urged by the Spirit of God to make the pledge of one thousand dollars, and I did so hoping that others, who were better able to give than I, would follow my example. I dared not leave the meeting without following the conviction I had, and I now I feel that I have done my duty, showing my faith by my works. —*June 7, 1911. (p. 947, par. 1)*

I have made some investments for Loma Linda to enable that institution to secure land adjoining the sanitarium that was for sale. Had this land been sold to unbelievers, and they had crowded in, the institution would have been placed at a disadvantage. I felt that we could not afford to run this risk. The land is now purchased, and to that extent we are safe from elements that might work trouble and confusion to our medical school. I could not rest until I had the assurance that we were safe from this possibility. This purchase may mean the keeping away from the institution a class of people who might have proved burdensome. Now that we have this land, a burden is rolled off my heart. —*September 28, 1911. (p. 970 all)*

Whenever I look at the buildings, the fields, and the orchards here at Loma Linda, I am thankful that we have this beautiful place, thankful for every foot of land that we control. By and by you will see, if you do not understand it now, that the securing of the land was essential. It may not appear to you now that it was necessary for us to secure so large a tract, but I am instructed that our work here must be carried forward on broad lines and in solid unity. That the will of the Lord may be done in this place, we must be in a position where we can understand His pleasure in regard to our words and actions, where we may be always helping forward that work which is most essential. During the night it was again impressed upon my mind that it was through the providence of God we obtained this place when we did. Also that the branching out and enlargement that we have done, and the development of the work as it stands today, is what the Lord would have us do. —*March 28, 1912. (p. 990, par. 3)*

As a people we cannot stand still. The work must grow as we move forward. We have now come to a time when there will be intensity of action on the part of some whose movements we do not now understand. How then shall we carry the work at such a time, when opportunities for advancement come unexpectedly and difficulties are constantly increasing. We must daily commit our ways to God in faith, and be learning continually of Christ Jesus. He will not leave us to walk in darkness, but will give us the enlightenment of the Holy Spirit.

Those who are bearing responsibilities in our institutions and in various branches of the Lord's work, need to be constant learners in the school of Christ. We must understand and know that the Lord is at the head of the work, although we do not always discern His overruling power. At all times it is our privilege to know that He is there, and to have the assurance that He will work with us if we will work with Him. But if one plans one thing and another plans another thing, and each endeavors to lead, we shall get things into confusion. We may avoid this if we will. We may carry this work intelligently, in the love and fear of God. If we will make up our minds to do this at any sacrifice, if we labor patiently, we shall not fail.

As I looked out of the window this morning after the fog had lifted, and saw the fields and the orchards in front of the institution, I felt thankful for all the land that is now in our possession. We are not to sell portions hastily to this one and to that, but we are to consider well who it is that we may sell to. Let every decision be made after prayer and faithful study. We need to cultivate the spirit of prayer, that all our plans may be laid wisely and in the fear of God. —*March 28, 1912. (p. 991, pars. 1-3)*

Work for W.C.T.U.

In the afternoon, Elder _____ gave an excellent discourse. Brother _____ is an able worker, and we hope he may labor for a time in this needy field. Now is a favorable time to work Redlands. The Woman's Christian Temperance Union recently held an important convention in Redlands, and Dr. _____ attended their meetings. She was introduced to the convention and by invitation spoke to them on the subject of healthful dress. She was well received, and has received many invitations to give lectures at various places. We trust the Lord will open the way before her, that she may be a help in removing the prejudice of some, that they may be willing to listen to the truth. —*May 20, 1907. (p. 359, par. 3)*

I am thankful that the Lord is leading you. I believe that the Lord has appointed you to do His work in His way. Let us in our work have faith in God and trust Him. While we may take pleasure in counseling with our brethren, an individual work is to be done which is beyond the power of any mind to comprehend.

I thank the Lord with heart, and soul, and voice that you have been a prominent and influential member of the Women's Christian Temperance Union. In the providence of God you have been led to the light, to obtain a knowledge of the truth.... This light and knowledge you need to bring into your work, as you associate with women whose hearts are softened by the Spirit of God, and who are searching for the truth as for hidden treasure. For twenty years I have seen that the light would come to the women workers in temperance lines. But with sadness I have discerned that many of them are becoming politicians, and that against God. They enter into questions and debates and theories that they have no need to touch. Christ said, "I am the light of the world: he that followeth Me shall not walk in darkness, but shall have the light of life." —*December 1, 1898. (p. 407, pars. 1, 2)*

The Lord, I fully believe, is leading you that you may keep the principles of temperance clear and distinct, in all their purity in connection with the truth for these last days. They that do His will shall know of the doctrine. The Lord designs that women shall learn of Him meekness and lowliness of heart, and co-operate with the greatest Teacher the world has ever known. When this is done, there will be no strife for the supremacy, no pride of opinion, for it will be realized that mind, and voice, and every jot of ability, are only lent talents, given by God to be used in His work, to accumulate for Him, and to be returned to the Giver with all the increase. We are expected to grow in capability, in influence, and in power, ever looking unto Jesus. And by beholding, we shall be changed into His likeness.

The woman's work is a power in our world, but it is lost when, with the Word of God before her, she sees a "Thus saith the Lord" and refuses to obey. The great and difficult thing for the soul to do is to part with its own supposed works of merit. It is not an easy matter to understand what it means to refuse self the best place of honor in the service of God.

All unconsciously we act out the attributes of our own character and the bias of our own mind in the very presence of God, in our prayer and worship, in our service, and fail to see that we are absolutely dependent upon the leading of the Holy Spirit. Self is expected to do a work that is simply out of its power to do. This is the great peril of woman's work in Christian Temperance lines.

The Lord does not bid you separate from the Woman's Christian Temperance Union. They need all the light you can give them. You are not to learn of them but of Jesus Christ. Flash all the light possible into their pathway. You can agree with them on the ground of the pure, elevating principles that first brought into existence the Woman's Christian Temperance Union. "Behold," said Christ, "I send you forth as lambs among wolves." If He sends His disciples on such a mission, will He not work through you to open the Scriptures to those who are in error? Cherish the fragrance of that love that Christ has revealed for fallen humanity, and by precept and example teach the truth as it is in Jesus. —*December 1, 1898. (p. 408, pars. 1-3)*

The Holy Spirit alone is able to develop in the human heart that which is acceptable in the sight of God. The Lord has given you capabilities and talents to be preserved uncorrupted in their simplicity. Through Jesus Christ you may do a good work. As souls shall be converted to the truth, have them unite with you in teaching these women who are willing to be taught, to live and labor intelligently and unitedly. —*December 1, 1898. (p. 409, par. 1)*

I am so glad, my sister, that you did not sever your connection with the Woman's Christian Temperance Union. You may have to sever this connection, but not yet, not yet. Hold your place. Speak the words given you by God, and the Lord will certainly work with you. You may see many things you do not approve of, but do not fail nor be discouraged. I hope and pray that you may be clothed daily with the righteousness of Christ.

My sister, let your heart repose in confidence in God. The Lord will be to you a present help in every time of need. He does not need to work through other minds in order to lead His chosen ones. He is desirous of communicating through those who seek Him with all the heart. While we put our entire trust in our Redeemer, we are perfectly

Work for W.C.T.U.

safe. We have a large work to do, and we are to have respect unto the recompense of reward. And more than this we are to use every God-given faculty that others, through our influence and Christlike example, may have the same respect that we have.

I hope, my sister, that you will have an influence in the Women's Christian Temperance Association to draw precious souls to the standard of truth. The Lord is drawing many to an examination of the truth, and you need not fail nor be discouraged. Sow beside all waters. These are good waters in which you can sow the seeds of truth, even if you do not dwell publicly upon the prominent features of our faith. It would not be wise to be too definite. The oil of grace revealed in your conscious and unconscious influence will make known that you have the light of life. This will shine forth to others in your direct, positive testimony upon subjects on which you can all agree, and this will have a telling influence. —*June 21, 1899. (p. 409, par. 2; p. 410, par. 1)*

I was greatly pleased with your letter, in which you gave me the history of your experience with the W.C.T.U. When I read it, I said, "Thank the Lord. That is seed-sowing which is of value." I am pleased, so much pleased. The Lord has certainly opened your way. Keep it open, if possible. A work can be accomplished by you. Preserve your strength for such efforts. Attend important gatherings when you can. These occasions will be very trying seasons, but when the Lord gives His loved ones a special work to do, He sends His angels to be round about them.

There are very many precious souls whom the Lord would have reached by the light of truth. Labor is to be put forth to help them to understand the Scriptures. I have felt an intense interest in the W.C.T.U. workers. These heroic women know what it means to have an individuality of their own. I desire so much that they shall triumph with the redeemed around the great white throne. My prayers shall be in your behalf that you may be given special opportunities to attend their large gatherings, and that your voice may be heard in defense of the truth.

I dare not give you advice in this important matter. You are on the ground and Christ is on the ground. Be assured that He will work with you and through you and by you.

It ought to be a great encouragement to you in your work to think of the compassion and tender love of God for those who are seeking and praying for light. We should hold convocations for prayer to ask the Lord to open the way that the truth may enter the stronghold where Satan has set up his throne, and dispel the shadow which he has cast athwart the pathway of those he is seeking to deceive and to destroy. We have the promise or rather, the assurance, "the effectual fervent prayer of a righteous man availeth much." —*December 1899. (p. 410 bottom of page; p. 411)*

Light has been given me that there are those with most precious talents and capabilities in the W.C.T.U. Much time and money has been absorbed among us in ways that bring no returns. Instead of this, some of our best talent should be set at work for the W.C.T.U., not as evangelists, but as those who fully appreciate the good that has been done by this body. We should seek to gain the confidence of the workers of the W.C.T.U., by harmonizing with them as far as possible. We are to let them see and understand that the foundation of the principles of our doctrine is the Word of God.

The necessity of working for the women of the W.C.T.U. has never been fully and squarely met. The problem has never received the consideration it ought to have received. If the workers in the W.C.T.U. can obtain the true faith, and set their feet in the right path, what a work will be done. But there is to be no driving on our part, no warfare, no use of the two-edged sword, which cuts every way. This people have been rich in good works.

When the light of present truth is given them through carefully prepared methods, when the golden oil is received into the willing hearts of our workers, the treasures of truth and grace will be communicated from one to another. By the women of the W.C.T.U. the law of God is misunderstood. If they can be enlightened in regard to this point, we shall see that their educated ability will do much more than it is now doing to create working forces for the advancement of truth and righteousness.

The Lord asks us, my brother, to seek His face. The work of the Holy Spirit must be felt in our hearts. Many who are standing aloof from Seventh-day Adventists are living more in accordance with the light they have received than are many Seventh-day Adventists. This may seem strange to you, but strange things will have to be demonstrated to show the foolishness of the wisdom of those who judge others who have not seen the light.

Much good would be done if some of the W.C.T.U. women were invited to our camp-meetings to take part in the meetings by teaching our sisters how to work. While at the meeting, they would be hearing and receiving as well as imparting. There is a great work to be done, and instead of presenting the features of our faith which are objectionable to unbelievers, let us say to them as Philip said to Nathaniel, "Come and see." We have had great light, great knowledge, and continual instruction, yet the word is given me for many of our people, "You are weighed in the balances, and are found wanting."

There are many ways in which we can work to reach those not of our faith. It would be well to return to the methods of presenting health and temperance that were adopted nearly thirty years ago. We need to trim our lamps and receive in them the holy oil from the two olive branches. When the power of the Spirit of God rests upon us, there will be a showing for our labors altogether different from that now seen.

Let us not represent truth and the situation of things as so formidable that those belonging to the W.C.T.U. will turn away in despair. There are vital truths upon which they have had very little light. They should be dealt with in tenderness, in love, and with respect for their good work. We are to guard against approaching them in such a way as to close doors whereby some, yes many, might be reached. Instead of condemning them, let us strive to reach their hearts—not through the learned arguments of ministers, but through the wise efforts of women of influence and tact who can devote time and thought to this line of work.

The Lord wants His people to follow other methods than to condemn wrong, even though their condemnation be just. He wants them to do something more than to hurl at their adversaries charges which do not convict, but only send those at whom they are made, farther from the truth—charges which make those in error point to the words written, and say, "You see, it is impossible to have any union with Seventh-day Adventists, for they will give us no chance to connect with them unless we believe just as they believe."

Let us remember that there is need of sanctified pens and sanctified tongues. When we as a people live as God would be pleased to have us live, we shall see the deep movings of His Spirit. Much will then be done for those who have never heard the truth. In our work for unbelievers we may expect to hear much that is not ordered by God. But let us remember that those who speak these words do not know any better. Let us pray for them, and approach them in discretion and with Christlike tenderness. Those who oppose the counsel of God against themselves need gentle dealing. God can at any time so move upon hearts by His Holy Spirit that they will be prepared to receive the truth and unite with His commandment-keeping people. —*April 18, 1900. (pp. 412-414)*

Be of good courage in the Lord. I pray that you will look constantly to God, and trust fully in Him. He will be your helper in every emergency.

I am deeply interested in the W.C.T.U. It is the Lord's pleasure that you should feel free to act in concert with them. It is by uniting with them in their labors that we shall be able to bring to these people an understanding of the claims of the fourth commandment. I believe there are many honest souls in this organization, who, when they are convinced of the claims of the Bible Sabbath, will obey the dictates of conscience.

In our earlier labors in the message, our camp-meetings were held in out-of-the-way places. Of late years, a change has been brought about in this respect and for this I am grateful. In our labors together, my husband and I always felt that it was our duty to demonstrate in every place where we held meetings, that we were fully in harmony with the workers in the temperance cause. We always laid this question before the people in plain lines. Invitations would come to us to speak in different places on the temperance question, and I always accepted these invitations if it was possible. This has been my experience not only in this country, but in Europe and Australia, and other places where I have labored.

I am sorry that there has not been a more lively interest among our people of late years to magnify this branch of the Lord's work. We cannot afford to loose one opportunity to unite with the temperance work in any place. Although the cause of temperance in foreign countries does not always advance as rapidly as we could wish, yet in some places decided success has attended the efforts of those who engaged in it. In Europe we found the people sound on this question. On one occasion, when I accepted an invitation to speak to a large audience on the subject of temperance, the people did me the honor of draping above the pulpit the American flag. My words were received with the deepest attention, and at the close of my talk a hearty vote of thanks was accorded me. I have never in all my work on this question had to accept one word of disrespect.

We need at this time to show a decided interest in the workers of the W.C.T.U. None who claim to have a part in the work of God should lose interest in the grand object of this organization in temperance lines. I am not afraid that you will lose your interest, or backslide from the truth because you interest yourself in this people who have taken such a noble stand for the temperance question, and I shall urge our people, and those not of our faith, to help us in carrying forward the work of Christian temperance.

I am being aroused anew on this subject. We have a work to do along this line besides that of speaking in public. We must present our principles in pamphlets and in our papers. We must use every possible means of arousing our people to their duty to get into connection with those who know not the truth. The success we have had in missionary work has been fully proportionate to the self-denying, self-sacrificing efforts we have made. The Lord alone knows how much we might have accomplished if as a people we had humbled ourselves before Him, and proclaimed the temperance truth in clear, straight lines. A large work of seed-sowing is yet to be done. The light of truth has flashed upon many minds who have not yet fully taken their stand, and these souls are waiting to see what next. The Lord's workers are to draw nigh to Him, and He will give them keener perceptions and broader views of His purpose and of their individual duty.

Look not to human agencies to learn your duty. Seek the Lord to know His will, and He well give you light. He is the One Who can truly estimate character. Christ bids His workers, "If any of you lack wisdom, let him ask of God, that giveth to all men liberally, and upbraideth not; and it shall be given him. But let him ask in faith, nothing wavering, for he that wavereth is like a wave of the sea, driven with the wind and tossed. For let not that man think that he shall receive any thing of the Lord." God bids us carry our difficulties and perplexities to Him. He presents for the acceptance of the believing soul the virtues of Christ's character. A way is opened for him to receive the truth as it is in Jesus, and to have that faith which works by love and purifies the soul....

Work for W.C.T.U. 231

Sister ———, look to Jesus, and make Him your Counselor. Go forward in faith with the work the Lord has pointed out to you. If wisely labored for, many of these women who have taken such a noble stand for the cause of temperance, will go still farther and will yield themselves to obedience to the commandments of God. A true missionary spirit will lead our workers to welcome these women to our meetings that they may hear the truth for this time.

We need to put away our narrowness of vision. We need to search the Scriptures, studying the works of Christ in His efforts to reach every class of people. Again and again Christ was charged with receiving sinners, and eating with them. But he said, "I came not to call the righteous, but sinners to repentance." This is the answer we may give to those who would criticize our works because they cannot reason from cause to effect.

Be encouraged to continue your work for the W.C.T.U. Unite with them in their good work as far as you can do so without compromising any principle of truth. Lead them to see that there is more light for them in the Word of God. God has shown you that it is your privilege to unite with these workers that you may give them a more intelligent understanding of the principles of His Word. —*September 5, 1907. (pp. 461-464)*

I feel very thankful that you have had the privilege of becoming better acquainted with the workers of the Women's Christian Temperance Union. Our workers should make special efforts to come in touch with this organization, and to connect with the workers in the temperance cause. This will prove a great help to our own people, and also to these women workers. If the present truth is presented to them in the simplicity of godliness, they will see and accept it. We must keep close to the Lord. If we are imbued with His Spirit, the light will shine forth. It is Christ in the life that will make the truths we advocate forcible, and will lead souls to accept Him.

While many of the workers in the W.C.T.U. have heard the truth of the third angel's message, there are many more who have never had it presented to them in its fullness. These women will not be condemned for not receiving that which they have not heard. I have been shown that if the Sabbath truth is presented to these, many will accept it. We should not neglect them, or treat them as if they were opposed to the cause of present truth. By showing ourselves interested in their work of temperance, we shall open the way to give them the light we have.

We need so much to study Christ's methods of labor. He traveled continually from place to place, ministerng to the temporal and spiritual needs of the multitudes that followed Him. He grasped every opportunity of presenting truth to the people, and the seeds of truth He dropped into the hearts of His hearers sprang up and brought forth fruit....

I have been shown that we have not labored as we should for the women of the W.C.T.U. They need patient, wise, Christlike efforts made for them. We can never do for them what God expects of us by standing apart from them to condemn. We need to give them the truth as it was revealed in the life Jesus.

Let no one hinder you from putting forth efforts to get the Sabbath truth before this class. Show them that you desire to connect with them in their work of temperance. Draw near to them, and in your association together, show them that you have a practical faith. And they, by coming to our meetings and being permitted to have a part in them, will learn the reasons of our faith.

At our camp-meetings we should make special efforts to reach the unbelieving, and to let the light shine forth amid the moral darkness. Consecration meetings should be held as well as discourses given. The living truths for this time should be preached. At the Los Angeles camp-meeting, opportunities should have been improved to make special efforts for the workers in the temperance cause. The tame way in which the temperance question is being handled by our people is not in harmony with the necessities of the times. The work of making known our belief in matters of temperance should now be entered into most heartily. When the W.C.T.U. workers see that we are in harmony with their temperance principles, they will be willing to listen to other points of our faith. As we present our principles on health reform, they will see that there is further light for them on the temperance question. We can then bring the Sabbath truth before them.

I cannot at this time write as fully as I desire, but I urge you, my sister, to let the light of health reform shine forth in clear, bright ways. The Lord will bless you in this work as He makes your knowledge of the truth a blessing to others. Lean hard upon God; trust fully in Him; walk in humility, realizing that the Lord is your helper, and your deliverer, your front guard and your rearward. —*September 19, 1907. (pp. 483-485)*

The Lord is good and greatly to be praised. I will not complain. I feel very sad over the state of things in Battle Creek. I am trying to do all that is possible to guard the flock of God from falling into error. God alone can keep them and through them work out His good pleasure. I am satisfied with the working of the Lord. If unbelief is multiplied, through the exercise of unbelief in the Testimonies, having done all we can do, we will talk faith, and work on the affirmative side of the question. If my name is cast out as evil, I am in excellent company. Those who would not receive Christ were dead in trespasses and sins. As they looked upon the evidences that He presented, by curing diseases and making the suffering ones rejoice in health, why did they not yield their unbelief? Because by such an action they held right on to their wicked purposes and said, He performed this wonderful work through the devil. This was the sin against the Holy Ghost. They had not forgiveness in this world, nor in the world to come.

What reason had Christ given them for making this statement? None at all. The Prince of life was seeking the lost sheep. At last the leaders of Israel put Him to death. What had He done? He had expressed to a rebellious world the love of God. And His death was the great freewill offering for sin. By it a fountain of mercy was opened to a world yet to be convinced of the wonderful sacrifice made in order that whoever believed in Christ should not perish, but have everlasting life. The preaching of the gospel gives sinners opportunity to receive the greatest gift ever proffered human beings. Those who refuse this gift reveal the highest contempt for God.

It is our privilege to be partakers of the divine nature. If we be falsified, if men give to the world a misstatement of the work that God has done through the humble instrument, dishonoring Christ by making a misrepresentation of Him, they are partakers of the shame and reproach upon me.

We understand the present feebleness and smallness of the work. We have had an experience. In doing the work God has given us, we may go trustingly forward, assured that He will be our efficiency. He will be with us in 1906, as He was with us in 1841, 1842, 1843, and 1844. Oh! what wonderful evidence we had then of the presence of God with us. In the earlier stages of our work, we had many difficulties to meet, and we gained many victories. If the Lord is leading us, we may go forward courageously assured that He will be with us as He was with us in past years, as we labored in feebleness, but under the miracle-working power of the Holy Spirit. He will be with us as He was with us when we had to meet the opposing influences of erroneous theories.

Many of the most successful undertakings made in behalf of the truth have at the beginning been small, and have cost many tears and prayers. At the beginning of our work, some brought in grave errors, and meeting these placed upon us much hard labor, and such difficulties as God's help alone could enable us to overcome. We prayed a great deal; often we wrestled whole nights in prayer. Then the light, precious light on Bible truth, would come upon the whole company assembled. All could understand the difficulties, and the truth of the Bible was comprehended and substantiated.

Thus we worked and thus we prayed. Errors were continually being brought in, but we went to God in prayer, and searched the Scriptures diligently. Year after year, after the passing of the time, many false theories were presented, but we collected our forces in favorable places, and continued in prayer, watching, and praying, and searching the Scriptures. Then light was given to the very youngest of those assembled, and the truth of the Word of God in regard to the position we were occupying, was plainly specified.

The time of respite granted us seemed short, too short to open to the world the great and wonderful things of God's law. The promises of God—how we laid hold upon them! We could not bear all the glory; our physical strength left us, and the power of God, like a halo of glory was over us. What praise went up to God. "Yet a little while, and He that shall come will come, and will not tarry." There was a tarrying time for us, but He, our Lord, knew the end from the beginning. It was no delay, and from year to year we worked and prayed and believed. The errors that were rushing in upon us, we met in the power of God and explained them. And the glory filled the room where we were assembled.

We had thought that the work would have been accomplished before this. But the light came from the Lord regarding the extension of the work. Jesus came and spake unto them, saying, "All power is given unto Me in heaven and in earth." This power we needed then in the early history of our work. "Go ye therefore, and teach all nations, baptizing them in the name of the Father, and of the Son, and of the Holy Ghost." Then we understood that there was a world to be warned. "Teaching them to observe all things whatsoever I have commanded you: and, lo, I am with you alway, even unto the end of the world." Here is our work, our commission. The truth was to go to every city in America, and we were to gather up our forces to proclaim the message in the regions beyond.

Had the work been done that God designed should be done, the condition of things in our world now would be very different. But the professing followers of Christ are asleep; the churches have not fulfilled the solemn charge laid upon them. Men placed as watchmen have been asleep at their post, and many refuse to wake up. They are not fulfilling the gospel commission.

After Christ had arisen from the dead, the angels said to the women, "Go quickly, and tell His disciples that He is risen from the dead; and, behold, He goeth before you into Galilee; there shall ye see Him: lo, I have told you." And they departed quickly from the sepulcher with fear and great joy and did run to bring His disciples word. And as they went to tell His disciples, behold, Jesus met them, saying, "All hail." And they came and held Him by the feet, and worshiped Him. Then said Jesus unto them, "Be not afraid: go tell My brethren that they go into Galilee, and there shall they see Me."

"Then the eleven disciples went away into Galilee, into a mountain where Jesus had appointed them. And when they saw Him, they worshiped Him: but some doubted." They doubted that He had risen from the dead, in spite of the most powerful facts in proof of it. The Jews did not deny the resurrection of Christ for want of evidence to prove it, nor did they hire soldiers to tell a lie because they believed the falsehood or could substantiate it. They did it to keep the people from knowing the truth. False teachers are always afraid to have the truth come before the people. This knowledge they wish to hide to keep the people from becoming acquainted with the facts. They desire preeminence, and the truth would spoil their history and their character.

Work for W.C.T.U. 235

There are many ways in which the truth has been withheld from the world that Christ has purchased with the price of His blood. But Christ has supreme authority over all, and power to give knowledge to all who desire it, and who seek it from God in His Word.

The sacred commission given us is to work for all nations. To turn sinners from iniquity is to be the great object of the followers of Christ. In various ways this work is to be done. In our camp-meetings a much more decided effort is to be put forth to accomplish the work. Short discourses right to the point are to be given, and those who hear are to be called to make a decision. The laborers are to be fervent in spirit. During the meetings our periodicals are to be distributed and sold.

Let all strive together to reach the object Christ has set before us. The gospel is to be translated into every tongue, and is to be preached to every creature. The divine presence of Christ will ever be with the true workers, enlightening their minds as they open the Scriptures to others. All who reach out for the Lord Jesus in their prayers, seeking for wisdom and efficiency, will be given success in their endeavors to win souls to righteousness. They will be God's light bearers, shining amidst the darkness of the world. —*January 19, 1908. (pp. 596-600)*

I have had much to write in regard to the shortness of time. Our work is soon to close, and we are now to place ourselves in working order in God's way. We are not to link ourselves up with those who are not wise to discern what is the will of God. We are to come out from among them and be separate. The end of all things is at hand, and the message of warning must be given. A spirit of anger is stirring the nations, and it will soon be too late to work for the Lord. Every conceivable deception will be brought in, and the enemy will work with masterly power. Stronger and stronger will be his efforts, until in heaven it is said, "It is finished." —*July 1905. (p. 185, par. 1)*

General Index

ACTS, book of, give careful study, 181
Advantages, brought to workers, 70, 109
    few in Australia, 121
    educational in different conferences, 138
Amusements, 170, 171
Ann Arbor, attendance at not necessary, 19
Anxiety, needless, uncalled for, 125

BATTLE CREEK, conditions in, 232
    judgments on institutions, why, 56
Bible, basis of all education, 142, 180, 182
    combined with, 193
    deeper knowledge of, 181, 183
    essential, 180, 182
    faithful teacher, 184
    guide to best workers, 152
    lesson book, 94
    man of counsel, 185
    study of, neglected, 94, 119, 124
    to be read and assimilated, 132
Bible Institute necessary, 99
Blend spiritual and physical, 192
Blessings, all may have, 126
Books, objectional, not to be used, 142
Boston to be worked, 46, 47

CALIFORNIA, Southern, as health resort, 157, 158
Camp-meetings, great blessing, 120
Cause, channels of light, 110, 111
    character, perfected, 130
    church, work of, 25
    imperiled by self-confident workers, 83
    of God, first, 213, 214
Centers, break up large, 143
Charge, solemn, 154, 180
Children, saved in God's way, 127
Christ, example of, 142
    the burden bearer, 120
    the great Medical Missionary, 134, 145, 169, 183
    the great standard for all teachers, 185, 186
"Christ's Object Lessons," 204-209
Cities, disasters befalling, 47
    medical missionary work, door to, 47
    men of character needed in, 50
    missionaries in laboring two and two, 50
    of Oakland and San Francisco, 50, 107
    to be worked, 46-49
    work for, kept before us for 20 years, 49

Commercialism, spirit of, 27, 28, 35, 87, 94, 96, 118
    work counter, 112
Commission, Gospel, not fulfilled, 48
Confession of sin, 110
Conference, Southern California, 22, 23, 26
Conscience for another, 135
Consecration, man measured by, 15
Conversion of souls, 156
Cooperation, essential, 102
Councils, worldlings invited to, 132
Counsel, following own, 106
    necessary, 98
    opposition to, 178
    very clear in, 214
Counselor, not of Lord, 85
    with fellow workers, 115
Crisis, coming, 76
Criticism, to avoid, 26, 115
    unkind, to be avoided, 49, 135, 161

DEBT and borrowing money, 201-204
Difficulties, to labor under, 109
Discipline, soul and body, 150
Display, nerve strain to, 144
Drugs, treated without, 55, 70, 151, 152, 192, 193, 195
    poisonous, 154, 158, 194
Duty, not to be defined by erring man, 91

ECONOMY, necessary, 77
    strictest, to be shown, 144
Educated workers, 143
Education, 178-183
    higher, defined, 19, 49, 178, 179
    so-called higher, 173
    the most valuable where found, 48
    to continue through life, 77
    well-balanced to be given, 76
    wrong, along some lines, 135
Educational advantages, 138, 164, 189
Elijah, earnest prayer of, 129, 130
    example of, 129
    life of, work of reform, 155
Employment in heaven, 133
Evangelists, faithful in every city, 69
Experience, early, recounted, 135, 233
    religious, needed, 122

FACTORIES, health food, in Southern states, 221

General Index

Facts, great, revealed, 130
Failure, in schools, 126, 169
Faith, greater need of, 115
Family changes, 125, 126
Fog of error, 130
Food, simple but good and palatable, 75

GLENDALE, sanitarium at, 10, 160
    sanitarium, purchase of, 10, 144, 160
Gospel, only antidote for sin, 65
    real end of, 54
Growth continual, in grace, 133
Guidance, divine, 108, 135

HARDSHIPS, unnecessary, 193
Harmony, in our institutions, 146
Haste in health food business, 112, 113
Healing, without drugs, 51, 55
Health, guarded, 162, 186, 187, 189
    institutions, wide missionary field, 152
    reform, reformation in, 216, 217
Heart, change needed, 85
Hedging up way for others, 106
Highest aim, what? 184
Hindrances presented, 106
Holy Spirit, counselor and guide, 137, 182
Hospitals, young men visit, 105
Human wisdom, mistakes made by, 108
Humility, grace of, 84, 85
    necessary, 114, 154

IMPROVEMENT of time, 139
Incident told at the beginning of Battle Creek Sanitarium, 123
Individuality maintained, 117
Indulgence of appetite, greatest evil, 154
Industries to be fostered, 170
Influence, great care in, 138
    of even one careless student, 169
    of godly lives, 118
    spiritual, needed, 111
Institutions, agencies divinely appointed, 88, 181, 182
    failures made, 156
    for education of children, 127
    to help instead of giving higher wages, 215, 216
Instruction, general, 109-137
    definite, 23
    found in Deuteronomy 4-11; 2 Peter 1; 154
    of Bible, to blend with medical instruction, 138

Investment, of means, 202, 203

JUDGMENT not given to men, 85

KNOWLEDGE, needed, will be given, 131

LEADERS, fully converted, 29
    special work of, 117
    Legal requirements, conforming to, 172
    Union Conference Training Schools to prepare for, 141, 142

Library in sanitariums, 73

Life, outdoor, for patients, 163, 164

Light, strong men against, 106
    true, misapplied, 131

Location of buildings, 49, 157, 163

Loma Linda
    Advantages, great, 39, 89, 121, 122, 128, 153
        ideal, 3, 6, 11, 18, 38, 192
    Amusements, 171
    Atmosphere, spiritual, required, 128
    Bakery small, 9, 219
    Bathroom, addition, 222
    Benefits of outdoor life, 157, 158, 192
    Business, manager, 150
        men, wise, 152
    Caution about enlarging work, 203, 204
    Center, educational, 7, 9, 14, 21, 39
        of work for Redlands, Riverside and San Bernardino, 61
    Channel of light, 151
    Charter for sanitarium and printing office, 175
    Church, need of, 13
    Commercialism, free from, 8, 217-219
    Competing with worldly medical schools, 171
    Cooperation of heaven, 128
    Cottages for teachers and students, 13
    Counsel from God, 33
    Counselors, wise, 27
    Criticism, spirit of, 8
    Debt, 202
    Dedication of, 7
    Deny self, 14
    Dependence upon God, 175
    Description of property, 1-5
    Determination, selfish, to be stopped, 128
    Dictatorial spirit condemned, 93
    Diplomas, 145
    Drugs, discarded, 3, 48, 51, 81, 192
    Economy, strictest, 78, 82

Loma Linda (Continued)
  Education, higher, 17, 178
    thorough in Bible truth, 8, 14
  Educators, carefully selected, 13
    men of talent, 13-15
  Elevator, need of, 199
  Facilities, enlarged, 128
  Financial help promised, 223
  Food factory, location of, 217
    not to be large, 203, 220
  Hardships, unnecessary, 193
  Health foods, 8, 221
  Hearts blended, 27
  Importance of work, 201
  Industries to be fostered, 170
  Influence, dependent upon, 176
    great care, 138
    of consecrated workers, 220
    of even one careless student, 169
  Inventions, costly, 82
  Institutions, agencies divinely appointed, 88, 181, 182
    to help instead of giving higher wages, 215, 216
  Instruction, 23, 109-138
  Land, additional, 128, 222, 223, 225
    essential, 20, 164
    use of, 222
  Leader, first, 81, 82
  Manager, 198, 219
  Means, for, 10
    freewill offerings, 11
    God's agencies, 20
    needed, 191, 196, 201
  Medical, course, not necessary for so many to take, 141, 142
    missionary center, 1-21
  Patients, work for, 158, 164, 187, 188
  Physical powers, keep perfect, students, 8, 76
  Physicians, ability of, 15
    efficient, 152
    learners of Christ, 153
    new ideas come to, 18
  Principles, hold-back, not to be, 2
  Proceeds from sale of "Ministry of Healing," 196, 210
  Purchase, instruction to, 1, 2, 37
    price, 1, 3, 196
    providential, 6, 7, 10, 192, 224
  Rational methods to be used, 3
  Relief must be given, 93

Loma Linda (Continued)
- Responsibilities shared, 113
- Sale of "Ministry of Healing," 199
- School, charter for medical, 15-17
    - connected with sanitarium, 7-9, 192
    - danger in worldly, 17
    - like schools of prophets, 11
    - of highest order, 11, 12, 17
    - strong for nurses and physicians, 7
- Simplicity stressed, 81, 82, 202
- Source of patients, 1, 36
- Spirit of self-control, 97, 98
- Students, end of their education, 126
    - not to finish in worldly schools, 173, 174
    - to confess Christ, how and when, 95
    - treatment of, 9
- Talents, best to be united to this school, 153
- Teachers, best to be employed, 105
    - to confess Christ, how and when, 95
    - work of, 168
- Teaching of health reform necessary, 80
- Vision of, 2, 4, 6-8, 12, 14, 188
- Words of instruction, 185
- Work, blended in sanitarium and school, 161
    - great, 20
    - not to be crippled for lack of room, 19, 105
    - not to be restricted, 105
    - very precious, 12, 105
- Workers, channels of light, 11, 129
    - union necessary for, 20
- Worldly schools, union with, 176

Los Angeles
- Constant labor needed in, 28
- Medical work in, 43
- Special field for sale of "Object Lessons," 42

MEANS, want of, 41
Medical course not necessary for so many, 141, 142
Medical institutions, rural districts for, 188
Medical missionary work, and evangelistic connected, 146
- as hand to body, bound up with gospel, 100, 103, 183
- economy and simplicity in, 78, 79, 144
- God's work, 53, 70
- in its infancy, 56
- in towns and villages, 146
- instructor, 139
- leaders of, in Battle Creek, 132

Medical Missionary Work (Continued)
    needed in Southern field, 101, 146
    not inferior, 72, 139, 166
    not one man centered, 100
    others jealous of, 74, 184, 185
    spiritual, 73, 145
    to be carried forward earnestly, 55
    to gospel as hand to body, 104
    united to gospel ministry, 57, 68, 103
Medical missionaries
    Christ the pattern of, 134, 156, 183
    every church member, 135
    taught in hospitals, 139
    thoroughly educated in Bible times, 143
Medical profession, atheists and skeptics in, 140, 167
Medical students in worldly schools, 74, 141
Men, of solid character needed, 107
    self-righteous influence of, 88
Message given at 1901 General Conference, 162
    of healing, 70, 134
    of the Lord upheld, 107
    of warning many, 130
    to all, 45
    to churches in Southern California, 58, 59, 62
    to leave cities, 159
    to men in position of trust, 33, 34
    to people in America, 199, 200
Midwives, 73, 190, 191
Ministry, young men not deterred from, 142
"Ministry of Healing," 204-210
Money, 196

NEGLECT of the Word of God, 184
Nurses, Bible instruction to, 149
    cheerful, kind and tender, 148-151
    earnest, devoted, successful missionaries, 147, 192
    if not rooted in truth, not employed, 149
    lady, 152
    medical missionary evangelists, 67, 147
    not regular course taken, 145
    pleasant and cheerful, 148
    use best remedies, 149, 192
    well trained, needed, 149, 192, 193
    well trained, to go to families, 149, 192

OFFICERS, church, 87
Opportunities, great, 124
Overwork to be avoided, 189

PATIENTS, outdoor exercise for, 188
    work for, 188
Perils of last days, 75
Physical powers, keep perfect, 8, 76
Physicians, best to be secured, 156
    following pattern of world, 177
    instruction for, 185
    lady, 152
    modesty of, 140, 167
    skillful, 133
    thousands with ability of, 15
    wise, needed, 152
    Picture of unclothed soul, 143
    Plans, to elbow fellow workers, 127
    yours against others, 125, 126
Pott's (Paradise Valley) Sanitarium,
    purchase of, 196
    reason for purchasing, 40, 43
Power, of God, guiding and controlling, 83
    saving, for medical students, 140
Prayer, acceptable, 109
    kinds of, 91
    need of, 120
    the key of, 114
Presence of Christ in sickroom, 146
President of Southern California Conference, 32, 33, 92-94, 114
Principle of true service, 110
Proclamation of Third Angel's Message, 204
Properties, at low prices, 160
    many suitable for sanitariums, 30
Publications to be greatly multiplied, 52
Purpose of sale of "Ministry of Healing" and "Christ's
    Object Lessons," 207, 209, 210

QUESTION of greatest importance, 126

REDLANDS to be worked, 1, 36, 37, 39, 201, 206
Relation to governmental laws, 172
Relief of schools, 198
Remedy for discontent, 127
Responsibilities, great, 151
    individual, 89, 90, 117
    misinterpreted, 86, 87
Restaurants, hygienic, 112
Restrict work, watchers sit to, 105

SALARIES, physicians, harmony in, necessary, 211, 212

Salaries (Continued)
    not to be too high, 210-212
Salary, high, stumbling block, 212
    self-sacrifice in matter of, 214, 215
Sanitariums, competent matron, 189
    helpers not exercise authority over others, 89, 97
    in country, 159, 163
    in many lands, 9, 158-160, 164
    in vicinity of Redlands and Riverside, 1, 160
    in vicinity of San Diego, 9, 10, 38
    intelligent men and women, 192
    men's work, 189
    minister to sinsick souls, 152
    needed in the South, 146
    not in cities, 50, 157-159, 164, 188
    not too many, 10
    object of, 152, 153, 157
    to teach the truth, 10, 45, 55, 60-62, 70, 88
    women's work in, 189, 190
Sanitarium, large, in Battle Creek, not in God's order, 158
    New England moved to Melrose, 46
    Paradise Valley (Pott's), 31, 39, 40, 43, 44, 160
San Bernardino, valley of, cities to be worked, 52
    work needed in, 28, 37, 201, 206
San Fernando, mistake made, 27
    purchase of school in order of God, 31, 38
Satan, advantages of, 122, 124
    at work, 120-122, 134
    linked with discordant spirits, 121
    pleased when we speak of his power, 119
Schools, agents divinely appointed, 88
    connected with sanitariums, 160-162, 193, 203
    educate evangelists and Christian business men, 142
    enemy works against, 88
    heaven interested in, 13
    large, not to be planned, 143
    necessary training in, 142, 168, 172
    of highest order, 11, 12, 141
    of prophets, 119
    special work for, 71
    training, our larger, 17
    treatment rooms connected with, 138
    worldly, danger in, 17
    worldly medical, 172
Scriptures, standard, 131
Selection of proper young persons, 150

Self-sufficiency, danger of, 110
Separation, a wall of, 96
    complete, 177
    from worldly teaching, 173
Sermon on mount, 124-129
Service, term of year, 108, 142-144
Shortness of time, 235
Souls, unclothed picture of, 143
Southern California, faithful workers needed in, 29
    importance of work in, 115, 157, 158
    missionary field, 28, 29, 158
    work for, 22-46
    work, past, present and future, 92
Speculations, rife, 153
Speech, talent of, 186
Spirit of carelessness, 155
    harsh and exacting, 136
Standard, high for medical students, 139, 167, 184
    high for sanitariums and schools, 81
    Store, bakery and health foods, 216-222
    health deform, 216, 217
    health food workers read carefully Vol. 7 in regard to, 216
    natural foods utilized, 221
    not conduct large business on, 218
    not for commercial channels, 217
Students, consecrated, needed, 165-167
    higher aim, spiritually, 184, 179, 180
    give practical education to, 142, 192
    in worldly schools, 168
    to be strict health reformers, 161
    to confess Christ, 35
    unruly, not to be retained, 170, 171
    work in Australia, 76
    work to be taken in Battle Creek, 162
Study, of Bible help to other studies, 169
    of Romans, 12, 99
Success wanted, not money, 213

TALENT, everyone used, 185
    of speech, 186
    varied, 102, 149, 150, 157
Teachers, 183-185
    best and well prepared, 13
    kind of, 80, 81, 141, 183, 184
    to confess Christ, 35
Temperance, to begin in our own hearts, 153
    workers to unite with, 229-231

General Index

Tested, our people, 177, 179
Time, account of, to be given, 166, 194
    to work the cities, 50
Treatment, kind of, 149
    rooms, feeders to sanitarium, 1
Training, great care in, 138
    thorough, in schools, 141, 142, 166
Translation, preparing for, 95
Truth, not to be blanketed, 106
    to be upheld in Battle Creek, 161
    withheld from the world, 235

UNBELIEF, result of cherishing, 118
Unequally yoked, 173-178
Unity, necessary, 89, 99, 102, 104, 147, 151
    of physicians and ministers, 63, 66, 67

VISION of, California, 30, 31, 41, 42, 149
    commercialism, 118, 218, 220
    men in positions of trust, 150, 152

WALL of separation placed by the Lord, 96
Washington, D.C., facilities needed in, 32
Weaklings, do not remain, 133
Wisdom, where obtained, 181, 185
Work, conducted after different order, 45
    directed by God, 53
    for everyone, 62, 68
    great for Los Angeles, 41, 42
    hindered by self-exalted men, 86
    if faithful, 134
    in Australia, 200
    in home for children, 126
    in New Bedford, 148
    in Washington, D.C., 147, 196
    individual, necessary, 125, 132, 150
    of health reform to be stressed, 143
    out-of-door, for patients, 188, 189
    surgical, to be done by skilled physicians, 139
    to teach sick, 150
    worldwide, 235
Workers, aged, not to be sent to unhealthful places, 162
    care of own health, 162
    harmonious characters needed in, 145
    higher plane, 155, 156
    women, 190
    kind of, needed, 83, 144
    message to, 154

Workers (Continued)
    need of, everywhere, 20
    not to be bound for several years, 54, 108, 142, 143
    to be chosen with care, 148
    unity of, in Southern California, 27
    warmhearted, unselfish, 144, 145, 151
Worldly schools, competing with, 171
W.C.T.U., attention to be called to "Ministry of Healing" and "Christ's Object Lessons," 208
    for 20 years have seen the light would come to, 225
    our best talent should work for, but not as evangelists, 228
    woman's work with, 225-228
    work for, in Redlands, 225

YOUNG men, to become successful evangelists, 67
    to connect with gospel workers, 105
Young people not to go to Battle Creek, 157

We invite you to view the complete
selection of titles we publish at:

www.TEACHServices.com

Scan with your mobile
device to go directly
to our website.

Please write or email us your praises, reactions, or
thoughts about this or any other book we publish at:

www.TEACHServices.com • (800) 367-1844

P.O. Box 954
Ringgold, GA 30736

info@TEACHServices.com

TEACH Services, Inc., titles may be purchased in bulk for
educational, business, fund-raising, or sales promotional use.
For information, please e-mail:

BulkSales@TEACHServices.com

Finally, if you are interested in seeing
your own book in print, please contact us at

publishing@TEACHServices.com

We would be happy to review your manuscript for free.

www.ingramcontent.com/pod-product-compliance
Lightning Source LLC
Chambersburg PA
CBHW070547160426
43199CB00014B/2407